Money Matters for Kids and Parents

A Step-by-Step Handbook based on

A True Story

Your Kid's** (and your) **Future Depends on these three (3) Money Matters:

1) *The importance of* ***Financial Literacy****...Freedom from Slavery to Work & Debt.*
2) *How to* ***Become Financially Free****...Sooner in life.*
3) ***Selecting College Wisely****...Getting your Child (or yourself) through the Right College with Little or No Debt - Including Elite and Ivy League Universities.*

FL = Financial Literacy

FF = Financial Freedom

Right College = An education that's priced sensibly and provides lifelong skills that translate into tangible earning power.

FF = Retirement on your terms.

By

Edward S. Rickter, *MBA, NCARB, ICC*

Architect, Technology Entrepreneur, Real Estate Developer, Educator

Cartoon Art work by Sean E. Rickter

Table of Contents

Money Matters for Kids and Parents (MMFK&P)

Released for publication: 11/11/2020

Author: Edward Scott Rickter

Published by: Edward Scott Rickter, dba, ESR-DESIGN-BUILD, GENERAL CONTRACTOR LICENSE SCHOOL, and Edward Scott Rickter, Real Estate Broker.
Printed by: Fresh Prints Design, Long Beach, CA 90807

ISBN: 978-0-578-67114-7

PROLOG

Purpose and Background behind this Book

The purpose of *Money Matters for Kids and Parents (MMFK&P)* is to teach financial literacy to kids, teenagers, young adults, and parents. This in turn maximizes the possibility of becoming wealthy and happier during one's lifetime. If you're not a kid or parent, that's OK. This book can help you too. Anyone who wishes to gain mastery over their money matters and/or pay for college wisely can benefit from reading and applying the principals in this book.

What do You Want to Be When You Grow Up?

Do You Know How to select the right college?

Do you know how to pay for your college education without staggering debt or getting ripped-off?

How do You know if that job or future career will Pay Enough?

How do you know it will make you happy or fulfilled?

Even if you start later in life, financial literacy will change your thinking and help empower you to reach your full potential, regardless of age. But the earlier you start, the better your chances of achieving greater wealth and soul satisfaction sooner in life. In fact, most people - possibly upwards of 95% - seldom achieve a degree of financial literacy or wealth that frees them from the bondage of working to pay bills and debt. We were destined to be more than that.

The Book's chapters provide insight into four critical topics involving money matters for kids and parents. This in turn equates to realizing financial intelligence, making better education choices, having better work options, making better spouse and friend choices, mastering money management, and ultimately, realizing your full potential. Other than survival, safety, and being with loved ones, this deep seated quest remains in the heart and soul of virtually every child, parent, and adult on earth. It's our birth right. Yet for the most part, schools, religion, parents, peers, friends, and most work environments provide little if any viable help in teaching financial literacy. This creates many problems later in life.

The Book's Key Topics are:

- The Purpose of Learning Financial Literacy
- The Five Steps of Financial Freedom in Detail. (Chapters 1-5)
- Getting Your Child through College - Including an Ivy League or other elite top tier university - with little or no debt. (Chapter 6)
- Summing it All Up. Make a Mentor list. Other FF Mentors and Teachers who can help you increase your financial intelligence and wealth. (Chapter 7)

All combined, these topics provide a foundation for realizing Financial Freedom (FF) much earlier and more abundantly than people who start later in their adult life or not at all. But even if you do start later in your life (like I did at around age 40), this book can still help you achieve financial freedom and/or pursue a higher education wisely. The only difference is <u>*when*</u> that occurs in your life.

An entire chapter deals with getting your child or yourself through college - even an elite or Ivy League University - with little or no debt. Considering that college costs are outrageously high and only going up each year, this is a *must-read* chapter to getting the right education and paying for it without staggering long term debt.

In essence, this book serves as a guide to help kids, parents - or anyone with a strong desire to grow - how to gain control over their money matters and pursue college education. Combined with other recommended financial literacy books referenced in later chapters, you truly *can transform your ability to build wealth and enjoy a fulfilling lifestyle!*

To Succeed in Life, you must learn how to realize your full potential.

*That in turn means (among other things), following your **heart's desire**, becoming **financially literate**, choosing the **right college**, and **paying** for it **wisely**!*

The ***TWO*** Primary Reasons for writing this Book...*You and Your kids*

The reasons for teaching financial literacy and how to select and pay for college wisely are two-fold:

1) *Realizing Financial Freedom, knowing which college to attend, and paying for it wisely are fundamental needs that affect the entire human race.* However, straight answers to those needs usually remain opaque or are seldom taught in great detail at home, in school, in the work force, or by our government. Self-serving interests are alive and well lurking behind the scenes in academia, the government, corporate cartels, major media sources, organized religion, and our families of origin.

The logical place to begin learning about money matters is at home, by exposing kids and parents to financial literacy fundamentals. The next logical place would be the K-12 and post secondary school system (i.e.; grade school, middle school, colleges and universities). Work environments, the media, and government have a major influence too - both good and bad. Unfortunately, our education system typically omits financial literacy courses and most parents struggle with money matters. Teaching their kids about money becomes a distant thought.

Meanwhile, our federal, state, and local governments over-spend by egregious amounts, while the media promotes consumer spending on every conceivable platform, billboard, bus, train, plane, and digital device. Consequently, millions of people don't find answers to these critical issues from sources they're exposed to the most. Exacerbating the problem are college tuition and book costs that have risen to outrageous levels over the past two generations. Consequently, we live in a world that promotes spending, minimizes saving, and encourages slavery to debt.

The answers are there, but you have to dig to find them. You need to read material, attend seminars, listen to honest and insightful media programs (which exist but require diligence to find), and have in-depth discussions with people that can fill the financial literacy gaps our society's institutions deliberately leave out. In this book, you will find *topic overviews and step-by-step* instructions. Both approaches are important to gaining mastery over your money. In some sections, the *Intro or Overview* may be sufficient. In other sections, you will need *specific details and steps.*

Either way, you can choose which method improves your comprehension the best. Upon completion, this book (and others I recommend) will provide a comprehensive reference library filled with real-world financial strategies you can apply to your own life beginning right now. *Therefore, you have to find answers and solutions to managing your money matters on your own through books like this and other related sources.*

2) *This author's background shares similarities with many middle class people in today's society.* I grew up in a middle class family. My self-employed parents were decent providers, but they did little to prepare me academically. A huge majority of people in society today live just days, weeks, or maybe a few months away from insolvency. This includes middle and upper class incomes, not just people in lower tier income brackets. That means virtually everyone is prone to running out of money, no matter how much of it they have, unless they truly practice financially literacy. Despite good middle class income, it included me for many years.

Most people work for either small companies, large corporations, the government, or are self-employed. I've worked in all those employment categories at one point or another in my life. This included nearly two decades of full-time employment in medium-to-large corporations, starting and operating companies as a self-employed business owner, working as an employee for small business owners, and working part-time as an adjunct instructor for schools, colleges and universities that were run by the state government or privately owned.

Like most working adults, I was running around like the mad hatter living from pay check to pay check, raising kids, holding a marriage together, driving in terrible traffic, and trying hard to realize my ambitions. I had good jobs and lots of nice assets, but I also had many liabilities. I always seemed to need more cash. It was a constant struggle. I wanted desperately to find a way through the money maze, but I kept putting it off so it didn't begin to happen for me until midway through life. I started seriously saving for retirement at around age forty. Instead of spending spare cash or plowing it back in my business, I started socking it away and placed much of it in tax-free or tax-deferred retirement accounts where my money was invested in low-risk stocks and bonds. Along the way, I found that I enjoyed helping other people learn new skills, which probably stemmed from doing it myself so many times throughout my life and career.

I eventually reached FF with a middle class income that was occasionally spiked with large cash flows from working as a real estate investor and technology entrepreneur. Not only did my wife and I reach FF, we put our youngest son through college at an Ivy League university with virtually no debt. As an architect, technologist, and entrepreneur, I am trained to see *both* the big picture and the details. Realizing FF requires both skills. It also requires two more things: A strong *desire to learn* and a *willingness to change*. Together, these two seemingly small but highly critical factors represent your "teachability index", which ultimately determines how far and how fast you learn and grow in life.

Learn to develop a high teachability index. Combining that with integrity, a good education, the law of attraction, timing, luck, hard work, your faith, your people network, and trusting your instincts, you'll be ready to accomplish the dreams and goals that lie deep in your heart.

If I did it, You can too.

How the Journey of Pursuing College and Financial Freedom Began for this Author

In the Spring of 1980 at the age of twenty seven, I graduated cum laude with a five-year nationally accredited architecture degree from California Polytechnic State University's School of Architecture and Environmental Design. Nestled in the picturesque hills of San Luis Obispo California, I entered Cal Poly at age twenty four and was six years older than most of my college peers. This fact seemed to matter more to my status conciseness mother than it did to me. What really mattered was, despite being older, I was finally prepared and got admitted to a highly competitive, top-tier architectural school and graduated with honors. For an aspiring building professional, it was a coveted credential that would last a lifetime.

I was unprepared for a four (or five) year college program straight from high school. Most of my grades were mediocre and I had almost no advanced high school courses under my belt. The only exception was straight "A's" in industrial arts courses during the three years of architecture classes I took under Mr. Copeland. He gave me a career purpose. Building design, engineering, construction, and finance are distinct skill sets on one hand, but they are closely related in real estate. Architecture and real estate development requires all these skills to be integrated and managed. Therefore, three months after graduating high school, I enrolled in junior college to make up missed high school courses. Then I began work as a part-time, and eventually full-time, drafting and engineering apprentice in the petro-chemical manufacturing industry. I had already taken plenty of architectural design courses. What I really needed I got at that job because it provided a solid math and engineering background prior to applying to architectural school in 1976. That in turn helped me get admitted on the first try, largely because architecture is so math and engineering centric.

Upon graduating in 1980, inflation was rampant. Mortgage and consumer loan interest rates varied from 15% to 22%. Bank CD's paid annual percentage rates that varied from 15% to 18% - just to park your money with them. My university costs were $10,000 for the three and half years I attended Cal Poly earning a five year nationally accredited architectural degree. My two year AA degree in 1976 from Long Beach City College (LBCC) took four years part-time to complete and cost about $2000. LBCC costs excluded rent, food, and books, but at Cal Poly they *were* included. Therefore, the majority of my college education totaled $12,000 by 1980. $3,000 of that was in the form of grants, and the $2000 at LBCC was paid with cash. The balance of $7000 was a government sponsored Sallie Mae student loan at 3% interest with a ten year pay-back period. Since most average consumer loan interest rates were 20% in 1980, I stayed with the 3% rate and took the full ten years to pay it off. I never missed one payment. By 1990, interest rates had dropped to roughly 8% to 10%, but that was still well above my 3% rate. I got a superb deal. Today, interest rates are low again, but college costs are astronomical. That same undergraduate college education in 2020/2021 could easily cost between $50,000 to $300,000, depending on the college.

Housing prices in California had just finished quadrupling during the mid-to-late 1970's due to a combined 1-2-3 punch of rising oil prices, the Viet Nam war inflation coming home to roost, and the population explosion in California that stripped housing supply. A generic 1200 square foot home in most Southern California middle class neighborhoods could be purchased for $20,000 to $40,000 in the mid 1970's. I know this first hand because my landlord at the time offered to sell me his 1000 SF house in North Long Beach, CA for $20,000 in 1976. Unfortunately, I couldn't afford it on my engineering salary of $800 per month. In 1976, all I could afford was food, a car payment, taxes, and $100 per month in rent for a four hundred square foot one bedroom apartment situated over a back alley garage in a seedy neighborhood. By the late 1970's, that home jumped to over $80,000. By the early 1980's, the price for that same mediocre 1000 SF house in a sub-par Southern California neighborhood was approaching $150,000.

The housing market was beyond white hot, and so was inflation. Price growth easily approached 20% per month, which translated to 240% per year. However ridiculous or unsustainable that seems, it remained a fact during my life in Southern California where I was born, raised, went to Wilson High School, Long Beach City College, and then Cal Poly University. Thirteen years later, I entered MBA School at California State University, Long Beach (CSULB) for my Masters in Business Administration with a dual concentration in Information Systems and Finance.

Thus, all my education came from California State operated schools, colleges, and universities. Some of my education was excellent. But many K-12 and college courses were utterly useless in the real world. Other than my MBA degree, my California State education provided virtually no courses in financial literacy. Even construction estimating was never offered at Cal Poly's School of Architecture and Environmental Design, which is still considered a top-tier architectural school in the western United States, even though it's located within a middle-tier state university. Thus, my first thoughts upon graduating Cal Poly later that day while driving back to LA along the California Coast were: "How could a poor slob like me ever afford a home in Southern California?"

That thought was especially looming in my mind since my 5th year architectural design thesis dealt with "Realizing the American Dream through Alternatives in Housing." I had a net worth of about $8000, which included my 1965 Fender Jaguar guitar (which I still own), a 1976 Guild Acoustic guitar, a 1970 gas-guzzling Dodge Charger 440 Six Pac that was (unfortunately) later traded for a boring but fuel efficient station wagon, several pairs of bell bottom pants, two Nikon F2 film cameras and lenses, a modular dark room, a drafting board, and my classic rock record collection. I was an intern architect working in a profession that paid notoriously low wages relative to the tremendous amount of knowledge, education, state licensing, and grueling long hours involved.

My solution to the low wage problem emerged three years later after I passed the grueling California architectural licensing exam in 1983 on my first attempt, worked two jobs, and switched architectural employers several times. All of those career maneuvers helped increase my annual income by nearly 100%, and allowed me to save enough money to buy my first home – a brand new manufactured home (AKA, a *mobile home)* - for $30,000. This included 1500 square feet of living area, three bedrooms, two baths, and a kitchen with ample counter tops. I didn't care if it was manufactured housing. It was mine, I was building future equity, and it was better than renting a cramped, run-down apartment in LA.

I placed my manufactured home on rented land high on a hill in an industrial area of Southern California known as Dominquez Hills, which is slightly north-west of Long Beach, CA. The mobile home park added the word *estates* to their name "*Dominquez Hills Estates*", much like a restaurant owner over-seasons mediocre meat to make it more acceptable to the public. But I was determined to customize my new home so it felt more like a site-built house and not the glorified trailer it really was. That meant drywall interiors instead of cheap paneling, exterior wood trellises, concrete porches, redwood decking, and a California redwood hot tub - all of which I built and installed myself. In hindsight, I was creating future sweat equity and marketability even though I wasn't fully aware of that fact at the time. I was simply following my heart's desire using what cash I had.

My initial mortgage interest rate in 1982 was 18%. In 1983, interest rates dropped slightly under President Reagan and Fed Chairman Paul Volker, so I re-financed my mobile home and got 14% APR, which was a great rate back then - especially for manufactured housing.

Who would have dreamed of 2.5% to 4% mortgage rates 40 years later? After three years, I sold the mobile home in two days for $55,000, and was earning almost twice the money most architects did by working for a large aerospace corporation as a *licensed architect* in the facility department at Garrett Air Research (now Allied Signal) in Torrance, California. No more would I work for puny wages at small oppressive mom and pop architectural firms.

All throughout the decade of the 1980's of active employment in the architecture, engineering, and construction (AEC) industry, I mastered new skill sets. This included mainframe and PC based computer aided design (CAD) software, customizing and building my own personal computers based on the Apple II and IBM AT, and learning new desktop applications like word processing, spread sheets, 3D CAD, BIM, and 3D animation. Life's unexpected opportunities and twists led me into other career tangents I never dreamed possible just a few years earlier during college. It resulted in gaining a serious competitive advantage and more income than had I remained a traditional architect slaving over a boring manual drafting table in a small or medium size AEC firm.

In 1984, I designed, built, and owned my first custom home by the age of thirty one. I drew the plans on an IBM mainframe using CADAM software, arranged a bank construction loan, and managed all construction which was completed in six months. My total cost in 1984 for land and construction for a 2800 square feet three story custom home was $225,000. The appraised value two months after completion was $400,000, which represented 78% equity growth in less than one year.

A few months after completion, I was offered a dream job with the largest AEC firm in the United States at CRSS in Houston, TX. I was hired as their Director of IBM/CADAM Operations. Eventually, I took over the entire Houston and Dallas architectural IT departments, which included Wang, Intergraph, IBM PC's, CADAM, and Microstation hardware and software platforms. After three years with CRSS, I returned to LA and started two businesses: 1) Designing and building custom homes and; 2) Operating a boutique CAD / IT training and sales business. I was beginning to realize my dreams.

By my late thirties, I began to yearn for more freedom from the ups and downs of running a business, working eighty hours a week, and risking my entire net worth every time I designed and built a new property. Hard work, vision, taking risks, and having the right education and credentials rewarded me with a six-figure income. My net worth approached well over a million dollars during the late 1980's and early 1990's. But I was also spending a lot of money on real estate mortgages, my business, German cars, and hobbies. I was stressed out. I needed a better financial road map. I also needed to learn more about the quality of life – not just the quantity of things acquired. Sometimes I felt just months away from insolvency.

At this point, I already had a basic understanding of financial statements and income tax ramifications, due to running my own business full time for almost a decade. But I needed more than that. I needed spending and investing control. I needed new marketing strategies. I needed to solidify my knowledge in accounting and finance. I needed to expand my IT knowledge beyond the realm of 3D CAD, and learn about networking protocols, relational data bases, enterprise software, and web programming. So, in 1993, I enrolled in MBA School at California State University, Long Beach, with a concentration in Information Systems, in order to gain more financial and technology literacy.

I also needed more discipline over my personal and business money matters. It was between 1993 and 1998 that the seeds of FF were planted deep in my soul. I closed my CAD business in 1997 and decided to work in industry again, in order to apply these new found skills without having to chase sales every week. The glory days of running a boutique CAD business were disappearing rapidly. I made good money for almost ten years, but the fun was gone. So was the good money.

One of the most exciting career twists I experienced landed me at DIRECTV in El Segundo, California, in 1997. I spent three years there during the initial Internet revolution, which was known as "Web One" or "Dot.Com One". I was a freshly minted MBA with a concentration in IT and finance. In addition to that, I was an experienced and licensed architect and had honed the skills of running my own business using state-of-the art 2D CAD, 3D CAD, and BIM, which is a form of highly advanced 3D and means "*Building Information Modeling*". I was initially hired to draw schematics of DIRECTV's sprawling broadcast networks that consisted of LAN's, WAN's, and MAN's" throughout Southern California and the U.S. Later, I mastered new information technologies like HTML, JAVA, ASP, SQL, Cisco router and switch protocols, and Ecommerce. I eventually became DIRECTV's Chief Intranet Architect within their IT department that consisted of 200 IT techies, and in turn, was part of DIRECTV's 2000 employee work force in the emerging world of satellite TV broadcasting.

DIRECTV was a well-funded tech start-up that was backed by Hughes Aircraft and General Motors. Their IT department was the largest in California at that time. Google and Amazon were in their infancy. Apple was barely escaping bankruptcy. Facebook and Twitter didn't exist. By 1998, DIRECTV grossed $100 million in sales *every ten days!* Yet, they were still ***not*** profitable. That made a big impact on me. My quest to help them become more productive with IT web applications began to pay off. I was awarded two CIO Magazine awards in 1999 and 2000 for producing two of the best corporate Intranet web sites in CIO Magazine's annual survey of the 50/50 best corporate web sites each year.

Working at DIRECT'V was tremendously rewarding. But it was also a critical lesson about how start-ups and market leaders don't always make profits. In other words, it's not just big sales figures that matter. In the long run, bottom line profitability matters even more. Like all start-ups during *Web One*, $100 million dollars in sales every ten days sounds fantastic. But it doesn't mean much if that company is losing money. Beware of financial double talk and accounting tricks. *EBTIDA is not a true measure of profitability. Companies that report high sales but no profits over a long period are hiding poor quality, poor service, bad management, declining market share, or wasteful spending practices. In the case of DIRECTV, once they cleaned house and got rid of bad managers and directors who spent foolishly on expenses, they began to realize true profitability. That same lesson applies to all companies *and* to each of us as individuals.

* EBTIDA = Earnings Before Taxes, Interest, Depreciation, and Amortization. EBTIDA is *not* a measure of true profitability. DIRECTV used this metric during my tenure because it masked the fact that they were losing money every month, despite grossing $100M every 10 days. When DIRECTV went public and became profitable by the early 2000's, they switched to "net income" as their profitability metric – just as Wall Street demands, and as it should have been earlier on.

By applying the same financial discipline used in business to my own personal life, I began to see a clearer picture in handling my money matters. But MBA School was not enough. Each time I visited a book store, I searched for authors who had mastered their personal finances or achieved their career goals. It was fun. It was tiring. It was inspirational. It was sobering. It meant I had a lot of work ahead of me. One of the early financial literacy books I read was called *Rich Dad Poor Dad* by Robert Kiyosaki. It was very easy to understand and made me aware I had been buying too many liabilities, not enough assets, and draining my cash reserves instead of investing more wisely. So by my early forties, I started seriously saving my excess job income and cut back on purchasing liabilities, such as buying cars every six months.

Prior to that, I invested in real estate, but not much else. Worse still, I didn't have any real FF plan in place. I needed more asset diversification and a personal financial road map. I was getting by on my earnings each month, but I had little if any money left over to save and invest for my future retirement fund - which became my FF fund.
Had I began saving seriously for FF at age 20, 25, 30, or 35, I could have been further ahead financially. But it was better than not starting at all, so with determined focus, I reached a state of FF by age 48. I didn't have to work if I didn't want to. But I did want to work in industry because it inspired me and meant I could save even more money for retirement. It also meant I'd have more Social Security built-up. Win-win-win!

I chose to remain in the workforce, but this time I began saving most of my excess job income instead of spending it. I placed a lot of my excess income in investment-grade (AA or AAA) corporate bonds. But I was still heavily invested in real estate when the financial crisis of 2008 hit and most of my bonds were in the financial sector. Yikes! Those were the two hardest hit industries when Leman Brothers went bankrupt on September 15th, 2008, the housing market collapsed, and the financial markets froze within days. The United States and Europe approached financial Armageddon. I was hit hard. I owned a lot of Leman Brother's mortgage-back bonds too.

I also owned four million dollars in real estate which was divided among five custom homes I had either built or purchased for investment and rental purposes - all with mortgages. Some went into foreclosure. I managed to avoid bankruptcy and hang on to the best property I had designed and built. Fortunately, that property retained its equity, continued to generate positive rental income, and provided a very nice roof over our heads due to the fact that it was over five thousand square feet and we could rent out several rooms we no longer needed to a tenant. Our home with the added bonus of rental income, plus part-time teaching and AEC consulting gigs, began to stabilize my finances.

My wife's full-time accounting job and my remaining investment grade corporate bonds (that paid 6% to 7% in interest) helped too. It took all of that and more to get through a major financial crisis that was second in magnitude only to the great depression of the 1930's. But full-time W-2 income for me personally was becoming a thing of the past since my older age and a devastated economy made it nearly impossible to find full-time work in the foreseeable future. Age discrimination in the work force is alive and well, despite constitutional protections to the contrary.

My financial freedom had been extended once again because this time I *had* to work to pay bills, put our son through college, and recoup my investment losses. Aside from the sizable equity we had in our million dollar home, I still had a lot of financial catching up to do.

As I approached my mid-to-late fifties, our financial picture steadily improved. I saved cash, re-diversified my bond and stock portfolio, stopped buying foreign cars, continued to teach and consult part-time, raised the rents on our rental unit, and applied early for Social Security. My forty year quest as an architect, builder, educator, and IT entrepreneur has been both agony and ecstasy. It's been as exhilarating as it's been demanding and challenging. It's hard to second guess if past actions were right or wrong, given what I knew then. In some cases, I'd definitely make different choices, but in other cases I wouldn't. Obliviously, had I started my FF quest earlier then age forty, and had I seized certain opportunities and avoided others, I could have been richer and FF sooner. What matters now is financially freedom was achieved, and in my case, it took a period of about one generation.

A paradigm shift in our recent lifestyle involved leaving the high cost state of California, selling our home and investment property, increasing our liquidity in securities and low risk CD's, and building a new custom estate in Dallas, Texas. By late November of 2019, those dreams were realized. It was one of the most ambitions endeavors we ever embarked on and took a tremendous energy toll. We had to constantly manage design details and maintain budgets for building a new home, selling our existing property (both of which were highly custom), moving a lifetime of assets half way across the country - all while dealing daily with lenders, vendors, shippers, and builders. Selling our primary home of 30+ years was the biggest asset we owned. As the listing broker, it translated into additional income instead of a selling expense. More importantly, it allowed us to free-up trapped equity. It also allowed us to stop managing rental property, which was becoming more and more difficult and expensive in California. Instead, I can focus on writing books, brokering and investing in real estate, teaching financial literacy, and part-time AEC consulting. Hobbies are involved too, like photography, flamenco guitar, and HO model railroads. There's also family and friends that are spread around the country and globe.

Life in the second largest city the United States had served a good purpose in our lives and careers. But the time had come to leave those opportunities behind, and along with them, intercity crime, rampant homelessness, over population, insane traffic, and high living costs. We now live on two acres of land surrounded by nature and wildlife in a brand new home we designed located forty five minutes away from a major metropolitan city. Except for high property taxes, the cost of living in Texas is affordable and the quality of life is high. We're debt free, other than a manageable mortgage at 2.625% APR fixed,. Everything else is owned free and clear and all expenses and credit cards are paid in full with cash. Income and expenses are managed just as carefully as before. Only now, passive income pays all the bills. The FF plan described in this book, and the chapter on getting a college education that is viable and priced sensibly, worked for myself, my wife, and our son in ways that were enormously beneficial. I hope this book severs as inspiration to help others too.

This is the true story of how it happened.

Intentionally Blank

CHAPTER 1

Step 1: Financial Freedom Fundamentals *(F^3)*

Introduction to Financial Freedom:

Freedom to live...or...Slavery to Work and Debt?

To Kids and Teens: *Are you interested in learning about why some people have money and others don't? Do you ever wonder why a price tag seems high or low? Do you want to learn how to make sound financial choices as you get older and have to earn a living?*

To Parents and Adults: *Do you have a road map for your current and future financial well being? And, if you do have adequate financial status right now, are you living life to your full potential? Or, are you among the living dead?*

To Everyone: *What does Financial Freedom (FF) really mean?*

Your journey to financial freedom begins with questions like these.

Think hard about the answers. Otherwise, you're walking through life in the dark.

The purpose of achieving Financial Freedom (FF) - also called Financial Independence (FI) or Retirement - is to freely choose what you want to DO and BE in your life without having to work for yourself or somebody else - unless you ***choose*** to. The concept is easy. Realizing FF takes time and hard work.

Obviously, it's normal to work for a company or in your own business during your career growth years. Even working later until you're in your sixties or seventies is not uncommon today. But after a certain point, you will need more than relying on job income to live. You will need freedom: Freedom to do what you love best; Freedom from debt; Freedom from toxic people; Freedom from driving to work in grid-lock traffic; Freedom to have your bills paid whether you work at a job or not; Freedom from other people's money controlling you; *and, if you DO want to work*; freedom to choose the type of work you like to do, and the amount of time you spend doing it.

Pursuing your dreams is a God-given desire that lies deep in our DNA. It's your birth right and mission in life that only YOU can protect and nurture.

Realizing FF doesn't happen overnight. The average work cycle for most adults begins in your early-to-mid twenties and ends around your late fifties to your mid sixties. That's thirty five to forty years of working! If you spend most of your money, you may not have enough left to live on during retirement. *Therefore, it's imperative to save and invest money while you still earn income from a job.* To do that successfully takes strategy, discipline, steady work, tenacity, various skill sets, education, a willingness to learn, a willingness to change, and time. Lots of time. FF is similar to retirement, but it differs in that FF is a goal you can attain at any age – not just old age - depending on your degree of commitment and financial inteligence.

Retirement often means working for thirty or forty years, and then piecing (or scrapping) together what's left of one's money and health. By then you hope you can squeeze out a few remaining good years (or decades) of joy in life. Statistically, this happens in unpredictable ways as humans get older. Some people have very good pensions and are able to live well in retirement. Many more do not.

That's because company-paid pensions, known as "defined benefit plans", cost too much and are virtually extinct today. The exception are public employee pensions and a small handful of large corporate pensions. People may live longer today, and death will always be an unknown future date. The key is being prepared. A large number of retirees live below the poverty line and/or require financial and medical assistance from family, charity, or the government. Social Security (SS) helps, but the roughly $100 to $4000 a month in benefits it may provide can be eaten up by monthly living expenses. Social Security is a good source of FF income, but it may not be enough by itself.

How do you begin? The way to start is by constantly thinking about your money matters. Why? Because thinking about your money turns into financial awareness. Financial awareness leads to learning about financial strategies, action, and determination. Financial strategy, action, and determination ultimately lead to financial intelligence. Financial intelligence ultimately leads to *financial freedom* (FF).

Financial Freedom means your bills are being paid and income is being generated ***passively***, rather than from *active* employment. An example of passive income would be your bank savings or other investments that generate interest, dividends, or rental cash flow. This type of money (passive income) is automatically generated in addition to your job income.

Once you build-up enough passive income, the interest, dividends, or rental cash flow can pay for most or all of your monthly expenditures necessary to have a place to live, eat, get medical care, travel, commute, play, practice your art, contribute your talent, or in essence, live the life you want to live without slavery to a job or debt. But first you need a paying job and you have to work and save wisely for a lot of years. That's why it's critical to learn about financial literacy as early as possible. It's also why choosing a viable and correctly priced college education for your kid (or yourself) is critical too. Just ask any recent four-year college graduate or two-year post graduate student how much their school loans are and you'll find that the amounts are staggering more often than not.

This *cycle* of "automatic revenue generation" (passive income) covering ***all*** your monthly bills (expenses) repeats itself every month for the rest of your life, freeing you to pursue your *soul* purpose and joy in life. That could mean quitting work, engaging in a hobby or passion, or pursuing any number of activities. Or, it could mean remaining in the work force on terms you're OK with and without the worry of inadequate job income because your bills are already being paid by passive income.

After reaching FF, income from a job is simply extra money you can spend, reinvest, save, donate, or do whatever you wish with. Careers can be fun and lucrative with the right company, salary, and position. A job, on the other hand, is usually something we endure begrudgingly in exchange for earning a pay check to live on.

Careers and jobs are both necessary to earn money. The difference between a satisfying, well paying career and a mediocre job involves a lot of variables, but a big component is having a good college education and seizing opportunities others miss seeing. Some people call FF "retirement", while others refer to it as "financial independence" (FI). For some, FF means inheritance. Some people obtain FF status overnight through marriage or winning the lotto. But essentially, they are all forms of financial freedom and boil down to the same destination. The key distinction is who's controlling the money: *You or someone else?*

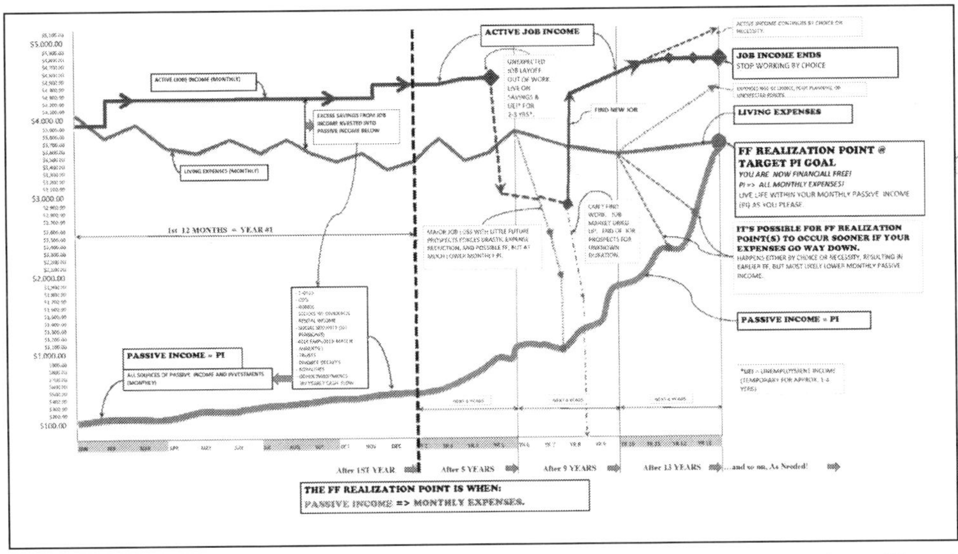

Above is a graph that illustrates how FF looks when plotted over time (X axis) in relation to money (Y axis). It shows the ***FF Realization Point.*** This will be explained in more detail later.

Answer: FF = FI

*** FF = Financial Freedom**

***FI = Financial Independence**

Quiz:

What does *FF mean?

What does *FI mean?

Are they the same or different?

For most people, financial freedom is achieved by earning money at a job or career over many years, spending less than you earn, and carefully placing that extra money in low-risk, low-cost investments that generate "free money". It might take five, ten, fifteen, twenty, or thirty years of working in a job and investing your savings to generate enough extra monthly cash flow that pays all your bills.

At that point, whether you continue to work at a job for money becomes a *choice,* not a *necessity*. However, it's imperative to learn to live within your means by not blowing the nest egg that's providing all this (free) cash flow. That means spending wisely and preserving your passive income sources. History is chalk full of lotto winners, entertainment celebrities, sports figures, and spoiled or financially naïve individuals that gained access to millions, spent it all, and ended up broke.

***FF = Financial Freedom**

***FI = Financial Independence**

***FF = FI**

***FF = Retirement on your terms, not societies rules or stigmas.**

**(Future changes in your lifestyle, unforeseen events, and sudden money emergences can always occur. Therefore, maintaining FF is just as important as reaching it. This is discussed in more detail in Chapter 5.)*

The Basic FF Concept…*FF in a Nut Shell*

Financial Freedom in a Nut Shell

Below are the Five Basic Steps to achieving Financial Freedom (FF). They represent the essence of what FF is all about. You need to learn, embrace, and faithfully execute them - no matter how long it takes! Read these five basic steps and remember them. You will learn more about each step in subsequent chapters and from other recommended teachings outside this book. Then, get to work and apply them to your life starting now!

1) **Step 1. Financial Freedom Fundamentals.** *Some estimates suggest that up to 95% of the world's population is financially illiterate. Therefore, you must establish financial objectives, understand common myths and realities about money, and learn fundamental definitions used in money matters related to finance and accounting throughout the world - including your own.*

2) **Step 2. Cost Control**. *Transform your spending habits and grab hold of costs using proven methods used in business. Spend less than you earn, then save and invest the difference (wisely and conservatively in step 4). Create a Personal Balance Sheet to establish your assets, liabilities, and net worth.*

3) **Step 3. Income Control.** *Earn (or legally obtain) money during a certain period of your working life. Establish all your active income and passive income sources. Create a Personal Income Statement to establish your revenue, expenses, and net income.*

4) **Step 4. Investment Control. Make your Money work for You**. *The money you save and invest generates "liquidity and free cash flow" (cash reserves, interest, dividends, capital gains), which, over time, will generate passive income that pays your bills.*

5) **Step 5. Reaching Financial Freedom.** *Integrating all the steps of your FF journey. Investing wisely, safely, and profitably. Choose to work, or NOT to, and eliminate toxic people in your life. You're now free to do what you love the rest of your life – all expenses paid - as long as you live within your means. Finding (or continuing) your passion in life.*

Coming Soon... Break time and a fun comic story!

Step 1: Financial Freedom Fundamentals - *The Intro*

FF *= Financial Freedom = The end of having to work for money, in order to financially survive and enjoy life. You can still work in a job for money, but it's a choice, not a necessity. It boils down to being able to choose when to work for money, and when not to, in order to survive financially.*
Age is irrelevant.

FI *= Financial Independence = FF*

Retirement *= FF, but usually at an older age, like 55 or 70.*

Therefore, FF = FI *= Retirement.*

Why study to become FF? *Answer: Financial illiteracy is rampant throughout the world primarily because it is not taught to us as children or young adults by parents, schools, or society. Thus, you have to diligently seek answers elsewhere on your own!*

How do I do the steps? *Answer: Each step is based on various "What, Why, Purpose, & How" arguments, followed by step-by-step homework exercises.*

Step 1 - More Details

What do FF, FI, and Retirement mean?
Essentially, they all mean the same thing. Financial Freedom (FF) is an innate desire and need that virtually every human being has. It means having (or generating) passive income (investments, endowments, non-work related income), in order to pay essential monthly bills - without having to perform "active" work (i.e. a job) unless you want to work.

How? It's more of a life-long process and way of valuing and funding the quality of your life - for the rest of your life - as opposed to a crash college course or book read.

If it takes a month to do step one, four months to complete step two, and a year, two, or three to get through the rest, so be it. The objective of learning FF is reaching FF....regardless of when. Obviously, when it comes to achieving FF, earlier is good. But life is hard and full of risks. Each of us must chart our own path relative to the strengths, weakness, talents, skills, and circumstances that make us unique human beings on one hand, and infinitely connected on the other.

Why learn about becoming FF? *Because Financial illiteracy is rampant.*
It's time to face reality and educate yourself about *your* money and Financial Literacy. The question remains: Why does the vast majority of the world's population remain illiterate about their money? Financial literacy education is a road that has been traveled and documented by many astute people throughout history. But it is not necessarily a well-traveled road because it is seldom ever taught to us as children or young adults. Therefore, you have to look hard to find sources of information that can truly teach you financial literacy in meaningful ways. Schools are often not in that mix. In fact, most schools don't teach (personal) financial literacy at all. Neither do most parents, religion, or work environments. It's up to YOU to seek the truth about managing money if you want to become FF.

***How do I do each step?**
Each step is based on various "*What, Why, Purpose, & How*" arguments, followed by homework exercises. For example, determining your *personal net worth* entails the exact same formula used in business, and serves nearly the exact same purpose. If you buy a car or a house, banks need to know your net worth. If you go bankrupt, or get a divorce, courts need to know your net worth for equitably asset distribution. If you establish a living trust, your net worth needs to be known to establish your "estate value" that goes into the trust. If you die, courts need to know your net worth for tax and inheritance distribution purposes. But even more important is: *You need to know your net worth while you're alive.* Therefore, you need to establish the true cash value of everything you own.

****A special note about the upcoming Steps 2 - 5:***
To become FF, you must first become financially aware (Step 1). Then you must follow a proven financial plan. To do that requires Cost Control (Step 2) and Income Control (Step 3). This teaches you how to calculate and track your assets, debts, net worth, income and expenses. Then, you need savings and investment control (Step 4). Finally, you need to learn how to put all the steps together (Step 5) to achieve and maintain FF. Thus, each step builds upon the previous one.

Step 2. Cost Control - *The Intro*

The Purpose of Cost Control, *or CC,* *is to reveal what your actual spending habits are really like. You will learn ways to control your spending, instead of spending controlling you.*

The 3 main parts of Cost Control are:

Part A: *Creating an inventory list of all the personal stuff (assets) you own.*

Part B: *Determining your total Net Worth by creating a Personal Balance Sheet. This shows you what you're really worth, up to the present moment, measured in cash.*

Note: Net Worth (NW) and Equity (E) mean the same thing.
The formula looks like this:

Net Worth (NW) = Assets(A) – Liabilities(L)

Or simply ... NW = A - L

Part C: *Spending Control: Tracking what you spend from now on.*

Learn to control your spending, rather than having your spending control you. To do that, you have to learn to track what you spend.

Step 3. Income Control - *The Intro*

The Purpose of Income Control (IC) *is to know how much money you earn and receive, and how much, if any, is left after you spend it each day, week, month, and year.*

The Three Main Parts of Income Control are:

Part A. *Create a* **list** *of all your personal* ***monthly Income (I) sources*** *and* ***Expense (E)*** *categories.*

Part B. ***Subtract*** *the exact amounts of money that you* ***spend as Expenses*** *from the money you* ***earn (or receive) as Income.*** *Therefore, subtract as follows:*
Income – Expenses = Your net income (before tax) each month. *If you receive a W2 pay check, taxes would typically be deducted by your employer.*

Part C. *(Optional)* ***Convert*** *$* ***dollar amounts*** *from part B* ***into*** *hours of human* ***time*** *= hours of your time used = your life force that is being used-up and cannot be replenished.*

Step 4. Investment Control - *The Intro*

Investment Control *(IC) means learning and implementing safe and profitable ways to invest the savings you generate from your earned income so it can grow bigger.*

Passive Income *has several meanings. For some, passive income means rental income from real estate only, while income from securities like stocks and bonds is called "investment income". For the purposes of this chapter, both investment categories are considered "passive income".*

IC and Passive Income are important because *you typically need your base savings (principal)* ***plus*** *the extra money generated from the investment (interest, dividends, rent, etc.) to live off of in the future when you become FF.*

Learning about investing takes time!

What about investment advisors and brokers*? Be careful. First, learn by reading FF books and asking tough questions before you hand over your money to an investment broker.*

Investments *are categorized by "****Asset Classes****" or "****Investment Vehicles****". They both mean the same thing. For example, stocks are an asset class. Bonds are another. Rental income from real estate is another asset class. Each has its own risk and reward.*

Step 5. Reaching Financial Freedom - *The Intro*

*FF is when: {Your Investment Income - Your Expenses} **=> 0***

The Purpose of Reaching Financial Freedom:

The purpose of Step 5 (reaching FF) is integrating all the previous steps of your FF journey (Steps 1-4) . This in turn allows you to realistically become financial free, and then ultimately maintain it for the rest of your life.

How to do Step 5? *Several approaches exist.*

1. One way is to write down in detail all your Expenses, Job Income, and Investment Income, compare the results, and review it often.

2. Another way is to create a visual graph (or chart) that shows your Expenses, Job Income, and Investment Income over time (visual version of #1 above).

3. The goal is to have (your Investment Income minus your Expenses) be equal to or greater than zero on a SUSTAINED basis.

Key Questions and Concepts in Step 5

How much money do you need to live on?
How much money you're saving and investing each year?
Interest Rates; (AKA "The Cost of Capital", "Return Rate", or "Yield").
How much more money you may need in case you run short?
The age you start saving?
The approximate age you begin to live entirely off your investments? (Begin FF)
How to calculate the answers to the above questions?

What FF Investment Formulas and Strategies to use:

FF Investment Method #1: Annual estimating approach.
FF Investment Method #2: Monthly estimating approach.

An Historical Look at Ancient Money Matters and the Influence of Technology on our lives.

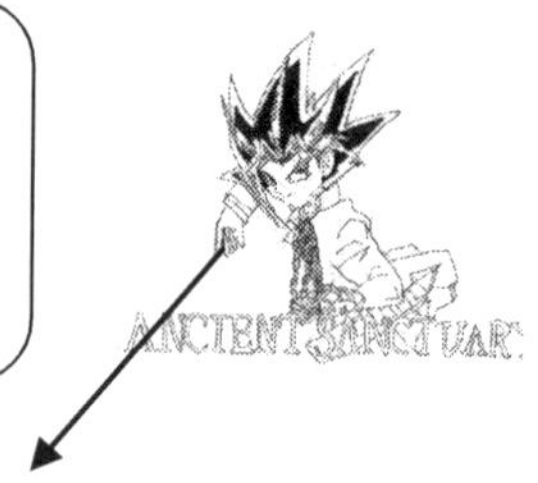

The importance of money matters existed well before the Greek and Roman empires. As Egyptian, Middle Eastern, Persian, European, Mongolian, Chinese, Japanese, and other ancient civilizations grew, financial literacy became increasingly important to building and sustaining those empires beyond war and pillaging conquests. That evolved into trading, buying and selling, which in turn necessitated currency exchange and establishing the value of goods and services.

Despite constant wars, finance and accounting fundamentals became more prevalent during the expansion of the Roman Empire, and later again during Mongolian and Chinese expansion conquests. Paralleling those events was the European Renaissance, as the expanding role of bankers like the Medici's helped finance tremendous advances in art, architecture, and infrastructure projects throughout Europe. 1500 years after the birth of Christ, money matters expanded on a global scale with bold and risky exploration conquests by Italian, Portuguese, Spanish, Dutch, and British empires - especially between the 1400's through the 1890's.

Modern day money matters began to take shape during the industrial age as British and American entrepreneurs paved the way during the late 19th and early 20th centuries. Bankers, railroad tycoons, oil barons, steam power, electricity generation - along with steel, auto, ship, and plane manufacturing - increased productivity, corporate profits, and personal fortunes unlike the world had ever seen. The British invented the double entry method of book keeping over 200 years ago, which is still the gold standard in modern day accounting.

The next quantum leap in money and technology advances occurred after World War II with the dawn of nuclear power, mainframe computers, and exponential industrial innovation on a scale that was unimaginable. Just several decades earlier, the world was thrown into the first global war (WWI), followed by a global financial depression a decade later in 1929. It took nearly25 years for stocks to recoup their value after the great depression - from 1929 to 1954.

Decades later, another revolution began in the mid 1970's with the dawn of the personal desk top computer, like the MIT's Altair heath kit computer and the Apple I and II personal computers. Then in 1981, IBM jumped into the personal computing market and exploded the desktop computer revolution wide open with the IBM XT and AT personal computers running Microsoft (MS) DOS. MS Windows eventually took the PC world by storm in 1992, which replaced DOS applications permanently. Another quantum leap occurred between 1989 through 1993 with the creation of the World Wide Web by British scientist Tim Burners Lee and the global expansion of the Internet.

But the secrets to wealth and power accumulation remained mostly in the hands of the rich, the elite, government entities, corporate cartels, and organized criminals. Seldom did it reach the masses in the form of education until the 20th century. "*Think and Grow Rich*" by Napoleon Hill was one such book published in 1937, which taught common people how to create wealth. It was far ahead of its time but didn't gain mass public attention until much later. Some conspiracy theories suggest that wealthy elites worked hard to have it removed from book shelves early on for fear of having their wealth secrets revealed.

Whether true or not, his book is still available after eighty million copies and remains one of the first publically available teachings on wealth creation in step-by-step fashion. More FF education in the form of books, TV shows, radio shows, and seminars began to surface in the latter half of the 20th century by a handful men and women who learned how to achieve financial freedom and wanted to teach those skills to others.

We are now living in the highly connected world of the Information Age. Physical boundaries are blurred and entire continents are bridged with networks, servers, workstations, desktop computers, laptops, phones, tablets, PDA's and infinite lines of software code. In free countries, and even many autocratic ones, information and research are readily available. History teaches most of what we need to know when we heed and embrace its endless wisdom. We have two eyes. Keep one looking ahead toward the future, and the other looking back to learn from history.

Developing the ability to see both the big picture, as well as the details, is a primary thrust behind this book. Mastering your Money Matters is also a skill that requires a combination of looking forward to your future, as well as looking back at what history teaches. Both hindsight and foresight are essential to mastering your money matters. This also applies to getting a college education that's priced sensibly and provides lifelong skills that equip you with real earning power.

What are you doing Billy? Playing with that tissue box again? You're almost in 7th grade! What are you going to do when you grow up?

I know what I am going to do! I am learning all I can about financial literacy, and later I want to learn how to apply it in my life as an adult.

Good grades in Middle school and High school are key. Then off to a top-tier university. And, I want very little or no debt after I graduate!

An Introduction to the FF Realization Point

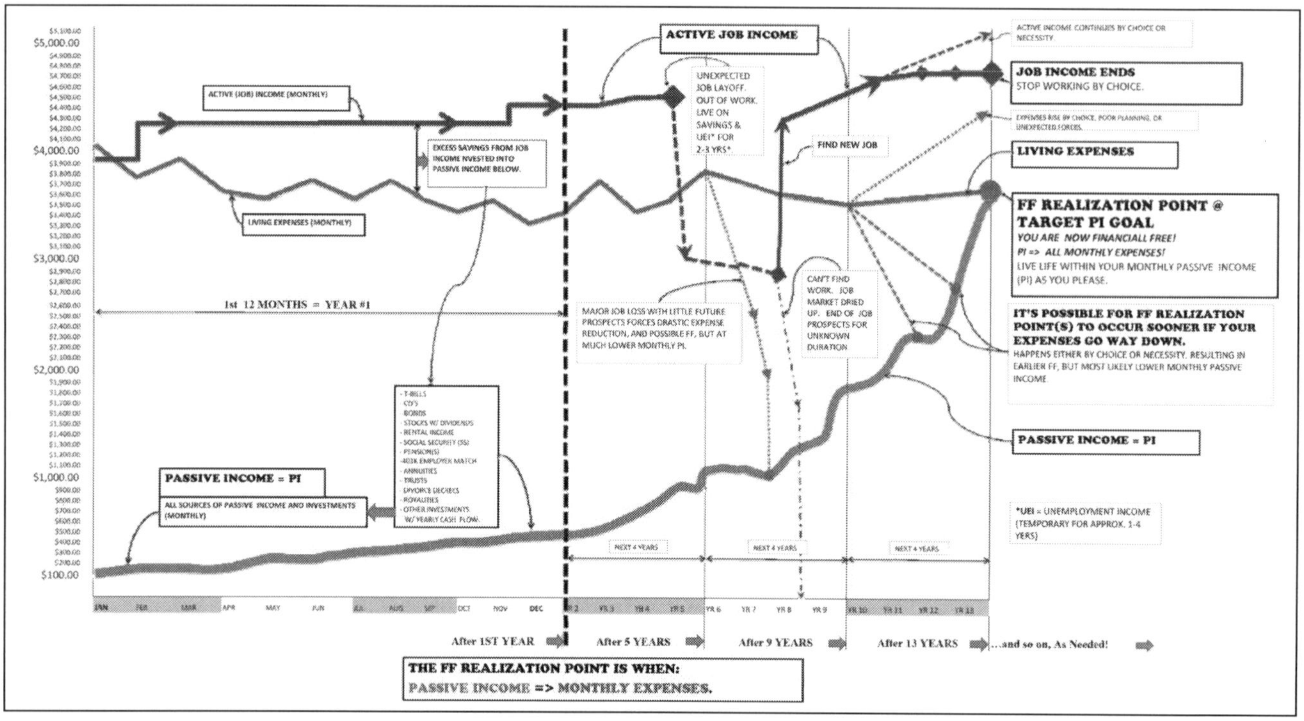

The FF Realization Point = The point in time in which You Become Financially Free (FF). This happens when _excess_ Job Income (top blue line) - which _when invested into Passive Income_ (bottom green curve) - equals or exceeds (all) your monthly Living Expenses...Permanently! (middle red curve).

History Teaches That:

To build a House without going broke or getting divorced, you need a good set of architectural and engineering plans.

To create and run a profitable and lasting business without going bankrupt, you need a good Business Plan.

To deal with people effectively, you need to know your strengths and weaknesses, and spend the time to correct your blind spots.

And, to succeed financially in life, you need a good Financial Plan and the right college education that's priced sensibly!

In the next chapter (Step 2), you will learn how to *calculate your true net worth* and how to *manage your spending* by thoroughly immersing yourself in Cost Control.

Next: Break time!
Time to rest your brain and read Sean's Cartoon Corner in ***APPENDIX A.***

Can you figure out the plot? Better yet, let your imagination run wild and think of your own story. Maybe one day you will be an artist, writer, business owner, or...? The key is to listen to your heart's desire, and ignore people's negative comments. Listen to your inner voice and follow your instincts.

See Appendix A.

CHAPTER 2

Step 2: Cost Control

Step 2. Cost Control - *Overview*

Questions:

What is the purpose of Cost Control = CC?
What are the 3 main components of Cost Control (Parts A, B, & C)?
Part A: What is an inventory list?
Part B: What does "Net Worth" and "Equity" mean?
What are Assets and Liabilities?
Part C: What does Spending Control mean?

Answers:

The Purpose of Cost Control: *Cost control will establish your real net worth (in dollars) at the present moment in time, and equally important, reveal your actual spending habits.*

The three main parts of Cost Control are:
Part A*: Creating an inventory list of your personal stuff (certain basic fixed assets).*
Part B*: Establishing your Net Worth by creating a Personal Balance Sheet (all assets and debts).*
Part C*: Spending Control: Tracking the money you spend from now on.*

Part A: An Inventory List: An inventory list is a written account of a portion of your most basic personal material possessions (known as fixed assets), like cloths, jewelry, tools, furniture, electronics, hobby items, etc. (Note: Your inventory list will not include cash, stocks, bonds, cars, real estate or businesses you may own. Those represent the balance of your total assets. Assets must be separated into two categories - "liquid" and "fixed". These other assets are added later to your personal balance sheet in Part B as separate line items.) Therefore, you're going to track only basic fixed assets in Part A.

Part B: Finding your Net Worth (NW) = your Equity (E). NW and E mean the same thing*.** Therefore, NW = E. Net Worth and Equity measure the absolute cash value of all the assets that you currently own, minus any loans (or debt) that you may have against those assets. Net Worth simply shows what you (or a business) are worth in cash, after adding up everything you own and subtracting all debts. How? Take your Inventory List (Part A), ***add all your cash, stocks, bonds, real estate, autos, and business equity (Part B), and then subtract any debts you may owe to people and banks. The formula has three parts: Assets, Liabilities, and Net Worth. The formula looks like this: ***Net Worth = Assets – Liabilities.*** *Simply put, NW = A - L.*

Assets and Liabilities
Assets = All your material possessions (inventory + liquid cash + autos + real estate + all else);
Liabilities = Any money you owe to others (usually this debt is against your assets);
Net Worth = The difference between the two: Therefore, *Net Worth = Assets - Liabilities.*

Part C: Spending Control: Track your spending using a Monthly Expense Report
The purpose of Spending Control is to track the money you spend each day, week, month and year. Why? So you can expose your spending patterns, make corrections, and then learn to control your spending, rather than spending controlling you.

<u>Step 2. Cost Control</u> - *The Details*

Parts A, B, and C: Creating an inventory list, a personal balance sheet, and a monthly expense report. *This will establish your true net worth at the present moment in time and reveal what your actual spending habits are really like. Some expenses are unavoidable, while others are self-induced. Only you can control "you" (and your spending).*

Why? All legitimate businesses, governments, institutions, and organizations produce balance sheets in order to see an accurate and up-to-date picture of their total assets (current and fixed), liabilities (current and fixed), and net worth (equity). This is done at least once a year, but more often every week, month or quarter. Creating your own inventory list, personal balance sheet, and monthly expense report is exactly the same process that a company or organization would use to gain accurate insight on their total assets, debts, and equity. Without it, they might go broke.

Therefore, just like a company, you need to know how much you are really worth if you: *Sold off all your possessions, paid off all your debts, and liquidated what's left into pure cash.* The money that is left would be *your total net worth* that has accumulated over your entire life time - up to the present moment - in liquid cash. This is a very sobering exercise because it reveals how much money you've accumulated in life, what you have to show for it, and how easily it gets spent.

Purpose? Becoming aware of your money habits enables you to live within your means by revealing how much you actually spend each month (expense report). Another reason is to measure the money that has entered your entire life up to the present moment, so you can accurately see the sum total of all assets and debts you've accumulated thus far (balance sheet). This in turn will reveal how well (or poorly) you're managing all the cash that enters and leaves your hands If you're married, do this exercise as if you're an individual for personal inventory items, cars, cash, retirement accounts, and securities. Take half the value for things that are jointly owned, like real estate, businesses, or joint bank accounts. Do the same for liabilities.

How?
First you need to tally up certain personal possessions you own and create a ***personal inventory list (Part A).***

Next, you'll transfer your inventory amount over to ***Part B***, and make a ***personal balance*** sheet that shows all of your assets, debts, and equity.

Finally, you'll create a ***monthly expense report*** (***Part C***) by itemizing and placing a cash figure on each and every spending category you have, in order to live your life as you currently do.

Over time, you can review your expense report regularly, make adjustments up or down, and eventually get to the point where you spend less than you earn. But remember this: It takes a lot of time and discipline to reach that point. That's why the earlier in life you begin, the further ahead you'll be as you get older.

Step 2, Part A: Create an inventory list of the following personal assets you own.

Include: Clothing, furniture, jewelry, electronics (audio, games, TV's, phones), guns, musical equipment, tools, books, kitchen and bath articles, garage items, sports gear, and personal hobby items.

Do Not include: Cash, stocks, bonds, retirement accounts, cars, boats, RV's, real estate, or businesses you own. Remember: those assets are added later to your balance sheet in Part B under separate line items. To do this fairly fast, identify large items first by walking around your home or apartment with a sheet of paper, write down the current date, list each asset, and then write down your best guess as to what they would be worth right now if you had to sell them fast for cash. Be realistic and honest with yourself. Use eBay, Amazon, or Craig's List as initial pricing guides. If you want more accuracy, include categories, descriptions, S/N's, what you initially paid, the approximate date you bought them, and a used market price based on research for like items that already sold (eBay, CL, Amazon, The Salvation Army, etc.)

Example #1:

Simple Inventory List. Itemize your personal articles into basic categories, sub-total, then grand total.

1. Clothing	**$2,500**
Shirts (25 @ $20 ea =500)	
Pants, (20 @ $25 ea =500)	
Suits (2 @ 500 ea=1,000)	
Shoes (5@50+1@250= 500)	
2. Computer H/S	**$1,500**
3. Hobby (photo)	**$4,000**
4. Furniture	**$3,500**
5. Jewelry	**$1,000**
==========================	
6. **Total Inventory:**	**$12,500**

Note: Typically there are two kinds of assets: 1) "current, or liquid assets" for things like cash, stocks, and bonds (securities), and; 2) "non-current or fixed assets" for things like property, plant and equipment; (i.e., your vehicles, real estate, boats, RV's, and businesses owned). In the manufacturing and retail business world, company inventory is listed as a "current asset" because it includes raw materials that are ultimately going to be used to make or sell a new product in the marketplace within a short amount of time (less than one year typically). However, your personal inventory is different. It should be listed as a fixed asset (non-current asset) because:

1) They are personal possessions and have more meaning to you than the general public.
2) They are not something you will manufacture or sell new to the public like a company would.
3) They may take longer than a year to liquidate into cash.
4) They might sell for a price that's far lower than you originally paid due to the unpredictable nature of selling used personal items to the general public.

Thus, your personal inventory will be harder to sell and liquidate into cash at full value because it's used, has wide ranging value in the market place, may not sell fast (or not sell at all), and for some items, might sell for a fraction of the price you originally paid. Thus, the current "street" value could be five to ten times less than what you paid new - especially for furniture and clothing items. Therefore, personal inventory must go on your balance sheet under "fixed or non-current assets" because they drop considerably in value and take longer to liquidate into cash (>1 year).

The below *Example Personal Inventory List* shows how detailed you can get if desired. You can include items like audio-video equipment, S/N's, art collections, hobby equipment, tools, or any other personal assets that are unique and necessary for you. (Remember - separate things like cash, stocks, bonds, investments, cars, boats, RV's, real estate, or a business you own, into individual line items that go directly on your balance sheet - not your inventory list.) After you itemize and establish current market values for your personal inventory items in Part A, you will transfer the total cash value of your inventory over to your Balance Sheet under the "Asset" line item called "Inventory"(shown in Part B).

Example #2:

Detailed Example of a Personal Inventory List. *{Step 2, Part A, cont'd}*
This example includes things like: Major category, sub-category, location code (for more than one home),description, Serial no., date (of purchase), cost 1 (if business), cost 2 (if personal), street price, category sub-totals, and total inventory total (on another sheet). Began in 1982 on Apple II. Now done with MS Excel.

AUDIO-VIDEO & ALARM EQUIPMENT

LC	CATEGORY	DESCRIPTION	SERIAL_NO	DATE	COST-BUSINESS	COST-PERSONAL	STREET PRICE
A	AMP	FISHER CA-276 150 W INTEGRATED AMPLIFIER	19374-8436	10/86		350.00	25.00
A	AMP	YAMAHA HTR-5280 500W 6.1 SURROUND AMP W/ 4YR WARR.	Y093740VX	9/23/01	565.00		400.00
A	AMP-CAR	PHILLIPS 100W CAR AMP (50W/CHANNEL)-FROM PORSCHE 911		8/1/86		50.00	25.00
A	AMP_MIXER	YAMAHA EMX2000 POWERED MIXER 8 CHANNEL 200W	PN02043	10/30/99	750.00		450.00
A	DVD	TOSHIBA DVD PROGRESSIVE SCAN SD-3750	18PL113016	10/24/01	216.00		150.00
A	VCR	JVC SVHS HR-S9500U	113M0935	11/26/99	725.00		200.00
A	VCR	RCA SVHS 725 VCR (MODEL VR725HF)	610630067	2/1/97		421.00	25.00
A	VCR	FISHER 3 HD STEREO VCR		1/1/85		275.00	10.00
A	DSS	SONY DSS 32 BIT SAT TV RECV. SAT-B3 W/DISH	8026870	6/1/98		200.00	50.00
A/B	DSS	HUGHES DSS 16 BIT SAT TV RECV. HIRD-B2 W/ DISH	B25343E200B3	3/1/98		0.00	50.00
A	STERO	SONY RX66 60W MINI STERO CD/TAPE/AMFM/RCA/IN-OUT	8884286	10/15/98	200.00		45.00
A	STERO	FISHER AM/FM TUNER FM-273	57244	1/1/85		175.00	20.00
A	STERO-CAR	ALPINE AM/FM CASSETT CAR STERO - 7163		8/1/86		200.00	20.00
A	ALARM-CAR	VIPER STEAL STOPPER 300 PC CAR ALARM		8/1/86		300.00	45.00
A	SYNTH	ROLAND JX-305 GROOVE SYNTHISIZER	ZL14022	10/30/99	756.00		450.00
A	TURNTABLE	TURNTABLE - GEMINI BELT DRIVE XL 400	GT8413742	10/30/99	108.00		50.00
A	MICROPHONE	SURE BETA56 GUITAR MIC W/ BOOM ARM ADJ. STAND	NA	10/31/99	180.00		130.00
A	MICROPHONE	SAMSON S1 VOICE MIC W/ ADJ. VERT. STAND	NA	10/31/99	60.00		50.00
A	CASSETTES	CASSETTE TAPES TOTAL 50	NA	N/A		100.00	25.00
A	RECORDER	CASSETTE RECORDER - PORTABLE SONY WALKMAN PROFESSIONAL	NA	5/1/95		212.00	35.00
A	VHSTAPES	VHS TAPES FOR VCR TOTAL=20	NA	N/A		200.00	25.00
A	CD	CD 'S - MUSIC TOTAL 10	NA				50.00
A	CABLES	MIC_CABLES - 25' SHIELDED CABLE-3 PRONG LOCK CONNECTOR	NA	N/A	40.00		25.00
A	CABLES	MIC_CABLES - 25' SHIELDED CABLE-3 PRONG LOCK CONNECTOR	NA	N/A	40.00		25.00
A	CABLES	SPEAKER_CABLES - 25' SHIELDED CABLE- RCA CONNECTOR	NA	N/A	40.00		25.00
A	CABLES	SPEAKER_CABLES - 25' SHIELDED CABLE-RCA CONNECTOR	NA	N/A	40.00		25.00
A	CABLES	INSTRUMENT CABLES - 25' SHIELDED NEUTRICK RCA CONNECTOR	NA	N/A	25.00		20.00
A	CABLES	INSTRUMENT CABLES - 25' SHIELDED NEUTRICK RCA CONNECTOR	NA	N/A	25.00		20.00
A	CABLES	A/V PATCH CORDS - 10 RCA A/V & 4 S-VIDEO	NA	N/A	150.00		50.00
A	SPEAKER	RCA 100W CENTER SPEAKER - 40-5011	NA	10/13/01	81.00		50.00
A	SPEAKER	BES SM 280 (R) SPEAKER	824109	11/1/86		350.00	150.00
A	SPEAKER	BES SM 280 (L) SPEAKER	827907	11/1/86		350.00	150.00
A	SPEAKER	VECTOR RESEARCH SPEAKER VS9	NA	1/1/85		320.00	75.00
A	SPEAKER	VECTOR RESEARCH SPEAKER VS9	NA	1/1/85		320.00	75.00
A	SPEAKER	ROLAND 12" 150W 8OHM SPEAKERS SST-151	ZK80840	10/30/99	217.00		150.00
A	SPEAKER	ROLAND 12" 150W 8OHM SPEAKERS SST-151	ZK80924	10/30/99	217.00		150.00
A	SPEAKER	SONY 6" 60W SPEAKERS	8884286	10/15/98	25.00		10.00
A	SPEAKER	SONY 6" 60W SPEAKERS	8884286	10/15/98	25.00		10.00
A	GUIT.SYSTH	ROLAND GR-20 GUITAR SYNTHISIZER (FOR GODIN GUITARS & OTHERS)		7/20/07	600.00		650.00
A	LOOPER	BOSS / ROLAND RC-2 LOOP BACK RECORDER & PLAYBACK FOR GUIT		3/31/08	155.00		200.00
A	DIG. DELAY	BOSS / ROLAND DC-20 DIGITAL DELAY FOR GUITAR		3/31/08	200.00		220.00
A	ON/OFF SW	BOSS / ROLAND ON/OFF FOOT SWITCH (FOR LOOPER ON/OFF CONTROL)		3/31/08	20.00		35.00
A	POWER/DISB	POWER SUPPY AND DISTRIBUTION HUB (5 DEVICES) -POWERS LOOPER, DELAY		3/31/08	38.00		35.00
A	AMP	CRATE 50W ACOUSTIC AMP		8/12/07	180.00		150.00
A	AMP	MARSHALL 100W SPEAKER BTM CAB & HEAD		12/15/05	1000.00		700.00
A	AMP	FENDER PASSPORT 100W AMP & MIXER - BOSE SPEAKER DESIGN		10/5/07	750.00		750.00
A	AMP	ROLAND JC-120 AMP		3/31/08	700.00		800.00
		SUB TOTAL - BUSINESS	$4,485.00				
		SUB TOTAL - PERSONAL	$3,823.00				
		TOTAL AUDIO/VIDEO....IORIG. COST	**$8,308.00**				
		TOTAL AUDIO/VIDEO....ISTREET VALUE		**$3,340.00**			

COMPUTER HARDWARE

LC	CATEGORY	DESCRIPTION	SERIAL_NO	DATE	COST-BUSINESS	COST-PERSONAL	STREET PRICE
A	MONITOR	RCA 52" PROJECTION HDTV MONITOR W/ 4 YR ONSITE WARR.	46230365	9/30/01	1866.00		1650.00
A	MONITOR	MITS.3305 33" MULIT-SYC MON., 1024,768		1/1/92	2200.00		200.00
A	CALCULATOR	HP-12C FINANCIAL CALCULATOR	3202B11185	12/1/91	75.00		50.00
A	TAPEBACKUP	IRWIN 250 MEG INT.TAPE BACKUP		3/1/92	250.00		5.00
A	TAPEBACKUP	IRWIN 250 MEG EXT. TAPE BACKUP		4/1/92	350.00		5.00
A	COMPUTER	DELL LATITUDE CPX J650GT LAPTOP 256MEG 10GIG CD 100BT FD CASE	GP6Z301	11/5/01	882.00		1000.00
A	COMPUTER	PENTIUM III 750MHZ 198 MRAM 40 GIG CD FD SPKRS 40G TAPE WIN2000	NA	1/0101	200.00		225.00
A	COMPUTER	PENTIUM II 233MHZ 128 MRAM 12 GIG FD SOUND WINNT	NA	1/1/98	800.00		75.00
A	COMPUTER	PC 486-50 1.4FD 64MG 1.2 GIG HD	OC486-03	10/1/91	3,500.00		25.00
A	COMPUTER	SGI 02 128MRAM 2 GIG 17" VIDEO CD WIN 95 IRIX 6.3 A/W ALIAS 8		7/1/97	6500.00		750.00
A	COMPUTER	SGI 02 128MRAM 2 GIG 17" VIDEO CD WIN 95 IRIX 6.3 A/W ALIAS 8		7/1/97	6500.00		750.00
A	COMPUTER	SGI 02 128MRAM 2 GIG 17" VIDEO CD WIN 95 IRIX 6.3 A/W ALIAS 8		7/1/97	6500.00		750.00
A	COMPUTER	SGI 02 128MRAM 24GIG 17" VIDEO CD WIN 95 IRIX 6.3 A/W ALIAS 8		7/1/97	6500.00		750.00
C	COMPUTER	AMD 350 MHZ 256MRAM 20 GIG WINNT DDWUSA.COM	NA	10/1/99	950.00		150.00
C	COMPUTER	AMD 400 MHZ 128MRAM 20 GIG WINNT ORACLE8I SVR	NA	10/1/99	700.00		100.00
C	COMPUTER	AMD 400 MHZ 128MRAM 30 GIG WIN2000 MEDIA7 SVR	NA	6/1/96	700.00		100.00
C	COMPUTER	FUTURE SERVER - ORACLE					
C	COMPUTER	FUTURE SERVER - EMAIL					
A	UPS	UPS -800RT APC POWER BACKUP		6/1/93		450.00	100.00
A	MONITOR	MONITOR ARM EXTIONSION 150LB		3/1/92	150.00		25.00
A	MONITOR	MITS.6915 16" MULIT-SYC MON.,1024,768	3501878	4/1/92	675.00		65.00
A	MONITOR	MITS.6915 16" MULIT-SYC MON.,1024,768	3501878	4/1/92	675.00		65.00
A	MONITOR	MITS.6915 16" MULIT-SYC MON.,1024,768	3501878	4/1/92	675.00		65.00

Step 2, Part B: ***Determine your total net worth: Create a Personal Balance Sheet.***

A balance sheet has (3) components: 1) Assets (what you own); 2) Liabilities (money you owe) and; 3) net worth (what's left after taking the difference between assets minus liabilities).
The formula is: ***Net Worth (NW) = Assets(A) – Liabilities(L)***, or just *NW = A - L*

The purpose of a balance sheet is to determine your ***net worth***. Net worth simply means the money (cash) you would have left if: *you added up all your earthly possessions, sold them for cash, and then paid off all your debts - including taxes*. The cash you would have remaining in this theoretical exercise is your true *net worth, measured in cash.*
Once you have created an inventory list and transferred it to your balance sheet, you can fine tune various categories over time. Do the inventory list prior to doing your balance sheet. It would be overwhelming to get lost in asset details too early, so it's better that you understand the big picture about balance sheets first - specifically your net worth - and then go back and fine tune various inventory and asset categories over time.

To create a personal balance sheet, transfer figures from your personal inventory list over to the Asset column on the balance sheet (see below). Then, list all the debts you owe like mortgages, auto loans, and credit cards and list those bills under the "Liabilities" category on the balance sheet. Finally, subtract your liabilities from your assets. The final answer is your Net Worth, or Equity.

Finance and accounting professionals often like to state net worth another way, which is: *Assets = Liabilities + Net Worth.* However, we will stick to the more straight forward formula of: ***NW = Equity = A - L.*** ***Let's look at some Balance Sheet examples below.***

Example #1:
Simple subtraction

1. Assets = ***$11,000.***
2. Liabilities = *(-$8,500)*
3. Therefore, NW = **$2,500** *(Your total equity or "net worth" as an individual.)*

Answer: *NW = A - L = 11,000 - $8,500 =* **$2,500**.

Example #2:
Typical Balance Sheet Format: Assets on left, Liabilities on right, Net Worth at bottom.

Balance Sheet

Assets =	A	Liabilities =	L
Cash	$2,000	School debt	50,000
Stocks	3,000	Car loan	12,000
Real Estate	0	Credit cards	10,000
Cars	20,000		
Inventory	12,500		
Total A = $37,500		**Total L = $72,000**	

Net Worth = A - L = {37,500 - 72,000} = **(-34,500)**

{Where total A = $37,500 and total L = $72,000}

Answer: NW = (-$34,500) = ***Negative Net Worth. Yikes!*** Can you see what's causing this? Hint: Look at the liability categories above on the right side column of the Balance Sheet.

Example #3:

The below example shows an average middle class couple that have been married for 15 years. They've acquired various car, real estate, retirement, and other assets. They've also accumulated liabilities against some of those assets. They have almost $1.2M in net worth acquired over their entire lifetime of hard work and sacrifice. Their balance sheet is quite good, though not necessarily exceptional. Could it have been better? Worse? Yes to both questions.

PERSONAL BALANCE SHEET

Months in Current Year	Period Ending for year	Excel File Name
9	**September 4, 2014**	PER_FIN_BALANCE_SHT_2014.XLS
	Enter as (MM/DD/YY)	

Billy Bob Bueford
Sally Bueford
INCLUDES PERSONAL ASSETS & LIBALITIES + BUSS. EQUITY
987Windy Lane
Atlanta, Georga

Legend

123	= Requires manual data entry
$123	= Automatically calculated cells = Sub totals
$123	= Automatically calculated cells = Totals
***	= Denotes business account. See company financi
	Note: Total business value is included here under "Net Worth of Business Owned" in Assets.

ASSETS

****

CURRENT ASSETS (CA)	
Cash and Equivlents	
BofA / Etrade business acounts	0.00
Wells Fargo Personal	2,000.00
Wells Fargo Trust	200.00
Other	0.00
Other	0.00
Sch E & W2 receivables	5,500.00
Wife receivables (W2)	3,500.00
	0.00
Etrade 401K - Billy	37,965.82
Etrade Roth IRA - Billy	46,854.41
Cash	45,000.00
Stocks/Securities	0.00
Kinecta Federal Credit Union	2,000.00
PWC 401K - Sally	45,000.00
TOTAL CA	***188,020.23***
NON-CURRENT ASSETS (NCA)	
Real Estate Owned	0.00
987 Windy Lane	1,250,000.00
(4800 sf x $203/sf = $974,400) - 2002	0.00
(4800 sf x $255/sf = $1,224,000) -2012	
Other	
Automobiles	
1994 Mercedes S400	6,500.00
2006 BMW 535i	15,400.00
1998 Ford SUV	5,000.00
Other	
Personal Property and Furniture	
Personal Property and Furniture	72,400.00
Net Worth of Business Owned	70,183.00
Other	0.00
TOTAL NCA	***1,419,483.00***
TOTAL ASSETS...	**$1,607,503.23**
CHECK SUM	1,607,503.23

LIABILITIES

****

II

CURRENT LIABILITIES (CL)	
Credit Cards	
Kinecta Credit Card ($500)	0.00
	0.00
Revolving Credit (< 1yr)	
Union Bank Credit Line - $25k	0.00
Insurance	
Auto Insurance	1,000.00
Home Owners Insurance	1,000.00
Payables - Sch E Mortgages+residence	3,000.00
Payables - Sch E Util, Maint, Reparis	900.00
Payables - Sch E Property Taxes	4,500.00
Other	
Son's College Partial Tution	5,000.00
Other	0.00
Other	0.00
TOTAL CL	***15,400.00***
NON-CURRENT LIABILITIES (NCL)	
Credit payable > 1 yr	
Other	0.00
Other Credit - Gas CC	400.00
Real Estate Loans - 1st Mortgage	
987 Windy Lane	407,000.00
Real Estate Loans - 2nd Mortgage	
	0.00
Citi Bank HELOC	Paid in full
Revolving Credit (>1yr)	
School Loans	
Wife's AA Degree	150.00
Misc	0.00
TOTAL NCL	***407,550.00***
TOTAL LIABILITIES	**$422,950.00**
CHECK SUM	422,950.00

NET WORTH = (ASSETS - LIABILITIES)	**$1,184,553**

Step 2, Part C: ***Track your spending with a Monthly Expense Report***

The ***method*** you use to ***track your monthly expenses*** (and your ***personal inventory and balance sheet),*** can be as simple as writing them down in a daily journal, or using a spread sheet like Microsoft Excel. There's also free spread sheet software created by Oracle, based on *OpenOffice.org*. *Corel corporation* also has very reasonably priced spreadsheet SW that doesn't require yearly subscriptions like MS Office now does.

You can also use inexpensive financial accounting software designed for personal and business use, like Intuit's Quicken or Quick Books. I started with a manual written method (Franklin Planner), then migrated to computer spreadsheets. Eventually I switched to an *RDBMS using Quicken software after about ten years of using the prior methods. I continue to use an older but very robust version of Quicken very successfully. Chasing software updates is a fool's game when what you're using meets 100% of your needs and runs perfectly fine. {Most software updates have bugs, waste time, and primarily reshuffle menus around to justify a new look or higher price}.

My recommendation would be to start with a quick paper and pencil list of major inventory items and costs. Do the same for a rough manual draft of your personal balance sheet to get a quick ball-park idea of your net worth. From that point, expand on those figures and transfer them to a computer spread sheet like Excel, or *RDBMS program like Quicken or Quick Books. Spread sheets exist for Mac's PC's, Linux, tablets, and smart phones. They're simple to learn and use. Free training tutorials are available online 24/7/360.

**RDBMS = Relational Data Base Management System.*

Expense Report Example
The basic format for an expense report is shown below. Use it as a starting point. Add or subtract expense categories as needed for your particular situation.

After that, you will transfer the individual expense line item amounts (items 1-10 below) to your Personal Income Statement in Step 3.

Inventory, Net Worth, and expense Tracking...

...Make it work for you!. Make it as personal and unique as yourself! But write it down!

Part C: Expense Report
How much $ I spend ea. month.

1. Food	**$550**
Groceries 300	
Restaurants 250	
2. College Loan (10y/,4.5%)	**520**
3. Car pmt + Insur.	**650**
4. Gas + Car Maint.	**350**
5. Rent	**1800**
6. Utilities (P/G/W)	**250**
7. Internet + Cell	**130**
8. Credit Card	**200**
9. Hobby+Enter+Misc	**200**
10. Total Expense =	**$4,650** /mo

Step 2, Part C: Spending Control: *Tracking the money you spend each day, week, month and year.*

As annoying as it seems at first, the only way to gain control of your spending is to consistently keep track of how much you spend each month. Credit card companies do this for free when you make purchases with their credit card. But cash (and other) purchases require receipts and tracking. Either way, you need to keep track of *ALL* your spending in a way that is both accurate yet not overly burdensome. You're going to win if you don't over spend. But to win means consistently tracking your spending each month, week (and sometimes each day). Write it down manually, or use a smart phone, tablet, PC, or laptop. Learn to use spreadsheet software. Ask for receipts each time you dine out or spend money. Then date those receipts, indicate what it was for (shoes, business travel, dinner), how you paid (cash, credit card, debit, card, check, etc.), and the amount ($48 including tip). Use those receipts to help build your monthly expense figures.

Create all the categories you spend money on - like rent, utilities, car payments, car insurance, car fuel, car maintenance, groceries, tolls, trains, airfare. eating at restaurants, internet fees, mortgages, property taxes, repairs, hobbies, travel, gifts, clothing, jewelry, maids, nannies, child support, kid's toys, loans, etc. Sub-total each category, and then total an entire month's worth of expenditures. Repeat this every month. Later, you will transfer these figures to your personal income statement in Step 3. When you spend money, you're also consuming a portion of the planet's resources, many of which have finite quantities. We all have to buy things to live. But excess consumption, or manufacturing, or building, increases waste and the carbon footprint on earth. Most of all, it consumes your cash and life force. It takes a lot of wasted cash before you learn how not to burn through it recklessly. **Let's look at some sample expense reports below.**

Example #1:
Grouped categories

1,5	***Food receipts, Rent***	***$2350***
2 - 4.	***College loan, car, insurance, gas and maintenance***	***$1,520***
6 - 9.	***Utilities, Internet, cell phone, credit cards, hobby/fun***	***$ 780***
10.	***Total Monthly Expenses (1-9) =***	***$4,650 / mo***

Example #2:
Detailed monthly expense report with category breakdown

1. Food	**$550**	
Groceries 300		
Restaurants 250		
2. College Loan (10y/,4.5%)	**520**	
3. Car pmt + Insur.	**650**	*(Car = $525/mo + Insurance = $125/mo)*
4. Gas + Car Maint.	**350**	
5. Rent	**1,800**	
6. Utilities (P/G/W)	**250**	*(Power=125/mo+ Gas=75/mo+Water=50/mo)*
7. Internet + Cell	**130**	*(Internet= $60/mo+Cell=70/mo)*
8. Credit Cards	**200**	*(Chase Visa+ BoA MasterCard)*
9. Hobby+Enter+Fun	**200**	
10. Total Expense =	***$4,650 /mo***	

Example #3:
Very detailed Expense Report with line-item categories for every expense item.
(It also shows Income too, which is a prelude to Step 3).

Below is a detailed example of a real monthly expense report (along with income) that was used during a period of unemployment. The expenses stayed about the same, but the income dropped by over half. The negative balance was paid from IRA savings for about three months until the rental house in city #1 was vacated due to no job prospects. Everything was then consolidated into city #2 household. After that, expenses stabilized and the monthly balance became positive.

Income & Expense Report (monthly)

MONEY IN (Every 2 weeks):			1,900.00	Note: May vary.
		Other Source:	0.00	
		Payroll:	0.00	
		BEGINNING BAL	$1,900.00	
Description/Category	**Min Due**		**Total Paid**	Comments
City #1:				
City Gas/Water/Trash:	180.00		180.00	avg-will vary
Gardening:	47.00		47.00	pay $95 every two months
RENT:	1,500.00		1,500.00	Some help with difference $200
PG&E:	75.00		75.00	avg - will vary
Water-North Coast:	27.00		27.00	varies. Pay ever two months
Recology of the North (trash svc):	21.59		21.59	pay ever two months $43.18
Comcast:	56.00		56.00	
Lawn Svc:	60.00		60.00	
Verizon Wireless:	53.00		53.00	May change after 12/15
Transportation: BART/Samtrans:	20.00		20.00	
Transportation - Auto - Gas:	50.00		50.00	
Transportation - Auto - Maint:	0.00		0.00	
FOOD/Groceries	225.00		225.00	will vary
Credit card #1:	100.00		100.00	varies
Credit card #2:	100.00		100.00	varies
Credit card #3:	75.00		75.00	varies
Education:	0.00		0.00	
Petty Cash:	120.00		120.00	varies. At around $30/week
OTHER - Medical:	0.00		0.00	
OTHER - Contingency:	60.00		60.00	personal/beauty/hair care/travel
SUB-TOTAL:			$2,769.59	
TOTAL EXPENSES		MONEY OUT:	$2,769.59	
		INCOME Avail:	1,900.00	
		Other Income:	0.00	
		LESS Total Expenses:	2,769.59	
		LESS (Savings):	0.00	
		LESS: Savings-rollforward:	$0.00	
		Ending Balance:	-$869.59	

Summarizing Parts A, B & C of Step 2:

***Step 2, Part A:* Personal Inventory List.** *Write down your personal assets (Clothing, furniture, hobbies, jewelry, tools, dishware, etc.). Keep cash, securities, cars, RV's, boats, real estate, and business ownership separate. Be honest with yourself. Use "real street prices" for current values. As previously noted, use Craig's List, eBay, TSA, or Amazon for reference.*

***Step2, Part B:* Personal Balance sheet.** *Transfer the total value of your Personal Inventory List over to your personal balance sheet. Then add any remaining special assets like cash, cars, RV's, real estate, or a business you own, in the Asset column of the balance sheet. Next, list all debts, credit card balances, and loans under "Liabilities" on the balance sheet. Finally, subtract Liabilities from Assets (Assets - Liabilities). This becomes your NET WORTH.*

Step2, Part C: *Track your spending with a* ***Monthly Expense Report.*** *Create all the categories you spend money on - like rent, utilities, car payments, car insurance, car fuel, etc. Sub-total each category, and then total an entire month's worth of expenditures. Repeat this every month. Later, you will transfer these figures to your personal income statement in Step 3*

Purpose:

Controlling one of the hardest things in life - spending your money!
These three sub-tasks seem daunting at first because it's not fun. You have to force yourself to get disciplined about it. The alternative is remaining in the dark about your true spending habits and net worth. Once you start, the light will begin to shine on how you actually spend your hard earned money, and more importantly, how you can better preserve both your cash and time (life force).

Let's now look at how all three of these parts relate to each other by comparing them side-by-side on the next page.

***Step 2: Cost Control Summary*:** **Part A:** Personal Inventory list; **Part B:** Personal Balance Sheet (Net Worth); **Part C**: Expense Report (What you spend money on each month to live your life).

Part A: Inventory List
My Inventory = My Stuff:

1. Clothing		**$2,500**
Shirts	500	
Pants,	500	
Suits	1,000	
Shoes	500	
2. Computer H/S		**$1,500**
3. Hobby		**$4,000**
4. Furniture		**$3,500**
5. Jewelry		**$1,000**
6. Total Inventory:		**$12,500**

Part B: Balance Sheet
Assets (A) & Liabilities (L)
My *NW = A - L*

Assets = A		Liabilities = L	
Cash	$2,000	School debt	50,000
Stocks	3,000	Car loan	12,000
Real Estate	0	Credit cards	10,000
Cars	20,000		
Inventory	12,500		
Tot.al A = $37,500		Total L = $72,000	

Net Worth (NW) = **A - L**
Where A = $37,500 & L = $72,000

NW = A-L = 37,500 - 72,000 = -34,500
NW = (-$34,500) = negative net worth

Part C: Expense Report
How much $ spent ea. month.

1. Food		**$550**
Groceries	300	
Restaurants	250	
2. College Loan (10y/,4.5%)		**520**
3. Car pmt + Insur.		**650**
4. Gas + Car Maint.		**350**
5. Rent		**1,800**
6. Utilities (P/G/W)		**250**
7. Internet + Cell		**130**
8. Credit Card		**200**
9. Hobby+Enter+Fun		**200**
10. Total Expense =		**$4,650** /mo

As you can see from the above figures, each part is interrelated. For example, each furniture item and electronic device you buy becomes part of your total inventory cost. That in turn becomes part of your net worth after adding cash, securities, vehicles, real estate, etc., and then subtracting all debts against them. Furthermore, each car you buy or school loan you incur becomes a monthly liability (if you don't pay cash) on your Expense Report in the form of a monthly bill. That in turn means earning money (actively or passively) to pay those monthly expenses . All the parts are relational - just like in nature or human relationships. Life is like a balanced equation: inputs on one side affect the outcome on the other side. There is no escape.
You are using up your precious time and cash when you spend money. Controlling spending is critical for obvious cash flow and survival reasons. Equally important is the fact that when it comes to your time, you only have a finite amount left and you don't get it back. It takes more time to earn more money.

There are basically ***three*** ways to increase your cash position: make more money, spend less (or no) money, or a combination of both. Spending less money that's already in hand is usually easier and faster than trying to generate more money. Both are necessary. But earning new money has to be taxed first, while existing money has typically already been taxed at the state and federal level. Every dollar you spend (or don't spend) has to include federal income tax (at a minimum), state tax (typically), and sales tax (usually). So you can't simply assume that what you actually pay is the total face value of any given purchase. Spending $100 means you have to ***earn*** approximately $134, due to sales tax, federal income tax, and state income taxes. (This example is based on an average sales tax rate of 8.5%, plus an additional 25% for federal and state income taxes.) The reason federal and state taxes are involved is because earning new money is taxable to the feds and state first. You get to spend what's left over. That's why your pay check has payroll deductions. You get taxed again with sales tax (in most states and countries) on that "already taxed" money each time you purchase something. When buying online, there's also shipping and tariff fees to consider.

Conservative spending accomplishes at least four magical things: *It saves money for your future; it conserves earth's resources; it reduces human stress; and any money saved has typically already been taxed, thus avoiding more effort to earn it.* It also reinforces wiser buying habits. Can you think of any more benefits?

Homework (very important): Using the example tables above, fill in your own money figures for Step 2, Parts A,B & C. (***Allow yourself at least a month or more to complete this step).***

CHAPTER 3

Step 3: Income Control

<u>Step 3. Income Control</u> - *Overview*

Questions:

What is the purpose of Income Control = IC?
What are the 3 main parts of IC (Part A, B, & C)?
Part A: What are Income and Expense categories?
Part B: What does {*Income - Expense*} mean?
Part C: What does "Hours of Life Force" mean? Why is it important?

Answers:

The Purpose of Income Control *is to know how much money you earn and receive, and how much, if any, is left over after you spend it each day, week, month, and year.*

The money you have left over needs to be used to build your FF savings fund. How? By saving and investing it (which is covered separately in Step 4). No IC, means no net income (NI). No NI means no savings. No savings means no money left to invest or use later in life. That means no FF (95% of the time). That means you're probably going to be poor or broke later in life.

The Three Main Parts of Income Control are:

Part A. *Create a* ***list*** *of all your personal* ***monthly Income (I)*** *and* ***Expense (E)*** *categories.*

Part B. ***Subtract*** *the exact amounts of money that you* ***spend as Expenses (E) - including taxes -*** *from the money you* ***earn (or receive) as Income (I)***. *The difference becomes your loss or gain (or break even), per month. Therefore, subtract as follows:*
*Your savings = {****Income - Expenses****} = {****I - E****}.*
Savings can also be called your "net monthly balance", or NMB..

Thus, {I - E} becomes your excess money that can be used to save, invest, and eventually live off of later in life.

Part C. ***Convert*** *$* ***dollar amounts*** *from part B* **into** *hours of human* **time** *= hours of your time used = your life force that is being used-up and cannot be replenished.*

Step 3. Income Control - *The Overview (Cont'd)*

Parts A, B & C Further Defined

Part A: ***Income Categories*** = Paycheck, bank interest, rental income, stocks & bonds, etc.
Expense Categories = Food, rent, mortgage, property taxes, clothing, cars, gas, etc.

Part B: The difference between {Income - Expenses} = Your Net Monthly Balance, or NMB. This is the money you have left over (if any) after paying your monthly bills. It's money that can be used to save and invest. It is the golden egg that produces more money when invested wisely. It becomes the money that allows you to become FF.

Part C: Hours of Life Force (HLF) is a way to convert money you've spent into ***Time Spent***.
Formula: HLF = Monthly expenditure (in $) per category / Your true hourly wage $/hr).

HLF Example: You spend $500 on new shoes. To convert that money spent into time spent, use the HLF formula = $ spent on $500 shoes / your true hourly wage.
Note: You must first define your true hourly wage, and not use your miss-leading "gross wage".

I.E., if your gross wage is $30/hr, after subtracting travel costs and time, it may be closer to $20/hr; (How the $30/hr becomes $20/hr is explained later in Part C). Therefore, your HLF = $500 / $20/hr = 25 hours of your time that have been used up and are gone forever! It's important to look at expenses not just in terms of money spent, but also life-hours spent, because unlike money, we can never get those hours back. Time is just as precious as money - sometimes more so.

The key is to realize that spending money also means using up our time on earth. Both money and time should be used as wisely as possible. We can make more money, but we can't always make up more time. We must learn to treat both ***money*** and ***time*** with equal respect.

Step 3: Income Control - *The Details*

Summary: Begin by establishing all your Income (I) sources (active income and passive income). Then transfer all your Expense (E) categories previously identified in Step 2, and subtract them from your Income. This forms the basis of your monthly "income and expense tracking control". It's extremely important because it reveals your true cash flow position each month. Finally, translate money spent into hours of time. Why? Spending money requires earning it first. Earning money takes a certain amount of your time, energy and skill. Time goes in one direction and you only get a finite amount of it in life.

Like Step 2, there are *three* parts to Step 3: Parts A, B, and C.

Part A.

Create a list of all your personal ***monthly income sources*** and ***expense categories***. (Note: Your expense categories will come from what you wrote down in Step 2 (Cost Control), so that's already done).

Part B. {*Two Methods)

Subtract the money you **spend** per month on **Expenses (E)** from the money you **earn (or receive) as Income (I).** The result becomes your "**Savings (S)**". It can also be called your "net monthly balance (NMB)". The math is simple and looks like this: **S = Income - Expenses.** ***Therefore, S =Income - Expenses = I - E. This = your monthly savings = "net monthly balance".***

Part C. Convert money amounts from Part B into hours of your *Personal Time* when spending money. The hours of your time used to earn money is related to your hours of life force (HLF) as a human being. Simply put, it's the amount of ***time*** you use each day to earn and spend cash.

Special note about How to do Part B {Two Methods}:
Part B, Method #1 uses a "cash-flow" style format for tracking income and expenses. Cash flow analysis is critical for all businesses, and is typically done on a semi-regular basis. It begins with any money on hand, and then tracks all sources of cash - including earned income, loan proceeds and investment income - and subtracts all expenses from that available cash. This method, while viable, is typically more useful for businesses than for personal finance purposes. However, it will be shown here to provide more financial insight and help reinforce basic money tracking principals.

Part B, Method #2 uses what's called a P&L format (P&L = Profit & Loss) that essentially equates to the same answer as Method #1, but is more in line with tracking income and expenses on a frequent basis for income and expense tracking. The P&L statement format works equally well for tracking personal finances, as it does for business accounting. Like Method #1, Method #2 is "**GAAP compliant", which means it's based on the best practices used in the accounting profession. Other names for a P&L statement are: "Profit and Loss", "Income Statement (IS)", Earnings Statement, and "Statement of Operations". They all mean the same thing and use the same format to measure income and spending.

***GAAP = Generally Accepted Accounting Principles. GAAP is an industry standard accounting format used in the U.S.by nearly all businesses,corporations,organizations,instutions,governments,and especially publicly traded companies. Why? To provide honest transparency in money earned and spent.*

In my experience, using Method #2 (P&L) is usually easier and simpler to understand for day-to-day income and expense tracking. In business, both Methods are used simultaneously to gain a 360 degree view of money flow. But for our purposes, Method #2 is sufficient by itself and will be given more attention.

Both methods require you to establish all the sources of money you earn and receive (Income (I)), and all the money you spend (Expenses (E)).

Both methods also require you to subtract Expenses (E) from Income (I), which becomes:
Income - Expenses = I - E. This establishes whether you are making money, losing money, or just breaking even. The ultimate goal is to spend less than you earn each month so you can start creating a savings surplus.

Let's begin learning about Income and Expense Control by examining the formulas and examples of all three Parts.

Part A.

*Create a list of all your personal **monthly income sources** and **expense categories**. (Note: Your expense categories will come from what you wrote down in Step 2 (Cost Control).*

1. Existing cash sources

Begin by identifying the amount of existing cash sources (***Beginning Cash Balance**) that you currently have stored in a bank, credit union, or other place. This is money that is readily available to pay your primary monthly bills with.
Let's assume your current checking account balance at your bank is $12,600. This equals ***All*** of your cash sources. It will also be referred to as your "beginning cash balance" for now.

Write it down here: ***$12,600 = My Beginning Cash Balance (BCB) at ABC Bank.***

***A Note about BCB:**
Beginning Cash Balance (BCB) = cash in the bank + other cash + marketable stocks, bonds and precious commodities that can be bought and sold through an established exchange, like the NY stock market, within a few days time. Start by adding up how much "liquid money" you have in the form of hard cash and *marketable* stocks, bonds, and precious metals like registered gold bullion. Total the amount of this "liquid money" and write it down. This would be considered your total "Beginning Cash Balance", or simply "*BCB*". This is also referred to as the lion share of your "current assets" on a balance sheet because these are assets that are equivalent to cash, and thus, are "currently available" for immediate cash transactions (like paying monthly bills).

2. Income sources

Next, create a list of all your monthly **Income (I)** sources that you earn or receive money from. **Income (I)** categories include, but are not limited to:

Your Paycheck from an employer.
Your Paycheck from your own business, like an S or C Corporation, if you draw a salary.
If you don't draw a salary, then your gross profit from your own business, like a sole proprietorship. This is the money left for you to live on, after you've paid all company expenses (including city, county, state, and federal taxes).
Interest on bonds and bank accounts, or dividends from stocks.
Net Rental Income (this means gross rent - vacancies - expenses). Very often negative if you're honest.
Loan proceeds (like a mortgage cash-out re-fi).
Other income: Tips, gifts, alimony, social security, pensions, disability, unemployment benefits (temporary).
Any other source of money you would receive during the year on a regular or irregular basis.

Let's assume your total income from working as a full-time employee is $3,500/mo.

Write it down here: ***$3,500 = My total Monthly Income from my job at Best Buyer Store.***

3. Expense categories

Next, write down your total monthly expenses that you identified in Step 2 (Cost Control).
Expense categories include, but are not limited to:

Food, rent, mortgage, property taxes, homeowners insurance, private mortgage insurance;
Utilities (Power, Water, Gas, Propane, Internet service);
Netflix and other content, paid TV subscriptions;
Clothing, jewelry, hobbies, health (Insurance premiums, co-pays, premium deductibles, doctor and hospital visits paid in cash, drug prescriptions);
Recreation (travel, lodging, food, parking, taxis);
Transportation (auto payments, gas, repairs, maintenance, DMV registration, smog);
All other expenses not listed above + those unique to your situation.

The monthly expense figures from Step 2 totaled \$4,650 and look like the following:

Step 2, *Part C*:
Expense Report Example
How much \$ spent ea. month.

1. Food		**\$550**
Groceries	300	
Restaurants	250	
2. College Loan (10y/,4.5%)		**520**
3. Car pmt + Insur.		**650**
4. Gas + Car Maint.		**350**
5. Rent		**1,800**
6. Utilities (P/G/W)		**250**
7. Internet + Cell		**130**
8. Credit Card		**200**
9. Hobby+Enter+Fun		**200**
10. Total Expense =		**\$4,650** /mo

However, let's assume your total monthly expenses are \$3,200 (instead of \$4,650).

Write it down here: ***\$3,200 = My total Monthly Expenses (to live my life and pay all bills)***

Summary of Part A.

\$12,600 = My beginning (current) cash balance in the bank
\$3,500 = My total Monthly Income
\$3,200 = My total Monthly Expenses

Remember, use income and expense categories based on your life as it is now (see examples listed in 2 and 3 above). Write them on a piece of paper, in a weekly planner, or use a computer spreadsheet. Create whatever is quick, easy, and accurate, but use it from now on.

You're now ready to do Part B.

Part B

Method #1 *Beginning and Ending Cash Balance, aka Net Monthly Balance (NMB)*

Example #1 *(Simplified version in Dollars)*

The NMB format typically spans a period of one year or less. It's based on simple arithmetic and looks like this in simple terms: ***Income - Expenses = Money left over*** *(each week, month, or year.)* Method #1, Part B is very similar to a company cash flow statement.

Use the NMB format below to ***write down the money you MAKE and SPEND each month***, based on the ***I and E*** categories from Part A. In other words, add up your total monthly ***I*** (income), and total monthly ***E*** (expenses), and then subtract the difference between the two as shown below.

Write these figures down on paper or in a software spreadsheet program, using the currency of your choice, such as Dollars, Euros, Yuan, Yen, etc. A summary of the output should look like this:

Example #1 (in Dollars)

Monthly Income and Expense Report for month (A): (Simplified format)

(I) Total Income for Month (A)	= $ 3500.00	(Mo. Income = I)
(E) Total Expenses for Month (A)	= $ 3200.00	(Mo. Expense = E)
***NMB** = (I) - (E) = $3500 - $3200	= ***$300.00****	(Net Mo. Balance = NMB)*

NMB = *Net Monthly Balance = I - E.
Surplus, loss, or break-even each month. In this case, there is a *surplus* NMB = *$300***.)

You could simply use the format above, and only account for actual expenses and income each month, and ignore any surpluses or break-even situations that occur. But, if you are running a negative cash flow each month, or you want to do this step in the most accurate accounting way possible to achieve FF, then you need to use an expanded format of this formula.

Like a company, personal spending continues every month during our lifetime, which means that the surplus, loss, or break even amount from the prior month's tabulation must be carried forward and accounted for in the next month's tabulation, as a beginning "cash balance".

This just means that your are starting next month with a money amount (beginning cash balance) equal to the prior month's "ending balance".

Therefore, you must include ***BCB*** in the formula as the beginning cash balance, and an ***ECB,*** or ending cash balance, at the end of the formula. This provides a much more accurate picture of your cash flow situation as it evolves month-to-month. Let's look at ***Example #2*** on the next page, which shows the more accurate version of using ***Method #1***.

Part B

Method #1 *(Cont'd.)*
Example #2 *(More accurate version in Dollars)*

In ***Example #2***, the process is almost the same as Example #1, but with the following nuances: ***First,*** write down the amount of total available cash (***BCB***) you have from all your existing sources like you did in Part A on Page 49. This includes savings, checking accounts, cash on hand, and any marketable securities like stocks and bonds. This equals your initial **B**eginning **C**ash **B**alance, or ***BCB***.

Next, figure out your current month's ***NMB*** like you did in Example #1 on the last page. ***Then,*** add or subtract the amount of ***NMB*** to the ***BCB*** you started with for that month. This becomes ***(BCB+NMB)*** and equals the **E**nding **C**ash **B**alance (or ***ECB***) for that month.

Finally, use that last figure (***ECB***) for the beginning of next month's ***BCB***. In other words, for next month's income and expense calculation, your beginning cash balance (BCB) of *$12,900* also ***equals*** last month's (ECB) ending cash balance of *$12,900.* Thus, each month's NMB affects the next month.

This is why the ***ECB for month A =*** the ***BCB for month B.*** You start each new month's calculation based on where you left off in the prior month.

Using the same figures from Example #1, the more accurate version of Example #2 is shown below. Note: The ***BCB*** of ***$12,600*** comes from ***Part A*** on Page 49.

Monthly Income and Expense Report for month (A): (More accurate format)

BCB = Beginning Cash Balance = $ 12,600 (BCB, as of 6/1/18)

(I) Total Income for Month (A) = $ 3500.00 (Mo. Income = I)
(E) Total Expenses for Month (A) = $ 3200.00 (Mo. Expense = E)

NMB = (I) - (E) = ***$300.00**** (Net Mo. Balance = NMB)
(**Surplus, loss, or break-even each month. In this case, there is a positive +$300 left.)

ECB = Ending Cash Balance → ***= $ 12,900**** (Ending Cash Bal. (ECB)
= $12,600 + $300 = (as of 6/30/18)

Therefore, ***ECB*** *for month A =* ***BCB*** + ***NMB*** = ***$12,600*** + ***$300*** = ***$12,900.00.***
Furthermore, the BCB for next month B = last month's ECB = $12,900.00

Thus, the total cash position (savings) increased by $300 during month A to $12,900. This process repeats itself every month. The goal is to generate as much positive NMB as possible each month. This becomes your future savings which you can invest to generate more money for FF.
In summary, Method #1, Example #2 shows two important things: 1) It shows your net monthly balance (NMB) each month plus; 2) It also shows that each month's NMB affects all future monthly figures because you are now tracking your cash position as it's accumulated and carried forward ***every*** month.

Part B

Method #1
Example #3 (in Euros)

Let's do another example using € Euros *(instead of dollars).*

Suppose you had €15,000 Euros saved up in all your liquid cash accounts. That means your BCB = €15,000 Euros. If your monthly Income (I) was €10,000 Euros, and your monthly Expenses (E) were €8,000 Euros, than you would have a €2,000 Euro surplus for that month; (I - E = €10,000 - €8,000 =€2,000 surplus).

Thus, the NMB = I-E = €10,000 - €8,000 = €2,000 Euros.

To determine your ending cash balance (ECB), you would ***add*** the €2,000 Euro NMB surplus to the € 15,000 Euro beginning balance (BCB). This would give you a €17,000 Euro ending cash balance (ECB); *Therefore, ECB = €15,000 BCB + €2,000 NMB =€17,000 Euro ECB.*

Placed in the previous table format, the above Euro example would look like the following:

Example #3 (in Euros)

(BCB) = Beginning Cash Balance	= € 15,000	(BCB, as of 7/1/18)
(I) Total Income for Month (June)	= € 10,000	(Mo. Income = I)
(E) Total Expenses for Month (June)	= € 8,000	(Mo. Expense = E)
NMB = (I) - (E) = Income – Expenses	= ***€ 2,000*****	(Net Mo. Balance = NMB)
(**Surplus, loss, or break-even each month. In this case, there is a positive +€ 2000 left.)		
^^ECB = Ending Cash Balance	= ***€ 17,000****	(Ending Cash Bal. (ECB) as of 7/31/18)

^^ The formula for ECB = *(Beginning Cash Balance + Net Mo. Balance) = BCB + NMB*

^^ *Therefore, ECB = { BCB +* ***NMB}*** *= {€15,000 +* ***€2,000****}* = **€17,000.**

Once again, a surplus NMB exists in the amount of € 2,000 Euros. That makes our ECB = € 17,000 Euros, which is up from € 15,000 at the beginning of the month.

Quiz: *Can you figure out what the beginning cash balance (BCB) for August 1st, 2018 should be?*
Hint: *BCB for August 1, 2018 = ECB for July 31, 2018.*
Answer*: BCB for 8/1/18 = ECB for 7/31/18 = €17,000 Euros.*

End Part B, Method #1

Part B

Method #2

Method #2: *Profit and Loss Statement, or P&L*

Method #2 uses what's called a "**GAAP compliant" P&L format (P&L = Profit & Loss Statement) that essentially equates to the same answer as Method #1, but is more in line with tracking income and expenses at a detailed level on a regular basis. Nearly all businesses and institutions use the P&L format. It's intuitive, easy to visualize, and provides line-item detail of expense categories. This makes it very suitable for personal income and expense tracking.

Begin by identifying all your income and expense categories from Step 2, and then write them down using pencil and paper. Better still, use software and your preferred digital device such as a tablet, laptop, desktop, or smart phone. If you use a computer, software like Microsoft Excel, Corel Quattro Pro, or OpenOffice Spreadsheet (free) are excellent ways to track and automate your work. Other names for an Income and Expense statement are: "Income Statement", "Profit and Loss", "P&L", "Earnings Statement", and (for big companies) "Statement of Operations". They all mean the same thing: *Money earned, money spent, and the difference between the two.*

Like Method #1 (NMB), the P&L concept spans a period of one year or less, and is based on simple arithmetic. It looks like this in simple terms: ***Income - Expenses = Money left over*** *(each week, month, or year.)*

Another way to express it would be:

* ∑ ***$ money earned*** **-** ∑ ***$ money spent and owed*** = ∑ ***$ left over*** *(or negative or zero)*

or, ***Total Income - Total Expenses (incl. taxes)*** = ***Net Income*** *(could be positive, negative, or zero.)*

Net Income and Net Monthly Balance are essentially the same concept. They're just two ways of expressing the same thing. The main difference is the P&L format allows for more detail to be visualized on the expense side. Also, NMB may not always include taxes, though it could if needed.

Don't be intimidated by the math symbols. Those are simply ways of expressing things like adding and subtracting in short hand. (See the definitions below).

The Greek* "∑" symbol stands for the word "Sigma". In mathematics, ∑ means "The summation of" or "The Total of" a given set of numbers or group of like items. For example, in the above P&L formula concept, "∑ *$ money spent and owed****" simply means "the total dollars spent in all categories of expenses and taxes", or simply, = "the sum of all expenses and taxes".*

***GAAP = Generally Accepted Accounting Principles. This was explained earlier. Here is another recap as a reminder. GAAP is an industry standard accounting format used in the U.S. for tracking income and expenses accurately and legally. Nearly all publicly traded companies, government agencies, and various organizations must comply with GAAP for accounting and tax purposes. Individual income tax filings are also rooted in GAPP to a large degree. For example, an individual who is a sole business owner must file a Schedule C on their IRS tax return each year. Schedule C is based on GAAP principals, and in particular, on the Profit and Loss structure that Method #2 goes into in detail on the next pages.*

Part B

Method #2

Below is the industry standard P&L format in its most basic form. The math is simple arithmetic. The P&L consists of 5 parts:

1. ***Total Revenue*** *(money earned or received);*
   (This is typically "after-tax" income for W2 wages, and "before-tax" for most other income.

2. ***COGS,*** *or "cost of goods sold" that must be purchased (Ignore).*
   (This is for business purposes only. Ignore this for personal use. Set #2 = $0).

3. ***Expenses -*** *The summation (or total) of all your personal living expenses.*

4. ***Your state and federal taxes.***
   (You estimate this initially throughout the year. When you do your taxes, it becomes an exact figure).

5. ***Net Income = NI:*** *The net amount of cash (if any) you have left over, after all income has been received, and all expenses and taxes have been paid. For personal use, this is your savings = excess money to save and invest. For a business, it's very similar. It's money used to: grow the business, make investments, stock pile cash, pay down debt, or pay back the owners.*

The Formula for Creating a Personal P&L:

- **The formula for a P&L looks like this in summary:** *(Solve for Net Income)*
  - **1. Total Revenue (W2 wages, investments, 1099 Income, company sales)**
    - *2. **- Less** COGS (ignore this for personal P&L's. Set to zero.)*
    - *3. **- Less** Expenses*
    - *4. **-Less** S&F* Taxes {*S&F = Combined State and Federal taxes}*

  - **5. Net Income = {1 - (2+3+4)}**

Part B

Method #2
Example #1 (Business Example)

Let's look at several simple examples of a P&L statement with some money figures plugged in. Since the beauty of the P&L format is its ability to be used to accurately monitor profit and loss for any type of business or personal situation, we'll look at both a business example and a personal finance example.

Example #1 *(Construction Business)*

The first example will be a business that is involved in building construction. The company builds residential homes and also engages in commercial retail construction.

1. Their total sales, or revenue, for 2017, were **$5,200,000**.

2. Their COGS, or cost of goods sold, were **$3,200,000**, and must be used in this case because it is a special type of cost many companies engaged in construction, manufacturing, and retail sales must deal with. It's a unique cost separate from administrate expenses and general overhead. The term COGS is also referred to as the "cost of sales". Another term for COGS is "direct costs". They all mean the same thing, which is the cost of material and labor "directly attributable" to the construction, manufacturing, or resale of a building, manufactured product, or consumer item sold in a store. In this case, the COGS, or direct building costs, amounted to $3,200,000, which specifically (and only) relates to construction materials and the "job-site" labor to install them. The remaining costs for a business, like administrative overhead expenses, are listed in #3 below.

3. Expenses, also referred to a administrative costs, were **$1,040,000**, and relate to the overhead administrative costs of running all business, like office rent, utilities, internet connections, office supplies, labor to run the office (separate from job-site labor), licenses, insurance, and payroll taxes.

4. State and Federal taxes were **$336,000.** *(This is estimated during the year using prior year tax figures. At tax filing time, exact figures are used based on current IRS tax tables that are published each year.*

5. The Net Income = ***NI = 1 - {2+3+4)*** =

NI = $5,200,000 - {$3,200,000+$1,040,000+$336,000}
= $5,200,000 - {$4,576,000} = $624,000

Answer: NI = $624,000 .

This is free and clear money that is left over after all bills and taxes were paid. It can be used for investing, growing the business, or saving cash . It could also be used to pay the owners (share holders) extra cash. Corporations call this a dividend.

Part B

Method #2
Example #1 (Business Example)- Cont'd.

Summary of Example #1 - Business P&L

- 1. **Total Company Sales** = **$5,200,000**
- 2. **COGS**, (aka, cost of goods sold, cost of sales, or direct costs) = **$3,200,000**
- 3. **Expenses**, (aka administrative costs) = **$1,040,000**
- 4. **Taxes** (Federal and State) = **$336,000**
- 5. **Net Income** = NI = 1 – (2+3+4) =

= $5,200,000 - {$3,200,000+$1,040,000+$336,000}
= $5,200,000 - {$4,576,000} = $624,000

This is the final answer: NI = **$624,000** /yr

This represents extra money the company made that year after all expenses and taxes were paid. It's free and clear surplus cash.

Next, let's look at an example of how to use the P&L format for your own personal finances.

Part B

Method #2
Example #2 (Personal P&L)

Example #2 *(Personal P&L for an Individual)*

A single person who recently graduated from college works for an accounting firm. She only receives a salary from the firm, and therefore has no other income sources right now. Therefore, her total revenue is the wages from her job.

1. Her salary was **$72,000** / year (gross salary before state and federal taxes are deducted).

2. COGS was **n/a. $0**

3. Her total expenses, including food, college loan, car, rent, utilities, etc., were **$55,800.** (*This figure comes from multiplying the monthly figure in Step 2 by 12 months. A recap is shown on the next page. Total yearly expenses = {$4,650/mo x 12} = $55,800 /yr.

4. State and Federal taxes: **15% Federal, and 5% State = 20%. {.20 x 72K} = $14,400**
For W2 payroll employees, tax figures come directly from your pay check, which in turn are based on what you filled out on your W4 IRS withholding form when you were hired. If you are self employed, or are a business owner in a corporation, LLC, or partnership, you may have to estimate this figure initially by using last year's tax return as a guide. The exact tax figures will be calculated when you file your taxes for that year.

5. Net Income = ***NI = 1 - { 2 + 3 + 4)*** = $72,000 - {0$+$55,800+$14,400} = **$1,800** /yr

Therefore, the answer is: NI = $1,800 / yr. *(or $150 / mo)**

This is what she has left over at year end to save and invest after all expenses and taxes are paid.

*Note:
This may seem like a modest amount of NI, but it's still free and clear money that's left after all bills and taxes are paid. Over time, it can grow quickly into a large FF fund if done every year. To accelerate that growth, she will need to reduce her expenses, increase her salary, or both, in order to increase her NI, which will increase her FF savings. That in turn will allow her to invest more savings wisely to become financially free sooner. But at this early stage in her career, it will take time. At this rate, she may need a good 25+ years - or longer - before she reaches FF. But maybe not. It depends on a number of factors, like interest rates, job advancements and/or declines, personal issues, the economy, government policies, and occasional luck - both good and bad.

Part B

Method #2
Example #2 (Personal P&L) Cont'd.

Example #2 *(Personal P&L for an Individual) - Summary format for Entire Year*

- 1. **Total Revenue** = her annual gross salary = **$72,000**
- 2. COGS = N/A = **$0**
- 3. ***Expenses**, (Total living from Expense Report) = **$55,800**
- 4. **Taxes** (Federal @15% and State @ 5%) = 20% x $72K = **$14,400**
- 5. **Net Income** = NI = 1 – (2+3+4) = **$1,800 / yr.**
  (= FF savings each year)

Personal P&L Summary

1. Revenue	**$72,000**
2. COGS = NA	**$ 0**
3. Expenses	**$55,800**
4. Taxes F&S	**$14,400**
5. Net Income	
= 1 - (2 + 3 + 4)	
= 72,000 - (0+55,800+14,400)	
= 72,000 - (70,200)	
= $1,800 / yr	
=====================	
5.Net Income =	**$1,800 / yr**

***Personal Expense Report**
How much $ she spends ea. mo.

1. Food	**$550**
Groceries 300	
Restaurants 250	
2. College Loan (10y/,4.5%)	**520**
3. Car pmt + Insur.	**650**
4. Gas + Car Maint.	**350**
5. Rent	**1,800**
6. Utilities (P/G/W)	**250**
7. Internet + Cell	**130**
8. Credit Card	**200**
9. Hobby+Fun+Misc	**200**
=====================	
10. Total Expense =	**$4,650** /mo
	x 12 mos.

	$55,800 /yr.

Part B

Method #2

Example #3 (Personal P&L) - Detailed Monthly Income and Expenses per category

Below is a Personal P&L that shows detailed dollar figures per every expense category. Use this and prior examples as a guide for making your own detailed P&L categories. (Read from top to bottom, left to right). This P&L was designed to be used monthly as well as yearly. It's an easy, fast, and accurate way to budget your income and expenses semi-automatically.

To make one yourself, use Excel, Quatro Pro, Open Office spreadsheet software to create 12 tabs for each month of the year, plus a 13th tab for the end of the year that would automatically total all 12 months (J-D). This allows you to see in detail how much money enters and leaves your life each month, along with a yearly total that is automatically generated.

Income & Expense Report (monthly)

MONEY IN (Monthly W2 Salary After S&F Taxes):			**4,392.00**
		Other Source:	0.00
		Payroll:	0.00
		BEGINNING BAL	**$4,392.00**
Expense Description/Category	**Min Due**		**Total Paid**
City #1:			
City Gas/Water/Trash:	180.00		180.00
Gardening:	47.00		47.00
RENT:	1,500.00		1,500.00
PG&E:	75.00		75.00
Water-North Coast:	27.00		27.00
Recology of the North (trash svc):	21.59		21.59
Comcast:	56.00		56.00
Lawn Svc:	60.00		60.00
Verizon Wireless:	53.00		53.00
Transportation: BART/Samtrans:	20.00		20.00
Transportation - Auto - Gas:	50.00		50.00
Transportation - Auto - Maint:	0.00		0.00
FOOD/Groceries	225.00		225.00
Credit card #1:	100.00		100.00
Credit card #2:	100.00		100.00
Credit card #3:	75.00		75.00
Education:	0.00		0.00
Petty Cash:	120.00		120.00
OTHER - Medical:	0.00		0.00
OTHER - Contingency:	60.00		60.00
SUB-TOTAL:			$2,769.59
TOTAL EXPENSES		MONEY OUT:	$2,769.59
		INCOME Avail:	4,392.00
		Other Income:	0.00
		LESS Total Expenses:	2,769.59
		LESS (Savings):	0.00
		LESS: Savings-rollforward:	$0.00
		Ending Balance:	**$1,622.41**

Part B

Method #2

Example #4 (Personal P&L) - Detailed Income and Expenses with multiple Income sources.

PERSONAL INCOME STATEMENT

Months in Current Year	Period Ending for year	Excel File Name
5	May 31, 2015	PER_FIN_P&L_2015.XLS
	Enter as (MM/DD/YY)	

All sources of Income for:
SCOTT DOE
MICHELLE DOE
INCLUDES SCH C, SCH E, W2, SCH B, ALL OTHER INOME SOURCES
4411 Key Largo Way
Palm Beach, FL

Legend
123 = Requires manual dat
$123 = Automatically calcul
$123 = Automatically calcul

	**	MONTHLY	SUB-TOTAL YR TO DATE	OTHER	YR. TO DATE TOTALS
	INCOME - SCH C (EBT) - ESR/DDW	$2,300.00	$11,500.00	$0.00	**$11,500.00**
	INCOME - SCH E (EBT) NET RENTAL	$300.00	$1,500.00	$0.00	**$1,500.00**
	INCOME - SD W2	$2,250.00	$11,250.00	$0.00	**$11,250.00**
	INCOME - INVESTMENT SCH B	$300.00	$1,500.00	$0.00	**$1,500.00**
	INCOME - MD	$5,000.00	$25,000.00	$0.00	**$25,000.00**
	INCOME - MISC	$0.00	$0.00	$0.00	**$0.00**
	TOTAL GROSS INCOME	**$10,150.00**	**$50,750.00**	**$0.00**	**$50,750.00**
	LESS RETURNS & ALLOWANCES	0.00	$0.00	$0.00	**$0.00**
I	TOTAL GROSS INCOME	**$10,150.00**	**$50,750.00**	**$0.00**	**$50,750.00**
	LESS ADJUSTMENTS, IF ANY				
	LESS…	$0.00	$0.00	$0.00	**$0.00**
	LESS…	0.00	$0.00	0.00	**$0.00**
II	TOTAL ADJUSTMENTS TO INCOME	$0.00	$0.00	$0.00	**$0.00**
III	**GROSS INCOME**	**$10,150.00**	**$50,750.00**	**$0.00**	**$50,750.00**
	OPERATING EXPENSES	MONTHLY	YR TO DATE		
	MORTGAGES / RENTS - PERSONAL	$0.00	$0.00	0.00	**$0.00**
	4411 Key Large Way	$650.00	$3,250.00	0.00	**$3,250.00**
		$0.00	$0.00	0.00	**$0.00**
	LEGAL & PROFESSIONAL FEES	$25.00	$125.00	0.00	**$125.00**
		$0.00	$0.00	0.00	**$0.00**
	UTILITIES	$0.00	$0.00	0.00	**$0.00**
	Electricty	$35.00	$175.00	0.00	**$175.00**
	Gas	$120.00	$600.00	0.00	**$600.00**
	Water	$10.00	$50.00	0.00	**$50.00**
	Gardening	$0.00	$0.00	0.00	**$0.00**
	Trash	$65.00	$325.00	0.00	**$325.00**
	Charter Cable	$190.00	$950.00	0.00	**$950.00**
		$0.00	$0.00	0.00	**$0.00**
		$0.00	$0.00	0.00	**$0.00**
	ENTERTAINMENT	$0.00	$0.00	0.00	**$0.00**
	Movies	$10.00	$50.00	0.00	**$50.00**
	Cable TV (see Utilities)	$0.00	$0.00	0.00	**$0.00**
	Music	$10.00	$50.00	0.00	**$50.00**
		$0.00	$0.00	0.00	**$0.00**
	REPAIRS & MAINTENANCE	$30.00	$150.00	0.00	**$150.00**
		$0.00	$0.00	0.00	**$0.00**
	MEDICAL	$0.00	$0.00	0.00	**$0.00**
	Doctor	$24.00	$120.00	0.00	**$120.00**
	Dentist	$25.00	$125.00	0.00	**$125.00**
	Eye Care	$26.00	$130.00	0.00	**$130.00**
	Prescriptions	$27.00	$135.00	0.00	**$135.00**
	AUTO	$0.00	$0.00	0.00	**$0.00**
	Gas	$375.00	$1,875.00	0.00	**$1,875.00**
	Maintenance	$130.00	$650.00	0.00	**$650.00**
	Registration	$45.00	$225.00	0.00	**$225.00**
	Auto Payments	$0.00	$0.00	0.00	**$0.00**
	FOOD	$0.00	$0.00	0.00	**$0.00**
	Groceries	$430.00	$2,150.00	0.00	**$2,150.00**
	Breakfast	$20.00	$100.00	0.00	**$100.00**
	Lunch	$30.00	$150.00	0.00	**$150.00**
	Dinner	$35.00	$175.00	0.00	**$175.00**
	Snacks	$20.00	$100.00	0.00	**$100.00**
	Vitamins	$15.00	$75.00	0.00	**$75.00**
	PHONE	$0.00	$0.00	0.00	**$0.00**
	SD Verizon Cell	$50.00	$250.00	0.00	**$250.00**
	MD Verizon Cell	$12.00	$60.00	0.00	**$60.00**
	Other	$0.00	$0.00	0.00	**$0.00**
IV	TOTAL OPERATING COSTS	**$2,409.00**	**$12,045.00**	**$0.00**	**$12,045.00**
V	**NET OPERATING INCOME** (NOI = EBT)	**$7,741.00**	**$38,705.00**	**$0.00**	**$38,705.00**

Expense to Income Ratio (Expenses / Gross Income)
Operating Margin (NOI / Gross Income)

Part C:

How to convert money expenditures into another valuable commodity: *Your Time*!

Introduction.
Another way to express it is: *How to determine your Hours of Life Force (HLF), measured in time.*

Why? Because a useful way to measure your happiness and quality of life is by the hours you have available and how you spend those hours. If it stands to reason that you assign a specific dollar value to each hour you work, then you should assign an equivalent value of each dollar you spend by how much time it took from your life to earn it. Time, energy, and skill become your "life force".
The expression "Hours of Life Force" (HLF) will be used to measure how much time in hours we use when we spend our money. It's ridiculous to do this for every expenditure, but it is very insightful on large or critical expenditures. It lets you see how much of your time in hours you trade for money.

Most of us have to work and earn a living for many years before we can retire or live financially free. Therefore, we need to trade our time for money for a good portion of our life. However, the degree and duration to which we do that is the bigger question. This gets into "quality of life" issues, which we all have to face at some point in our lives. Better to face and embrace it now, than have it hit you like a run-a-way locomotive or rogue wave later in life. Think of the term "mid-life crisis". It's a point in life, usually between the age of forty and fifty, when our body and mind questions our quality of life thus far, and the soul cries out for meaningful answers to straighten it all out. The formula for *Hours of Life Force (HLF)* is shown below. It's explained in detail later in the chapter.

HLF = ($ Money Spent ÷ THR).

The HLF formula is analogous to business school case studies where factories determine how much time and money is involved to produce an item, based on employee salaries, hours worked, and productivity gains. The concepts of HLF and THR are also derived from this author's professional experiences working in business for fifty years, and from personal insights gained over the course of six decades earning and spending money. The purpose behind HLF and THR is largely based on how earning and spending money equates to either joyous or non-fulfilling outcomes. This in turn provides the realization that money and time are inextricabily related to each other in both work and in personal pursuits. Equally important is the realization that personal choice plays a large role because most money predicaments are self-induced. The goal of this formula is to not only further embrace financial literacy, but to also examine your *quality of life*. It helps reveal the correlation between your time, your job, your salary, spending money, and how well or poorly you do all those things - including how you spend your available time on earth earning money and living your life. Like financial teachings throughout history, this concept is neither new nor proprietary. Rather, the origins trace back to before the beginning of the industrial revolution, and well before European, Asian, South American, and North American empires, which today all embrace financial balance sheets, P&L statements, cash flow statements, and time-value-of-money analysis, in virtually the exact same way. Financial literacy, time valuation, and quality of life issues are universal truths. They are the equivalent of the financial laws of physics that apply equally and impartially to all human beings on earth, just like the law of gravity, the laws of thermodynamics, and spiritual laws.

So, in order to calculate your HLF when spending money (especially large amounts of it), we first have to calculate what your true hourly rate is. Therefore, let's go to the following page and learn how eye opening it is to see what you really make per hour, by calculating your "True Hourly Rate", or **THR**.

Part C

How to determine your True Hourly Rate, or THR.

Calculating Your True Hourly Rate, or *THR*.

The best way to learn the concept and precise formula of your THR is by example. Let's look at the following example which typifies a person who earns a wage close to fifty thousand dollars a year, and has to commute by car one hour (each way) from home in rush hour traffic within a large city.

THR Example:
Suppose your gross hourly wage is ***$23.00 / hr***. (before taxes), but after gas and commuting time, it's reduced to ***$17.32 / hr*** (before taxes). Therefore, your true hourly rate ***(THR) = $17.32 /hr.*** before taxes, (*not $23 / hr*.) ***How did that happen?*** Simply math and honesty.

When you drive to work each day, you're spending your time, plus money for gas, car, insurance, and maintenance. You typically receive no pay for these expenditures, and seldom can you avoid this additional time and expense related to commuting to and from work.

Let's look at the math just for the driving time and gas involved. Assume gas costs $3.50 per gallon. Assume the average R/T commute to work is 20 miles each way, multiplied by (2) = 40 miles per day. Your SUV gets 24 miles per gallon on the open freeway, but in bump-to-bumper traffic and grid-locked streets, it averages out to around 13 miles per gallon.

That burns up 3.08 gallons of gas per day; (40 mi / 13 mi /gallon = 3.08 gallons), and costs $10.78 in gas per day: (3.08 gallons x $3.50 /gal = $10.78 / day in gas). In one week, you spend five times that amount, so gas costs you: {5 x $10.78 = $53.90} per week. On a monthly basis, that equals four times that amount, or: {4 x $53.90 = ***$215.60 / mo.***}.

Now let's look at your unpaid time traveling to work.
Assume one hour each way = two hours per day (<u>*not including*</u> traffic delays and prep-time at home). Two hours per day = 10 hours per week; (2 hrs. ea. day x 5 days per week = 10 hours).

In one month, it's four times that: (4 weeks x 10 hrs./ week = ***40 hrs. per mo. of unpaid travel time***).

Therefore, you're spending an additional 40 hours (per month) of your time *unpaid*, **plus** $215.60 in fuel costs *un-reimbursed*. Those figures don't include higher insurance and maintenance costs, which we'll ignore for now.

At forty hours per week, your average monthly salary is: 4 weeks x 40 hrs/wk x $23 /hr. = $3,680.00 / mo. (four weeks). To arrive at your ***true*** hourly rate, you must add unpaid travel time to your total hours worked, and subtract gas expense from your monthly salary. Therefore, if $3,680 represents four weeks at 160 hrs of work at $23/hr, then you have to adjust it as follows:

Your salary is fixed at $3,680, but the time worked with 40 additional hours of commuting shoots up to 200 hours (160 hours of work / mo. + 40 hours of commute time per mo. = 200 hrs /mo.). That drops your hourly job wage to $18.40 / hr; ($3,680 per mo. / 200 hrs. mo. = $18.40 / hr).

We're not done yet! Look at the next page ...

Part C

How to determine your True Hourly Rate, or THR, cont'd.

Next, you must subtract your fuel costs from your monthly salary since you have to spend it to get to work. We'll only consider the cost of fuel in this example. In reality, there would be other costs like freeway toll fees, parking fees, traffic tickets, oil, wear and tear maintenance, higher insurance due to more commuting, and so on.

From the previous page, we determined one month of fuel costs $215.60. Since most employers don't (typically) reimburse employees for gas, you have to subtract that from your gross salary. That results in the following calculation: ***$3,680 /mo - $215.60 / mo. = $3,464.40 / mo. reduced salary*** due to fuel costs for driving to work every four weeks.

At this point, your true hourly rate (THR) equals your real reduced salary (after subtracting gas expense), divided by the real increase in work hours (due to job-related commute time).

That looks like the following: ***Real reduced salary / real increase in hours worked***. Substituting real figures, we get the following answer for the THR:

Answer:

THR = $3,464.40 per mo. ÷ 200 hrs per mo. = $17.32 /hour.

Therefore, your True Hourly Rate = ***THR = $17.32 / hr.*** *(not $23.00 / hr.)*

And don't forget that the above THR of $17.32 is before state and federal income taxes, which reduces your hourly rate even further.

Yikes!

This is the time to step back and consider alternatives, like telecommuting, getting a job closer to home, moving closer to work (usually very expensive), cheaper transportation (usually takes too long or not available), moving to a lower cost city or state, or any combination of these alternatives.

In reality, most people remain stuck in their work commute for long periods of time because it's not easy to switch jobs quickly - especially when you have steady work that offers decent benefits and/or have a family to support every day. It's a trade-off: the better the pay and benefits, the less worrisome commute time and fuel costs become. But for many people, it becomes an endless trap of schlepping through life chasing the dime. Still, the alternative of having *no income* is worse. Grinning and bearing down becomes necessary for everyone during certain periods in our lives. However, this exercise is meant as a wake-up call to face financial reality, and an opportunity to get energized about realizing FF sooner.

Part C.

Now that you know how to calculate your ***THR ($17.32),*** you can accurately calculate your ***HLF*** when spending money. As introduced earlier, the formula is simple and looks like the following:

HLF =($ Money Spent ÷ THR)

Why do this? Because money spent = your time spent, and your time is as precious as money. In some cases, time is more valuable than money. Think of every purchase as an expenditure of both ***money and time***. Why? Because it is. The difference is, money you can regain, but time is a one way street. When it's gone, that's it. We all have an unknown, yet finite amount of time available to us in life. *Spending money* means you also have to *spend time* to earn it. That's OK, but spending blindly is what you want to avoid. Don't do this for every purchase. Do it when you're faced with a large money transaction. Do it for the excess things you don't need, but buy anyway. Do it to gain your power back.

HLF Example:
You spend $250.00 on a pair of sun glasses, so ***$ Money Spent = $250*** (after tax) and ***THR = $17.32*** (from prior example). Therefore, ***HLF*** *=($ Money Spent ÷ THR.) =* ***$250 / $17.32 = 14.43 hours.*** This means 14.43 hours of your time is now used up and gone in order to have those sun glasses. Was it worth it? For me, the answer is typically no because I lose sunglasses regularly. But since I bought cheap sun glasses my entire life, I treated myself to a nice pair of genuine Rey Bans for once (which got lost). But, the real question to ask is: "When we spend money, is it worth the time it takes to earn that money?" Many times that answer is simply "yes". Other times it's a definite "no". Sometimes it's "I have no idea", or "I don't care", or "I am going to take a chance anyway and buy it." It takes a lot of honesty and soul searching to become realistic about this issue. It takes time, motivation, and brutal honesty to face ourselves. To stop doing unhealthy things, we have to be willing to change our ways. Tracking expenses and calculating things like THR and HLF is fundamental and necessary for nearly all businesses, organizations, and institutions throughout the world. They might go by different names, like *"Expense Tracking", "Cost Analysis", and "Time Management",* but they are fundamentally the same concepts used in the business world. They're just as important on an individual basis too.

In summary, this little exercise will help you see how much you are actually *spending* each month in terms of not just *money*, but also *time*. This in turn will reveal ***how*** you are actually ***living*** and *spending both your money and time on earth*. But, unlike money, you can't get that time back. If we're lucky, we might get a second or third chance. But time has still elapsed and we grow older each year. How we spend the time we have available on earth is as critical as how we spend our money.

You seldom here someone on their death bed say: *"If only I had more money right now".* Usually, a person might say: *"If only I had more time", or; "If only I spent my time more wisely", or; "If only I had spent more time with you".*

A note about Time: *This simple calculation will provide a foundation for the rest of the FF program. In one way or another, it's also a critical concept in other systems or books that teach financial literacy. It has to be done, no matter how much you dislike the idea initially. Eventually, you will learn to do it automatically, and see it as a powerful tool to control your financially destiny. It requires discipline and consistency. Start one day at a time. It becomes more doable, and not so overwhelming, over "time".*

CHAPTER 4

Step 4: Investment Control

Step 4. Investment Control - *Overview*

Questions:

Next Page

What does Investment Control (IC) mean?
What does "Passive Income" mean?
Why are IC and Passive Income so important?
Does learning about IC take time, or can I do it fairly quickly?
What about investment advisors? Should I use one, invest myself, or do both?
What kinds of Investments should I consider for my FF savings fund?

Answers:

Investment Control (IC) means learning and implementing safe and profitable ways to invest the savings you generate from your earned income. Over time, it will grow larger by generating "free" money that you don't have to work for. Remember: Savings from earned income is called net income, or NI. Net income is the extra money you have available (after expenses & taxes) to invest with. You can also invest "pre-tax" dollars inside IRS qualified retirement accounts - like IRA's, 401k's, 403b's, annuities, and life insurance policies. In those cases, your cash grows "tax-deferred" which means it's taxed later. You also get a tax deduction for that year when you make contributions. Cash inside retirement accounts (IRA's, Roth IRA's, 401k's,403b's) can also be invested in stocks and bonds. But eventually your money gets taxed when you start taking it out later in life. Taxes must always be paid. It's just a matter of when and how much. The exceptions to paying tax upon withdrawal are Roth IRA's and Roth 401k's, which are funded with "after-tax" income. That means you pay income tax upfront. There's no tax due upon withdrawal because it's already been paid prior to contributing to the Roth IRA or Roth 401k.

Passive Income has several meanings. For some, passive income means rental income from real estate only, while income from securities like stocks and bonds is called "investment income". For the purposes of this chapter, both investment categories will be considered "passive income". It is simply the extra money that is generated from all your "non-job" types of investments. Note: It's called passive income because you do not have to actually work for it. Instead, you "passively" watch it being generated over time - even while you sleep or do little-to- nothing to physically earn it. The primary concern is to **choose** and **monitor** your investments wisely and not get too greedy. That's the art and science of investing. Easy to say. Harder to achieve. Knowledge is power. Knowledge is your best friend. Gain knowledge first.

IC and Passive Income are important because you typically need your <u>base savings</u> (principal) **plus** the <u>extra money</u> generated from the investment (interest, dividends, rent, etc.) to live off of in the future when you become FF. Without investing , your savings alone probably will not be enough for you to achieve FF because it will not grow any larger on its own. However, it's important to leave some percentage of your savings in cash for immediate access and unknown emergencies. *Therefore*, you don't want to invest all your savings (NI), but you should invest a reasonable portion of it so it will grow beyond the base amount you start with. Growing your excess money, without physically working and being careful as to what you invest in, is the main idea behind all sound investing principals since the beginning of civilization. (Overview cont'd on next page.)

Questions:

What does Investment Control (IC) mean ?
What does "Passive Income" mean?
Why are IC and Passive Income so important?

Previous Page

Does learning about IC take time, or can I do it fairly quickly?
What about investment advisors? Should I use one, invest myself, or do both?
What kinds of Investments should I consider for my FF savings fund?

Answers: *cont'd.*

Learning about investing takes time. It can be done quickly too, but you will probably lose money very fast. To invest wisely means to earn passive income and **not** lose your base "savings amount", which is called your "principal". Over time, the long term goal is to make more money than you started out with, and measure it against industry standard growth rates.

What about investment advisors and brokers? Be very careful. Learn to ask lots of questions before you hand over your hard earned money to an investment broker. A good way to begin (after studying some investment basics), is to interview at least half a dozen well known investment brokers without committing to anyone. If you find one you feel comfortable with, open an account (known as a "managed account"), and give them a trial run. You can later switch to another broker at any time if you're unsatisfied. If you're unsure about the big "managed brokerage firms", consider opening a free, low-cost, self-managed online investment account with a broker like E*TRADE or Ameritrade. The worst thing you can do is hand over all your money to a sales-driven, high commission-based investment broker without exploring more options. Many retail brokers, like Edward Jones, et al, are notorious for pushing products that benefit their balance sheets, and charging IRA and 401K fees when other firms provide them for free. Whether you make money or lose it, they charge you fees. In my case, Edward Jones did just that. They had a revolving door of arrogant sales advisors who either pushed trades I didn't want, or looked mystified about substantial bond losses I incurred based on their recommendations. They pretended to care. In reality, EJ's sales advisors are under tremendous pressure to make sales quotas for the firm. When they don't meet those quotas, they get tossed out and replaced with another sales troll. The cycle then repeats itself. After a decade of that nonsense, (aside from a few good investment experiences early on), I moved my entire portfolio over to E*TRADE eight years ago and have never looked back.

Investments are categorized by "Asset Classes", also known as "Investment Vehicles". Asset classes are different investment choices to pick from, in order to grow your money, such as stocks, bonds, or annuities. Asset classes should have solid reputations and not be too speculative - especially as you approach fifty or older - unless you have a stomach for high risk. People have different levels of risk tolerance, which leads to differences in opinions over what to invest in. A safe starting point for FF investing would be the following choices: *investment grade bonds (A or better), an S&P indexed mutual fund, dividend stocks from companies with solid financials and high cash flow, U.S. Treasury Bonds, and bank or credit union CD accounts when the interest rates offered are above market.*

Step 4. Investment Control - *Overview, cont'd.*

The money you save and invest needs to generate "liquidity and free cash flow" (bank interest, stock dividends, rental income, U.S. Savings Bonds, investment grade corporate bonds, etc.). Eventually over enough time, these sources of invested savings will generate enough (passive income) that pays your bills so you don't have to work unless you choose to. That is FF in a nut shell. In this step, we'll focus on the pros and cons of various investment types that make sense for an FF program. There will always be more than one choice. Often, it's a mix of assets you end up investing in. For example, a good FF investment strategy might be investment grade bonds, small and large cap dividend paying stocks, an S&P indexed mutual fund, a small amount of growth stocks, real estate, and credit union CD's (Certificates of Deposit). Together with a steady job, spending wisely, and saving money, investing wisely is the life blood of all FF programs. It requires a lot of study. Allow yourself ample time - as in many months and years - to learn and apply sound principals. This is where other book readings I've outlined can help you learn a great deal more about the truth of wise investing - including people like Warren Buffett and the Columbia Professor who taught him named Benjamin Graham.

Do not simply go out and hire an investment manager, no matter how big or well known. Do your homework first. They will gladly take your money and often lose it, and you will still owe them a commission and be ignorant about how to invest your money. I switched to E*TRADE after years of dismal service and losses under a "managed account" with Edward Jones. Switching to a "self-managed account" like E*TRADE is not for everyone, but it worked for me and helped turn around my portfolio and investing experience substantially. I good friend of mine had a similar dismal experience with another large retail brokerage firm who was managing his money and losing it every quarter. He switched to a self-managed investing broker and his portfolio increased over 50%. On the other hand, my daughter is pleased with her retail investment broker and is comfortable with the fees they charge her for managing her account. To each their own. Below are a few excellent books about stock and bond investing. Each author is well known - if not famous - for the insights they provide and the successes they've achieved over many decades.

The book by Jeremy Siegel called "Stocks for the Long Run", and "The Intelligent Investor" by Ben Graham with Jason Zweig, go very deep into "value-based" stock and bond investing based on buying stocks and bonds for dividend and capital appreciation (total return),and holding them long term. In another book called: "Snow Ball; Warren Buffett and the Business of Life" The author (Alice Schroder) explains why Mr. Buffett's well-researched stock investing method was successful for over half a century. Thorough research, due diligence, timing, and integrity were key to that success.

Few people are motivated to do this kind of rigorous analysis, so they rely on investment advisers. That works occasionally, but often it's the worst way to learn about investing. Mr. Buffett, and his partner Charlie Munger, understand this principal well. You have to know a lot about who it is you're placing your money with. You have to learn how to place the "right" value on the things you buy and sell. You have to roll up your sleeves and study the financials of the firms you plan to invest in. That's what Buffett and Munger did and they aren't alone. Most successful investment experts follow that strategy too. It's a formula that's proven. Learning how to do it successfully, however, takes time. Don't expect silver bullets or instant success. It takes months or years to build a successful portfolio.

Step 4. Investment Control - *The Details*

Finding your Risk Tolerance

The first thing to establish when it comes to investing is your risk tolerance. Every investment choice you make comes with risk. For an FF investment account, the goal should be generating more money with *moderate-to-low risk* of losing your principal. As stated earlier, suitable examples for FF investing might include, but are not limited to: *dividend stocks, S&P 500 indexed mutual funds, investment grade bonds, U.S. Treasury Bonds, bank certificates of deposits, aka "CD's", bank savings accounts, certain types of real estate investing, and certain fixed annuities.* Investment types will be discussed in more detail later in the chapter.

Asset classes have different levels of risk, rates of return (interest paid to you), and minimum dollar amounts needed to enter the game. Investing is like gambling at times: There *is* a minimum buy-in. But unlike pure gambling in Las Vegas, Atlantic City, Monte-Carlo, Macau China, or on a Native American reservation, you can reduce a significant amount of risk by doing adequate due-diligence on who and what you invest in. That's virtually impossible (except for blackjack) in any of the above gambling casinos because the gaming industry thrives on "house advantage" by remaining "opaque"; (i.e. secrecy). Companies that sell their stock to the public can't do that. Often called "equities" in investment circles, publicly traded corporations who sell their stock to the public are highly regulated by a branch of the federal government (SEC) which forces them to publish all their financial statements to the public for free according to very strict rules. The SEC (usually) insures transparent, honest, and accurate reporting, in order to protect the public from financial fraud.

This simply means you or I can go online and pull-up the financial statements (P&L, balance sheet, cash flow) of any Wall Street traded company for free. This is where you gain insight into a company's true financial position. It almost never comes from listening to the main stream media. You have to learn what to look for and that takes time and requires study. You also have to learn how to place a value on the things you buy - including stocks, bonds, annuities, and especially real estate. You have to control your emotions. You also have to know your risk tolerance. All of these skill sets sound like common sense, but they are not easily acquired or executed. Consequently, people lose money all the time when investing. It's also why many people get fleeced by investment brokers and scam artists. Think: *Madoff, Enron, WorldCom, Edward Jones, Ponzi, Lehman, et al.*

How do you find your level of risk: Low, Moderate, or High?

Finding your risk tolerance takes honest introspection and knowledge about what you're going to invest in. Everyone hates to lose money, but we're all different when it comes to how much risk we can endure to earn that money. The definitions below will help you find which risk category you fit into.

High risk tolerance people: People who are willing to make large bets on risky investments *because they focus more on the potential of winning lots of money, rather than losing it.* A high risk person seldom deviates from this type of thinking. They may lose money at times, but soon, they're right back at taking considerable risk in hopes of earning fast and large financial rewards. For them, the thrill of winning over powers the fear of loss.

Moderate risk tolerance people: People who focus on making reasonable amounts of money, but with a keen eye on the potential of losing money; (their principal). I am generally in the moderate risk category when buying stocks and bonds. Moderate risk people are fairly conservative in general, but not to the extent of low risk people. They may even take bigger risks on occasion. For example, I take bigger risks when it comes to real estate investing due to my background in that profession. The strategy of moderate-risk investing involves a little of both high and low risk elements by choosing an asset class ranging from low to average returns, with a good *(but not guaranteed)* probability of ***not*** losing principal. Consistent cash flow is another desirable objective for this risk category, such as investment grade bonds, dividend stocks, certain fixed annuities, and above-market CD's.

Low risk tolerance people: People who *focus almost entirely on the pain of losing money*, compared to making it. Low-risk people are fine making modest amounts of money, but only if there's ***no*** loss of principal. Otherwise, they're worried sick. The strategy of low-risk investing involves choosing an asset class that may offer a very low return, but is virtually guaranteed *never* to lose principal. Think: Bank CD's and US Bonds.

Step 4. Investment Control

Investment Vehicles to Choose From, *aka, Asset Classes*

Learning about ***Investment Vehicle**s* is next. Choose one (or more) that fit(s) your ***risk tolerance*** and can reliably achieve your short and long term financial objectives. For an FF program, that primarily means steady income and principal preservation, even though risk will always be present. Inflation protection (i.e. Gold) is another consideration. Listed below are common investment vehicles (asset classes) to evaluate when the right conditions prevail. Some examples are *not* recommended for FF due to the high risk of principal loss and/or unpredictable cash flow potential. Pros and cons are given for each one.

Bonds - Government and Investment Grade Corporate Bonds *(Low risk, low to moderate returns (3%-7%); Very low returns in low interest rate environments(.02%-1.5%) like those between 2019 - 2020).*

Large Cap Stocks = Capital appreciation only (no dividend) *(Moderate risk; returns vary from negative to moderate. Generally, large cap stocks result in slow but steady price growth over many years).*

Growth Stocks = Capital appreciation (w/wo dividends) *(High risk; returns vary widely between negative and high. Growth stocks yield both high returns and disastrous losses depending on how strong and profitable the company is, coupled with where the company is located in the world).*

Dividend Stocks = Income + appreciation *(Moderate to high risk; guaranteed income via cash dividend despite any capital loss (monthly, quarterly or bi-annually); Low to moderate return (1.5%-7%)).*

Stocks bundled inside an indexed mutual fund *(Low to moderate risk; Moderate but steady growth rate with capital gain potential over the long term if the fund is well managed and tied to a reliable stock index like the Vanguard VOO S&P500). Returns may vary between 2%-7%, with 4.5% as average).*

Real Estate Investing - Rental Income and Capital Gains *(High risk of principal loss, capital intensive, time intensive. Returns vary widely from negative to very high, depending on location and price paid).*

US Treasury Bonds, Bank Savings Accounts, Bank or Credit Union CD's *(Virtually risk free (99%); Low to moderate returns(1% -3%, and extremely low between 2010 and 2020; (i.e. .25%-1.5%)).*

Fixed Annuities - Indexed and non-indexed *(98% risk free for principal, high buy-in risk ($100K+) and long term commitment risk(7-10 years). Returns vary widely from very low (<1%-3%) when rates are low, to above average CD rates(4%-5%), to higher yields(6%-8%) in high interest rate environments).*

****Variable Annuities - Indexed or non-indexed.*** *(High risk of principal loss, high buy-in risk ($100K+), long term commitment risk (7-10 years); Returns vary from low to negative when the stock market goes down, to very high returns(7%-10%) when the market is up. Akin to gambling with stocks).*

****Investing in start-up businesses*** *(Very high risk of principal loss, high stress; Returns vary widely. They range from low to extremely high gains, to catastrophic losses).*

Buying gold, silver, and other commodities. *Gold is more of an insurance policy against future inflation or paper money devaluation, than it is an investment with a reliable rate of return. Buying and holding physical gold or silver may (and sometimes may not) provide such protection. You may have to hold it for many years. *In contrast, trading (buying) in gold or silver paper certificates without actually possessing it, is risky and unpredictable if the primary goal is to generate cash flow or quick gains that never occur.*

** Not recommended for FF. Variable annuities, start-up businesses, or trading in gold certificates involves high risk of principal loss.*

Step 4. Investment Control

Dividend Stocks; Growth Stocks; Stock Mutual Funds

No matter how carefully you adhere to your risk tolerance or select an asset class, the economy and luck play a big role. Think back over the last 100 years to the following events: The beginning of IRS income tax in 1913, WWI, the 1929 stock market crash, the 1930's great depression that followed, WWII, the energy crisis during the 1st and 2nd oil embargos of the 1970's and resulting hyper inflation that lasted until the mid 1980's, the savings and loan/real estate/stock market crash of 1987, the 2001 "Web One" Internet crash, the 2008 housing collapse and resulting financial crisis that lasted over five years - and now in 2020- the COVID-19 global pandemic accompanied by world-wide government mandated lock-downs that are destroying businesses and causing global economic mayhem unlike the world has ever seen. National and global economic forces can throw the best laid plans into crisis mode, so you have to have backup plans and remain alert.

Let's look at Dividend Stocks, which is an example of an asset that pays you income, regardless of the stock rising, falling, or staying the same. Dividend stocks are regular publically traded stocks that also pay you cash. A dividend stock will pay you money when you buy the company's stock, just like a bank pays you interest on a savings account or certificate of deposit. So, whether the stock goes up or down, you will still receive your dividend, which is a rate of interest called the "dividend yield". For example, a stock that cost $20.00 per share that pays an annual dividend of 4%, would pay you $.80 per share per year ($20.00 x .04 = $.80). If you bought $5,000 of that stock, then you would receive $200.00 in dividends per year ($5000 x .04 = $200.00 / yr). If that stock happened to increase in value over that same year, to say $25 per share, then you would also enjoy a gain in appreciation of the stock by $5.00 per share, in addition to the dividend. In this example, the capital appreciation would be the number of shares bought multiplied by the per share increase from when you bought it.

Studying stock profiles (Google or Yahoo Finance) and learning about investors who have achieved successful track records over many years and decades will increase your knowledge about risk, reward, and valuation. Why? Publicly traded company history and financial information is abundant on the internet. Historical data is a great teacher. It doesn't lie. The facts are difficult to hide. This helps you make wiser decisions on what to buy, and what *not to buy in the future!* That same axiom applies to selling investments. Sometimes you make money just by avoiding hasty sell orders and waiting. Other times, the reverse is true. Learning, experience, due diligence, patience, rationality, and time are your best friends. For example, if you bought $5000 of shares at $20/share, that would equal 250 shares ($5,000 /$20 per share = 250 shares). 250 shares x $5.00 increase in share price equals a $1,250 price increase since you bought it. That's what capital appreciation is. It's good to have capital appreciation, or "*capital gains*" as it's usually called. But you can just as easily lose money on stocks as make it.

The following page shows a detailed example of a dividend stock from AT&T, why it's a good alternative to bonds or CD's in low interest rate environments like 2020, and how all the technical jargon works. However, successful stock buying and selling also depends on what price you initially buy the stock at. For example, in 2012 when I bought my initial shares of ATT stock, it increased almost 90% over seven years while paying almost 5% in dividends. Then in 2019, the stock decreased by over 30%, but still paid a good dividend of 7%. What did I do? First I got depressed. Then I did nothing. Why? It cost me zero money to hold the stock and not sell it. Meanwhile, I still make free money on ATT's generous dividend, which they've paid consistently over thirty years.

Step 4. Investment Control

Dividend Stock Example - AT&T

Below is an example of a stock (ATT) that pays between 4.75% to 7% in dividends. I own a lot of ATT stock because of the following features:

1) AT&T is a $221B telecom giant capable of huge cash flows, consistent profits, and staying power.
1) AT&T (with Verizon) dominates the market and has never lowered their dividend in over thirty years.
2) 4.75% to 6.74 % is a decent return on investment - especially in an ultra low interest rate environment like we've had in the past decade (2010 - 2020). High grade bonds can't even compare right now. Neither can most CD's. To be conservative, I've used the lower yield range (4.75%), which is explained below.

The term ***"Div/ yield 0.49/4.75"*** expresses how much money you get paid per share and what that equates to as an annual interest rate. In this case, the left number ***"0.49"*** means you get 49 cents per share ($.49/share) paid every 3 months. The right number ***"4.75"*** expresses your dividend (money) as an interest rate earned per year. In this case, it's 4.75%. The yield, or interest rate, is always expressed annually, while the dividend amount is typically paid quarterly, unless there's a note to the contrary - like bi-annually, or monthly. Since the dividend is paid to you four times per year, it's necessary to make a simple math adjustment so that the interest rate is calculated correctly on an annual basis (and not a quarterly basis) . Therefore, the interest rate, (yield), is arrived at by doing the following: ***Dividend yield = yearly dividend $ amount per share per year / stock price***. This means we have to multiple the quarterly dividend ($.49) by four (4) to get the total dividend per year = (4 x $.49) = $1.96 /year/share.

To summarize, the dividend yield is simply calculated as follows:

Annual dividend yield = (yearly dividend) / (stock price). Doing the math results in the below figures: $1.96 / $41.25 per share = .0475 = 4.75%. That's considerably more than what A+ bonds currently pay.

AT&T Inc. (NYSE:T)
41.25
+0.07 (0.17%)

Range	41.20 - 41.52
52 week	35.91 - 43.89
Open	41.48
Vol / Avg.	19.15M/21.12M
Mkt cap	253.75B

Div/yield	0.49/4.75
EPS	2.10
Shares	6.14B
Beta	0.39
Inst. own	55%

Next, let's look at some other types of ways to buy stocks: *Growth Stocks, Mutual Stock Funds, and Technical investing.*

Step 4. Investment Control

Growth Stocks (large cap value*, with or without dividends).

*The term "large cap value" stands for "large market capitalization value", which is a classification given to publically traded corporations with market values in excess of $10 billion.

A successful FF stock investment strategy that works for many - including myself - is to pick a combination of both dividend paying stocks, and a few stocks for their growth appreciation potential. One example is Amazon, which I bought purely for appreciation potential at $790 per share in late 2016. By mid 2018, it increased to around $1700 per share. Amazon is currently trading above $3000 a share as of late 2020. I bet and won. But I researched their earnings by studying Amazon's financials. Amazon was poised to keep making more money due to Amazon Prime's massive cash flow from their streaming server farms and dominate Ecommerce position. However, that kind of gain - while exciting - is not common. It's actually uncommon. Still, Amazon's stock price remains high even after the COVID-19 stock market crash in March of 2020. Market crashes are good stock price tests, and Amazon managed to pass the test well. Its' stock price dropped around 13% and then bounced back to its pre-crash price of nearly $2000 per share within days. Meanwhile, the overall stock market on March 23, 2020 went down approximately 25% to 30% with some stocks dropping by 50%. Some stocks still haven't recovered. Oil giant Exxon is one example.

Amazon could continue to go up, down, or stay flat. I am willing to bet it's going up further over the next few years due to their phenomenal business model and dominate ecommerce market share. The time to buy is when prices are low. That takes faith and guts. My wife did just that when stock prices were artificially depressed due to COVID-19. She bought more Amazon at $1800 per share, and it soon shot-up even higher to $3000 within several months. Even I was surprised it went that high so quick. Netflix and Adobe continue to perform well due to massive cash flow resulting form their subscription-based Internet services. Doing homework, timing, and taking calculated risks pays off. There's lots of things to consider. Still, a thin line often exists between gambling and investing. Don't take it lightly.

Indexed Stock Mutual Funds

Another widely used, relatively safe, and reasonably profitable place to put your investment dollars stock-wise, is in what's called an "indexed mutual fund". You have to do some soul searching and independent research to find which ones would be suited to your risk tolerance and investment goals. The one I chose is called the Vanguard S&P 500 Indexed Mutual Fund. It has gone up about 15% over eighteen months. My son is a financial analyst at Disney and graduated from the Wharton Business school. He did some research and recommended it to me.

An indexed mutual fund is simply a group of stocks lumped together into one big pool or "fund" of stocks. That fund has an average stock price and projected growth rate that closely mirrors a particular stock index, like the S&P 500 Stock Index, or the Dow Jones Industrials average stock index. The S&P 500 index uses 500 companies to arrive at an average stock price value. The Dow Industrial Average uses only 30 companies, which is far less predictable and more volatile. Stock mutual funds that are tied to the S&P 500 stock index have been performing more predictably over the past decade because of these facts.

Step 4. Investment Control

Technical Investing - High risk, high stakes stock market gambling?

Indexed stock funds and dividend stocks aren't for everyone, especially if you crave higher returns and are willing to take bigger risks. I have a long-time friend who has a high risk tolerance for many things in life. This includes stock trading, which he loves to do by buying and selling fairly large dollar amounts of stocks on a regular basis. In fact, after he fired his last sales-driven "high-profile" stock broker three years ago, he finally started making big gains.
How? He joined a stock club that enhanced his own research. He then created a stock "watch list" and analyzed various stock prices over the past 12, 36, and 60 months. You can do this yourself using Google or Yahoo Finance. When a stock tip looks promising, he often invests large sums of cash on stocks that look poised to increase, and takes the commensurate risk of purchasing that stock in the hope of it going up in a short (or medium) time frame. If it doesn't perform well, he holds it for a certain period, sells it, and reinvests that money back into another stock. Some stocks he lets ride and keeps long-term.

This is sometimes called "technical investing". In reality, it's a combination of intelligent investing and gambling, but it's based on timing and well researched figures and facts, not just pure luck. He's lost money some months, but on average over the past 48 months, his stock portfolio increased in value by over 67%. He started with a principal amount of $600,000 and grew it in value to $1,000,000 during that four year period. He also has a cast iron stomach for risk taking (i.e. high risk tolerance). Some days he's up $30,000. Other days he's down $20,000. He's retired and enjoys spending time managing his portfolio daily, but not everyone can or wants to do that.

In mid 2019, sensing a possible market correction, he sold all his stock and put the cash in liquid CD's that paid 2%. In late 2019, he was hungry for some action again, but this time he only reinvested 20% of his total portfolio back into the stock market. Three months later, in March of 2020, the COVID-19 virus took a massive toll on everyone's investment portfolios around the world - including his 20%. He was uncertain about what to do, so he did nothing. That decision paid off. The remaining 80% of his money was already safe and continued to earn interest regardless of irrational stock market gyrations. After three weeks, his stocks were back up 20%+. He got out in mid 2020 with a gain of 67% again. By October of 2020, and being in the high risk tolerance category, he jumped back in, but with only 20% of his total cash as before. Was it luck or wisdom? A little of both? One thing I know for sure - and I've known him for over forty years - is he's very good about being realistic and following his gut instincts. His gut was telling him back in 2019 that the U.S. stock market might be headed for a big correction in the near future. He followed his gut, on one hand, and got out. Months later, he yielded to his desire to make more money since the stock market remained hot. But, he never forgot how hard it was to earn money as a self-employed auto mechanic and finish carpenter. Having worked hard his entire life, his realistic side protected him by limiting his risk to 20% of his total portfolio each time he jumped back in the market.

The take away on this example is this: While 67% sounds great, growing a self-managed or fully managed stock portfolio and earning 7% is hard enough, let alone 17% annually over four straight years. It's not typical and can't be taken lightly. It takes high risk tolerance, discipline, research, experience, consistency, courage, and some luck, to pull-off a 67% increase over four years, which equates to 16.76% growth per year. 7% used to be a reliable historical average. Today, 2% to 5% is now more common. Lots of people break even or lose money in the stock market daily. Just ask around, but don't believe everything you hear either. Some returns are calculated wrong or exaggerated - by brokers and investors alike.

Step 4. Investment Control

Long Term versus Short Term Investing

Conventional investment wisdom teaches that you should research and buy stocks carefully, and then hold those stocks for the long term, in order to make long term money via capital gains and any dividends they pay. Buying and then selling stocks too frequently can lead to rapid investment losses due to commissions, market swings, and acting on emotion rather than rational decisions. My friend knows this, but unlike me, only occasionally buys and holds stocks for the long run. He isn't afraid to cut some loose, and reinvest the money in a better performing stock. I, on the other hand, deplore stressing over my portfolio frequently and simply want it to generate modest but consistent cash flow each year without losing (much) principal or sleep. The trick is figuring out which stocks to buy, which to sell, which to hold, and when to pull the trigger. That takes lots of experience and goes beyond the intent of this chapter. This is where other recommended books can help, like on page sixty nine in this chapter, and also in Chapter 7: *Making a Mentor List*.

In summary, aside from a very small percentage of growth stocks like Amazon, a safe and robust FF investment strategy might consist of asset classes comprised of investment grade bonds (A- or better), dividend paying stocks, an S&P indexed mutual fund, CD's, and real estate. For the most part, that's what has worked for me over the past thirty years. You can never stop learning because investing is part science, part art, part timing, part self control, and part luck. It constantly evolves and fluxuates on one hand, yet is very predictable on the other. When all the parts come together in unison, you win more often. But equally important is winning over the long term. Other than people like my friend who has a high risk appetite and laser focus on stock buying and selling, short term trading is generally very risky and unsuitable for people investing in an FF program.

You have to learn, experiment, and re-evaluate what works for you. To get started, you might consider allocating 20% of your total savings towards dividend stocks, 50% towards an S&P 500 indexed mutual fund, 20% in bank CD's, and the remainder in emergency cash. Over time, you'll learn to readjust those percentages to suit your risk tolerance, financial needs, investing opportunities, and age.

Step 4. Investment Control

Real Estate Investing.

One thing is certain: while real estate can be potentially profitable, it can also be highly risky, stressful, and cash intensive. Many fortunes have been lost in real estate ventures that have gone bad due to poor estimating, poor construction, bad design, partners breaking up, zoning law changes, and economy downturns. The great depression of the 1930's, the real estate bust that followed IRS tax changes in the late 1980's, the great recession of the 2008-2012 housing melt-down and bank crisis, and most recently - the COVID-19 global pandemic crisis - are four vivid examples of external forces wreaking havoc on the real estate market.

As an architect, general contractor, real estate broker, and real estate investor, I speak from experience. Real Estate investing is an asset class *not* to take lightly. Real estate can be a great wealth building asset, but it involves many things to succeed. It requires knowledge, time, hard work, dealing with government regulations, market timing, cash, and perseverance to successfully make a profit over the long term. The following page shows two examples of investing in real estate. The first example illustrates what's involved in attempting to make short term capital gains; (i.e.: buy and flip a house for profit). The second example illustrates buying real estate for long term rental cash flow purposes. Each has its own risks and rewards.

The *"buy, fix, and flip"* example shows a loss, due to paying too much and unaccounted carrying costs related to owning real estate while trying to sell it. In contrast, the real estate rental example shows a positive cash flow. Lots of hidden costs are involved when renting a building to the public. Achieving a positive rental cash flow requires a lot more than just paint, carpet, and throwing up a rent sign. It takes wise purchasing, prudent management, careful tenant screening, and thorough tracking of all costs. It looks simple. The execution is not.

The primary ways to earn (or lose) money in real estate are:

1) Buying existing residential or commercial property, fixing it up, and selling it for profit.

2) Buying existing residential or commercial property and renting it out for positive monthly cash flow.

3) Buying residential property to live in as a primary residence and holding it as an investment. The property may (or may not) appreciate over time. If it does increase in value, equity can be "tapped" by taking out loans against the home. It can also serve as a major capital gains investment that has up to a *$500,000 tax-free IRS exemption for a married couple if the home is later sold, providing it was occupied as a primary residence for two out of the past five years.
*($250,000 tax free exemption for single tax payers).

4) Buying raw land and holding it for future appreciation, in order to sell it for a profit.

5) Buying raw land and constructing new residential or commercial buildings for rent or for re-sale.

6) Buying raw land and renting the land to commercial, industrial, government, or residential developers. The developers never own the land. Instead, the developers (tenants) pay rent for the land, and they typically have to pay all building construction costs located on it. The land owner almost always trumps the building owner if a default occurs. If the company or person who rented the land later defaults, they also lose all the buildings that were constructed on that land. Think of Hong Kong: The British Empire had a 99 year land lease with the Chinese government and constructed many expensive buildings between 1897 to 1997 in Hong Kong harbor. But China still owned the land underneath and took back both the land and the buildings in 1997 when the lease ended and was not renewed. This was the risk the British government took in spite of billions of pounds in construction costs that were later forfeited. Ultimately, the revenues generated and ROI far exceeded the costs. The high risk of never owning the land was worth taking because the cash flow and profits were so high over a century of time.

Step 4. Investment Control -

More Real Estate Investment Examples, *cont'd.*

This page provides real estate investing excerpts from *Achieving Financial Freedom...in 5 Basic Steps.* Shown are step-by-step breakdowns of both "fix & flip" and "rental cash flow" investments.

Real Estate Example #1: *Buy, Fix and Flip*

Below, a loss occurs on a "buy, fix, and flip" property due to high purchase and carrying costs. Furthermore, the property location limits the re-selling price. It's very easy to lose money on flips due to poor due diligence, bad construction management, unrealistic financial projections, the economy changing, or a combination of all these forces.

Financial statement of a fix and flip real estate investment, held one year:

Selling price = flip price = $553,925
Less cost basis (orig. price) = (-$508,500)

Gross profit $ 45,425
Less Carry costs (-$58,077)
(Mortgage interest, insur., prop.taxes, util.,repairs,remodel work, city permits,)

Profit / Loss before tax (-12,652) Loss

Seller's principal reduction +6,468 (credit)

Total Project Cost (-$560,109) ◄
(-$508,500) + (- 58,077) + 6,468 = $560,109)

Actual Net Cash Flow (-$6,184) Loss
$553,925 - ($560,109) = (-$6,184)

Where's the beef?

Example of various Development Cost Categories.

Total Project Costs - New, Existing or Remodel			Annual $ / SF
Retreieve Automatically? "Y" or "N".................		N	
	Enter Manually	..&/or Automatically	
Purchase Price (land+bldg) →	-$508,500		$87.72
Land (if new development)			$0.00
Const. Costs (new or exist)	$0.00	**$0.00**	$0.00
Architecture/Engineering	$0.00		$0.00
Permits/Fees	$0.00		$0.00
Testing/Surveys	$0.00		$0.00
Legal Expense	$0.00		$0.00
Builder's Risk Insurance	$0.00		$0.00
Advertising/Marketing	$0.00		$0.00
Office/Rental Furnishings	-$58,077		$0.00
Closing Costs			$0.00
Interest Carry →			$0.00
Principal Reduction →	+$6,468		$0.00
		$0.00	$0.00
Total Project Costs →	**-$560,109**		

Debt Service Example. Debt Service means there is a bank or investor loan on the property. This in turn means there will be a monthly mortgage payment on the property that has to be paid before the owner can realize any "true" positive cash flow. Refer to the line item below under "Development Financials" that reads "Mortgage Payment (P&I) @ $299.78 / mo.

Also refer to the next page on the "Real Estate Rental Feasibility Analysis". Look for "Debt Service" at Row CF8. The same mortgage payment figure shows up.

Development Financial Variables			
(With Leverage = Financing)			Annual
		Annual	$/SF
Amortization Period - Months		360	
Interest Rate		6.00%	
	Total Project Costs	$50,000.00	
	Equity/Cash down	$0.00	
Loan Amount		$50,000.00	
Mortgage Payment (P&I)		($299.78)	
Loan to Value Ratio (LTV)		100.00%	
Operating Expenses/Net SF		($2.29)	
Vacancy/Collection Loss %		8.33%	
Gross Rents/Net SF/Mo		$1.49	

Development Financials	Monthly	Annual
Mortgage Payment (P&I)	($299.78) ←	($3,597.30)
Capitz. Gross Rents (Mkt.Value)		
Capitalization Rate		
Cur. Market Value/Gross SF		
Projected Gross Income	$850.00	$10,200.00
Break-even = Min.Cash Flow in $	$479.19	$5,750.30
(ebit=pmt.tot.dev.=cf3=cf8+cf4+cf6)	----------	----------
Projected Pos.Cash Flow	$370.81	$4,449.70

Step 4. Investment Control - *The Details, cont'd.*

More Real Estate Investment Examples, *cont'd.*

Real Estate Example #2: ***Buy for Rental Income***

REAL ESTATE RENTAL FEASIBILITY ANALYSIS: NOI, BTCF, ATCF, & ROI				Latest update: 2/18/2017			
Statement of Cash Flow				**Monthly $**	**$/SF/Mo**	**Annual $**	**$/SF/Year**
CF1	*Gross Rents*			$850.00	$1.49	$10,200.00	$17.89
CF2	Other Income			$0.00	$0.00	$0.00	$0.00
CF3	Total Gross Income			$850.00	$1.49	$10,200.00	$17.89
CF4		*Vacancy / Collect Loss*	(8%/yr)	($70.83)	($0.12)	($850.00)	($1.49)
CF5	Effective Gross Income			$779.17	$1.37	$9,350.00	$16.40
CF6		*Operating Expenses**		($108.58)	($0.19)	($1,303.00)	($2.29)
CF7	*Net Operating Income (NOI = EBIT)*			$670.58	$1.18	$8,047.00	$14.12
CF8		Debt Service		($299.78)	($0.53)	($3,597.30)	($6.31)
CF9	*Before Tax Cash Flow (BTCF)*			$370.81	$0.65	$4,449.70	$7.81
CF10	Tax Rate: Combined State & Fed		30.00%	($111.24)	($0.20)	($1,334.91)	($2.34)
CF11	*After Tax Cash Flow (ATCF)*		0.70	$259.57	$0.46	$3,114.79	$5.46

The above table shows a rental cash flow analysis projection that could be for either residential or commercial tenants. To read the cash flow projection report, begin at the top left at "CF1", and then work your way down to row CF11.

As you go down each row, look to the right and read the column headings for: "Monthly $", $/SF/Mo", "Annual $, and "$/SF/Year".

In this example, the landlord will theoretically be making money after all expenses and taxes (CF11), totaling $259.57 / month and $3,114.79 / year. Rows CF9 and CF11 show positive numbers in black, which means they generate positive cash for the owner.

Also notice that potential vacancies have been accounted for in row CF4, at about 8% vacancy loss. Other rental expenses shown are: Debt service (bank loan) in CF8, and State and Federal taxes in CF10 at a conservative 30% average tax rate.

End of Step 4: Investment Control.

CHAPTER 5

Step 5: Reaching Financial Freedom

Step 5. Reaching Financial Freedom - *Overview*

Questions:

What is the purpose of Step 5, "Reaching Financial Freedom?
How do I actually execute Step 5?
What are the Key Concepts and Questions in Step 5?
What FF Investment Formulas and Strategies should I use?

Answers:

The Purpose of Reaching Financial Freedom:
The purpose of Step 5 (reaching FF) is integrating all the previous steps of your FF journey (Steps 1-4). This in turn allows you to realistically and permanently become financial free, and then ultimately maintain it for the rest of your life.

How do I actually execute Step 5?
By creating a FF Summary Form that shows your Living Expenses, Job Income, and Investment Income expressed together over time. The FF Summary quickly and accurately shows your current FF progress and how much more work (in terms of time, job income, and investment income) you have left to do.

What are the Key Concepts and Questions in Step 5?
How much money you need to live on per month when you retire and have no job.

How much money you're saving and investing right now for retirement.

The range of realistic and achievable interest rates you should be considering for your investments. This is called your "rate of return", "cost of capital", or simply "return".

How much more money you may need in case you underestimate certain living costs.

What age should you start saving? The sooner the better, but remember: It's never too late.

What age do you want to retire at?

How do you calculate the answers to the above concepts and questions using financial strategies and formulas that are time tested and reliable?

(Overview Cont'd on next page)

Step 5. Reaching Financial Freedom *Overview (cont'd.)*

Questions: *(cont'd.)*

What is the purpose of Step 5, "Reaching Financial Freedom?
How do I actually execute Step 5?
What are the Key Concepts and Questions in Step 5?
What FF Investment Formulas and Strategies should I use?

Answers: *(cont'd.)*

What FF Investment Formulas and Strategies to use:
Two fundamental FF formulas will be discussed:

FF Investment Method #1: ***Annual*** *estimating approach,* based on five factors below:

1) Decide how much money you need for living expenses (each year at retirement);

2) Decide on a realistic COC = cost of capital = the interest rate for investing your money;

3) Estimate how many years you will save money (for retirement);

4) Calculate your approximate total retirement nest egg;

5) Calculate approximately how much you need to save each year.

FF Investment Method #2: ***Monthly*** *estimating approach*, based on ***one or many*** monthly income streams as the financial goal.

1) Calculate your ***present and future monthly Passive Income*** (PI) from all Investments. Do this by adding all your monthly (PI) sources: {Investments (Stocks, bonds, annuities) + Pensions + Social Security + Rental Income + any interest on cash or other source}.

2) Estimate your anticipated monthly expenses, and compare that to your passive income in answer #1) above. When your PI equals or is greater than #2) expenses, you have reached a state of Financial Freedom. The key is to then maintain and safeguard it for life. See #3.

3) Create a FF Summary Form by documenting your (current active) job income, expenses, and investment income in one of several ways: Keep a simple journal of each month's job income, expenses, and passive income, and/or: plot those figures on a graph to see your FF progress visually over time. The ultimate goal is maintaining your FF status by consistently monitoring #1 and #2, which means living within your (PI) and expense targets.

Step 5. Reaching Financial Freedom - *The Details*

Purpose: Step 5 is about integrating all the previous steps of your FF journey, arriving at financial freedom, and maintaining it for the rest of your life. It's about living your life the way you want to - free from job slavery, crippling debt, and money worries - so you can pursue your dreams and desires (legally and within your financial limits).

FF doesn't always mean you will be debt free or job free, though "debt free" is always good and "job free" may be a choice rather than a necessity. It means your bills are 100% covered (or very close to 100%) by passive income, which frees you to pursue your dreams, or, simply continue working or doing what you may currently love to do in life.

How?

In Step 5 you're going to apply the FF Formula. *You'll be piecing together the FF formula and plugging in your FF variables from Steps 1-4, in a FF Summary Form, or on a visual chart. From there, you'll work the plan every day, month, and year like a determined hungry tiger.*

Key Concepts Covered in Chapter 5.

How much money do you think you can realistically live on per month when you retire and have no job? How much are you saving right now for retirement? How much more will you need? What age will you start saving? What age do you want to retire at? How do you calculate these answers using financial strategies and formulas that are time tested and reliable?

Determining your future {FF / Retirement} nest egg involves saving and investing money (now) while you're still working, and then using (living on) that money later in life when you retire and no longer work. To accurately determine how much retirement savings you'll need requires a realistic estimate of three key factors.

Some factors occur in the future and must be estimated. Others are determined in the present moment. The three factors are:

1) How much money is needed to live on during retirement?
2) The interest rate on your investments, called the Cost of Capital?
3) Time Duration: The age you start saving and the age you retire at?

*There is more than one way to calculate the answer to the above retirement variables. Two methods are presented here: **FF Investment Method #1** and **FF Investment Method #2.** The choice is yours as to which method fits better with your life style and job situation (Explained later). Other strategies exist within the financial world, and it would behoove you to explore them at times. In the final analysis, they all require some (or all) of the variables listed here, and they all end up with fundamentally solving for the same solution - the income and nest egg needed for FF on terms that are realistic and suited to your lifestyle.*

FF Investment Method #1:

FF Investment Method #1 is a quick estimating approach that determines your future retirement money needs, based on a reasonably accurate approximation of five key variables listed below:

1) How much money you think you need for living expenses each year at retirement;

2) Estimating a realistic COC = Cost of Capital = an interest rate you "hope" to realistically receive - now and in the future - on your invested money;

3) Estimating how many years you will save money for retirement;

4) Calculating your approximate total retirement nest egg, and;

5) Calculating approximately how much you need to save each year to fund your FF nest egg.

Details of each key variable

1) Estimate your future Retirement Income. Estimate a future annual "before-tax" income amount that you think would cover all your living expenses once you retire. Note: This is where most people make big mistakes. Be very careful. You need to have a firm grasp on your expenses to do this right. This future annual retirement figure can vary widely. Start by estimating a monthly income that is about 5% to 20% more than you may need. This gives you a cushion for mistakes and also helps cover future inflation. Convert that monthly income into an annual salary by multiplying it by 12.

Monthly income examples might be: $3000 per month, $4500 per month, and $7000 per month. These are all "before tax" incomes. They equate to $36,000, $54,000, and $84,000 per year respectively; {12x3000 = $36K/yr; 12x$4500 = $54K/yr. ; 12x$7000 = $84K/yr.}
If you need more or less money during retirement, adjust the annual figures up or down accordingly. These are typical income ranges that millions of people in the United States and other G-20 countries live on during their retirement years. If you're not sure, start with the lowest estimate of $36,000 a year, which is $3000 per month before taxes. Re-run the numbers until you start to feel comfortable.

2) Estimate an adequate but realistic Cost of Capital (COC). This simply means you must estimate a realistic interest rate that you can expect to receive today on the money you invest for your future retirement. That means the money you invest today will be saved and used to pay bills after you stop working. Therefore, *Your COC* is an estimated interest rate that you could realistically achieve by investing your money today, while waiting to receive the proceeds later in the future.
For example, if you buy a $10,000 bond today that pays 4% annually as of right now, and you hold it for 20 years, then 4% is what you will earn each year for the next 20 years on $10,000. That equates to .04 x $10,000 x 20 years = $8,000 in earned interest over a 20 year period. In twenty years, you will end up with your $10,000 back, plus an extra $8,000 in earned dividends (interest income).

Therefore, your cost of capital (COC) in this example is .04 = 4%, which historically isn't that high for investment purposes. However, it remains relatively good in a low interest rate environment like the one that exists today (2020/2021). ***Note,*** however, that this is where many investors end up short in tough times - including massive university endowment funds, multibillion dollar public pension funds, financial advisors, big-name brokers, and FF gurus. Why? *Because they were overly optimistic and estimated the COC wrong by being **too high***. When people estimate COC rates like 8%, 10%, and 12%, and instead end up with 2%, 4%, or 5%, future cash flows from investments fall drastically short. Then pandemonium sets in.

3) Estimate the Time Duration (how long) that you will save and invest money. Estimate a *beginning year* and an *ending year for saving and investing* In other words, make your best guess-estimate of when you will start saving and investing, and when you will stop working and retire (or simple become FF). This means you will start saving at some point in time, and retire at another point in time.

For example, suppose you start saving at age 30. You estimate your FF retirement age at 65. This gives you 35 years to save and invest money for your retirement nest egg (65 years - 30 years = 35 years). That may be too little, too much, or just right. It will depend on many variables. The critical variables are discussed in this section, but they need to be analyzed and re-calculated many times before you start to see clearly and estimate realistically over time.

4) Compute the total FF Nest Egg you're going to need for retirement, based on steps #1) and #2). After computing the answers to steps #1) and #2), divide the annual income of step #1) by the COC in step #2). This is a rough estimate of your needed retirement capital. The figure may be larger than what you need for now, due to compounding interest, which is ignored for now and explained later. There are various ways to calculate this very accurately, including the effects of compounded interest, but that goes beyond the basic intent of this chapter. For now, this formula is easy, quick, and close enough to serve as an initial target. Example: Step 1 retirement annual income = $36,000. Step 2 COC = 4% = .04 (4%/100 = .04). Therefore, $36,000 / .04 = $900,000. This approximates your entire nest egg that's needed to generate $36,000 per year at 4% (.04) interest, before taking into account compounding interest, which would yield even more money.

***NOTE:** You will still have your $900,000 principal to tap into for spending, but doing so too quickly lowers the principal balance (the $900K) and thus will reduce the $36K passive income. One rule of thumb in the investment community is to draw down your principal at a rate of around 3% to 5% per year so you don't take too much (of your principal) too fast.*

5) Compute the approximate amount of money you will need to save each year, based on answers from #1), #2), #3), and #4).
This final step for ***FF Investment Method #1*** entails taking your ***Total FF Nest Egg*** dollar amount from Step 4, and dividing it by the ***Total Time Duration*** (number of years) you have saved and invested. Using the numbers from above, the formula is a rough, but reasonably accurate approximation which looks like the following:

Step #4 / Step #3 = ***Total FF Nest Egg / Total Time Duratio***n (# years you saved and invested) = $900,000 / 35 years = $25, 714 per year that must be saved for 35 years, in order to reach $900,000 for retirement at age 65. The $900,000 will always generate $36,000 per year at 4%, without touching the principal. (Note: The effects of compounding interest is also involved, but is ignored for these examples. Thus, you'll likely have more money in the end, which provides a buffer or hedge against underestimating your future FF projected income and nest egg.

Furthermore, the $900K could also be used a little at a time each year - such as 5% to 10% - in order to pay for unexpected bills, gifts, hobbies, or additional living costs. In reality, the $900K could also be much lower (i.e.; cut in half or reduced by one third), and you still might have plenty of money to live comfortably if you manage your expenses well. For example, if you only saved half that amount (50% of $900K), you would have at least $450,000 saved after 35 years. Note: You would typically have more money after 35 years than $900K (or $450K), due to the effects of compounding interest. At 4%, $450,000 would generate $18,000 per year in interest the first year.

If the interest were added back to the principal each year, the next year's income would increase a little more. That's because the base principal amount keeps increasing. That's the power of compounding interest. If you took each year's interest and spent it, then the principal balance (i.e. $450K) remains constant and no interest compounding takes effect.

You might use some of the $450K as cash for living expenses. Cutting the $450K in half gives you $225,000 to invest, which would generate $9,000 per year at 4% (.04 x $225,000 = $9000). The remaining $225,000 principal could still be saved until needed, or used a little each year.

At this point, using $225K at 4% from the example above, you would be down to $9000 per year, but you would also have the remaining $225K principal, which still gives you spending options. If you spent less, the remaining $225K (or whatever amount) would last even longer. Likewise, if you spent more each year, the remaining principal would be used up quicker.

However, as previously stated, the final nest egg would actually be larger than either $900K or even $450K, due to the compounding effects of interest on interest. FF Investment Method #1 is an approximation method only, but it gets you in the right ball park fairly quickly. Furthermore, it's conservative enough to allow for estimating mistakes, taxes, inflation, and unknown expenses that invariably arise in the future.

Examples of Investment Method #1, using different figures for variables 1-5.

Example 1A:
$4500 per month estimated living costs at FF/retirement age = $54,000 / year (before tax).
COC = 5% = .05
40 years for saving and investing; (start saving at age 22, end at age 62; 62-22 = 40 years)
Total FF nest egg needed = $54000 / .05 = $1,080,000
Required yearly savings to reach nest egg (conservatively); 1,080,000 / 40yrs = $27,000 / yr.

Example 1B:
$3000 per month estimated living costs at FF/retirement age = $36,000 / year (before tax).
COC = 6% = .06
35 years for saving and investing: (start at age 25, end at age 60; 60-25 = 35 years).
Total FF nest egg needed = $36000 / .06 = $600,000
Required yearly savings to reach nest egg (conservatively); $600,000 / 35 yrs = $17,143 / yr.

Example 1C:
$7000 per month estimated living costs at FF/retirement age = $84,000 / year (before tax).
COC = 7% = .07
45 years for saving and investing: (start at age 23, end at age 68; 68-23 = 45 years).
Total FF nest egg needed = $84000 / .07 = $1,200,000
Required yearly savings to reach nest egg (conservatively); $1,200,000 / 45 yrs = $26,667 / yr.

Example 1D:
This is an example of split (i.e. "two") income streams due to starting your FF savings fund later in life at around age 40 (like me). It includes taking SS four years early at age 62, in order to help make up the lost investment opportunity. The retirement parameters and income split (two income sources) for Example 1D are shown on the next page.

Example 1D, cont'd. *(Two income sources)*
Estimated FF Mo. Income: $3800 per month needed at FF/retirement age = $45,600 / year (before tax). Since the FF income stream is split, the total nest egg needed at 4% (see below) is $604,200. Otherwise, the total nest egg @ 4% would need to be $1.14M ($45.6K/.04), which is extremely hard when starting at age 40.
Income split: 53% ($24,168) will come from investment savings. The remaining 47% ($21,432) will come from Social Security. (Combined total = $45,600).
COC = 4% = .04
22 years for saving and investing: Start at age 40, and end at age 62; Thus, (62 - 40) = 22 years.
Investment nest egg needed @ 53% = {.53x$45,600/.04} = {$24,168 / .04} = $604,200.
Required yearly savings to reach 53% of total needed (conservatively); $604,200 / 22 yrs = $27,464 /yr.

Add Social Security: Start SS at age 62 (instead of 66) with 25% reduction and meeting minimum work history requirements needed for Social Security eligibility. We'll assume taking SS at age 62 equates to $1800 per month, which is $21,600 per year, instead of $2,400 at age 66. Taking SS four years early reduces SS benefits 25%, or 75% of full value; ($2,400 x .75 = $1,800). However, it also results in $86,400 of extra income that otherwise would be forfeited; {48 mos. x $1800/mo. = $86,400 extra income between ages 62 - 66}.
See below to compute Breakeven Analysis when taking SS early at 62, versus age 66.
Breakeven Analysis on taking SS at age 62 versus age 66:
Waiting until age 66 to take SS would take 12 years to break even; {$7,200 more/yr. at age 66 ($2400-$1800=$600 more per mo. at age 66) / $600 x 12 = $7,200 more/yr when taking SS at age 66}; BUT WAIT: (4 year early gain at age 62) / (extra SS waiting till age 66) = ($86,400 / $7,200) = Breakeven. {$86,400 / $7,200 = 12 years}.Thus, it takes 12 years to recoup the forfeited $86,400 in SS by waiting until 66 for SS.
Required yearly savings needed to reach the remaining 47% using SS = $0. However, it does require working and paying your half (or all when self-employed) of 15.3% in SS and Medicare taxes until age 62.

Total Income at retirement for Example 1D from two income streams:
Yearly Investment Income = $27,464/yr.; SS Income at age 62 = $21,600/yr.; Combined total = $49,064/yr.
Monthly Income = $49,064 / 12 = $4,088.67; Round up to $4,089 / mo.
{This is slightly more than the estimated $3,800 / mo., due to rounding up SS to $21.6K/yr. vs. $21.432K.}

Summary of Method #1 approach.
In ***Examples 1A through 1D***, saving $17K to $27K per year after all living expenses and taxes are paid, might be doable for some people, but it could be too much for other folks, especially when typical salaries range between $40,000 to $85,000 a year. Realistically, a person might have to earn $100,000 a year or more (before taxes) and/or have relatively low living expenses, in order to be able to save $17K to $27K per year after all taxes, living expenses, and bills have been paid. However, 401K contribution matching helps considerably when companies offer employer matching 401K retirement plans. Take advantage of them. Method #1 will resonate with some people, but not others. It's inherent in the nature of estimating and modeling future outcomes, just like most approaches to solving math, engineering, and finance problems often have multiple formulas or methodologies that attempt to arrive at similar or exact solutions as a means of cross checking. Method #1 is more of a long term, "lump-sum" based approach. It might work well for those with very stable, long term, well-paying jobs that last many years - often with the same employer. It's much easier to accurately plan for the future with that type of income stability and long term financial consistency using Investment Method #1.

Investment Method #2, which is explained next, is another alternative. The final answers are fundamentally the same for either method. Only the approach differs. Both methods work, but each has its own nuance. One is more yearly based (Method #1), while the other is more monthly based (Method #2). Method #2 is geared toward month-to-month cash flow monitoring. It breaks down the FF components and expresses them on a monthly basis. This could be well suited to those with widely varying paychecks and cash flow, like entrepreneurs, people in sales, people with 1099 salaries, and part-time workers, to name a few. Next, let's look at FF Investment Method #2 in detail.

FF Investment Method #2:

FF Investment Method #2 shares similarities with Method #1, but instead of an annual money focus, it's more centered on *monthly income and expenses*. It involves calculating your present and future monthly Passive Income (PI) from Your Ongoing Invested Capital (similar to Method #1). In other words, your PI is compared regularly against your living expenses each month, in addition to annually.

The goal is to grow your monthly PI until it *equals or surpasses* your current and future monthly living expenses. When that occurs, you have technically reached a state of FF.

How?
Add-up all your Passive Monthly Investment Income, and compare it to anticipated Monthly Retirement Expenses.

FF Investment Method #2 uses ***one or many*** monthly income streams as the financial goal. The income could be from one source - like a mutual stock fund, or many sources - like stock dividends, bond dividends, Social Security, pensions, rental income, annuities, interest on CD's, or more.

Like Method #1, some or all of Method #2 income is generated from passive and portfolio investments based on how much money (capital) you have invested and your rate of return (COC).
Both methods can have multiple income sources and rates of return the more diverse your investment portfolio becomes. The calculated answer is then compared to an estimated amount of monthly living expenses needed at retirement age. Multiplying by twelve gives you the yearly totals.

Optionally, the results can be placed on a chart to better visualize the progress of monthly passive income vs. living expenses. When passive income surpasses monthly expenses, you are technically financially free. Your living expenses are automatically paid by passive investment income *without* having to work at a job (unless you like working and want to continue doing so).

Let's look at some examples of **FF Investment Method #2**.

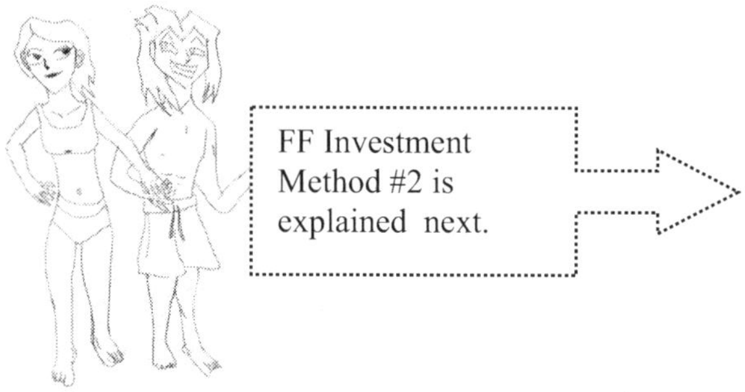

Examples of FF Investment Method #2

Example 2A: *(Using two sources of monthly passive income)*

Two Monthly Income Sources: *$10,000 Bond* + *Social Security @ $800 / Mo, age 62.*
Bond features: $10K invested, 5% dividend, AA rated, expires in 20 years.

How to calculate: Calculate the bond monthly payment per below, then add the SS monthly payment to that answer in Step 5a below.

Step 1a. Use the amount of capital you currently have saved for bond investing: = $10,000.00

Step 2a. Determine your rate of return = COC. For Bonds, this = annual yield = 5% = .05

Step 3a. Use a 12 month payment cycle. = Divide by 12

Step 4a. Plug in the bond variables above into the below FF formula:

$$\frac{\text{Capital x COC}}{12} = \text{monthly investment income} = \frac{\text{Step 1a x Step 2a}}{12} = \frac{\$10{,}000 \text{ x } .05}{12} = \$41.67 / mo.$$

Step 5a. Add-up both income sources: Bond @ ***$41.67***/mo. + SS @ ***$800.00*** = ***$841.67 / mo.***

Thus, the Final Answer is: *$841.67 total monthly passive income (bond + SS).*
$841,67 in monthly FF income is a good beginning. For some, this could be as good as it ever gets. I've seen rental applications from prospective tenants wanting to rent my properties with such figures. However, this figure could be higher with better FF planning. Obviously, that involves many changes, the least of which means starting your financial planning as earlier in life as possible.

That in turn means making more income, spending less, or a combination of both. That involves major life changes and choices, which is possible but highly dependent and where you're at in life *age wise, location wise, health wise, relationship wise, job wise, education wise*, and last but not least, *the degree to which you're willing to change yourself*, in order to improve your situation.

On the next page, Example 2B illustrates how increasing your investment to $130,000, using a slightly higher COC of 6%, and having higher Social Security income changes the outcome considerably for the better.

Examples of FF Investment Method #2

Example 2B. *(Using two sources of monthly passive income with higher figures)*

Revise Dual Monthly Income Sources as follows:

Two Monthly Income Sources: *$130,000 Bond(s)* + *Social Security @ $1660 / Mo, age 62.*

Step 1b. Capital = *$130,000 Bond, 6% dividend, AA rated, expires in 20 years.* = $130,000

Step 2b. COC = 6% = .06

Step 3b. 12 month payment cycle. = Divide by 12

Step 4b. $\frac{\text{Capital x COC}}{12}$ = monthly investment income = $\frac{\$130{,}000 \text{ x } .06}{12}$ = *$650.00 / mo.*

Step 5b. Add-up both revised income sources: Bond @ $**650/mo**. + SS @ **$1660/mo**. = ***$2310/mo.***

The revised results total ***$2310 /*** month, which is much better than $841.67. It could still be higher with better planning. On the other hand this may be an amount that's as good as it gets for the foreseeable future. Either way, you can always try to add more money to your investment fund, reduce expenses, or start investing earlier. You should always brainstorm potential ways that could increase your monthly FF cash flow position, such as reducing debt, finding better bank or credit union interest rates, investing in real estate rental income, tweaking your stock or bond portfolio, maxing out your employer matching 401K plans, moving to a lower cost city, state, or country, etc.

Next, we'll summarize all the results using a simple formula for the Financial Freedom Realization Point so you can quickly see your FF investment progress each month and year.

The Financial Freedom Realization Point *(FFRP)*

The Golden Reward at the end of (mandatory) employment = FF Realization Point.

The formula for the FF Realization Point, or FFRP, has a very simple mathematical structure. The following three variables are involved, all of which are determined from the prior steps in this book:

A. Monthly Job income - Your income from working as an employee or business owner. (From Chpt. 3) *Example: $4300/mo. = Job income = A*

B. Monthly Expenses - Precise monthly living expenses with allowances for necessities, fun and hobbies, social time, and unforeseen expenses.
(From Chpt. 2) *Example: $3800/mo. = Expenses = B*

C. Monthly Investment Income - Passive and portfolio monthly income, such as interest, dividends, rental income, royalties, Social Security, pensions, annuities, IRA, Roth IRA, 401K distributions, etc.
(From Chpt. 4) *Example: $3850/mo. = Investment Income = C*

Monthly Investment Income in Part C above represents "free cash flow" from all your investments and work efforts, which are made possible from *excess* active income (A) that is saved and invested, plus any SS, pensions, or retirement distributions you may be eligible for at retirement age.

The FF Realization Point Formula:

(It Represents ***When*** you initially become FF)

FF occurs when: C – B >= 0

Here's Why:

{When your Passive Income (PI) is equal to, or greater than, ***ALL*** of your Living Expenses on a consistent monthly basis, your bills can be paid from passive income rather than job income.}

...or simply:

FF = { PI => Expenses }

...or in other words:

FF occurs when: C – B >= 0

Next, let's look at some examples of applying the FF formula using the FF Summary Form.

Examples of applying the FF Formula using the FF Summary Form.

FF occurs when: C – B >= 0

Example #1.

Years 2010 to 2016

A. Mo. Job Income = $4300/mo
B. Mo. Expenses = $3800/mo
C. Mo. Passive Income (PI) = $3850/mo

Answer:

FF = C - B => 0
FF = $3850 - $3800 = $50/mo.
FF? Y/N — Answer = Yes. FF = $50 excess

Note: Job income (A) @ $4300/mo is now optional.

Years 2020 - 2022

Fill in Your Figures

Your Mo. Job Income A.__________
Your Mo. Expenses B.__________
Your Mo. PI C.__________

Answer: **FF = C - B => 0**
C - B = $ ________/mo.
FF? Y/N — Y or N? Excess/Shortage?

Notes:

Example #2.

Years 2010 to 2016

A. Mo. Job Income = $8700/mo
B. Mo. Expenses = $8000/mo
C. Mo. Passive Income (PI) = $4000/mo

Answer:

FF = C - B => 0
FF = $4000 - $8000 = *(-$4000)/mo.*
Answer = No. FF = *(-4000)* short

Note: Job income (A) @ $8700/mo. is still necessary. This person has good income, but high expenses too. They have to work longer and increase their Investment Income (C) up to $8000, and/or reduce Expenses (B) to be equal or less than $4000/mo. Doing both is best.

Years 2023 - 2025

Fill in Your Figures

Your Mo. Job Income A.__________
Your Mo. Expenses B.__________
Your Mo. PI C.__________

Answer: **FF = C - B => 0**
C - B = $ ________/mo.
FF? Y/N — Y or N? Excess/Shortage?

Notes:

Example #3.

Years 2010 to 2016

A. Mo. Job Income = $3000/mo
B. Mo. Expenses = $2500/mo
C. Mo. Passive Income (PI) = $3500/mo

Answer:

FF = C - B => 0
FF = $3500 - $2500 = $1000/mo.
Answer = Yes. FF = $1000 excess

Note: Job income (A) @ $3000/mo. is now optional. This person has the lowest job income, but the highest excess FF amount due to good Investment Income and low expenses.

Years 2026 - 2030 and beyond

Fill in Your Figures

Your Mo. Job Income A.__________
Your Mo. Expenses B.__________
Your Mo. PI C.__________

Answer: **FF = C - B => 0**
C - B = $ ________/mo.
FF? Y/N — Y or N? Excess/Shortage?

Notes:

The FF Formula Stresses Three Important Concepts:

{FF occurs when C – B >= 0}

A.) Continue working and earning job income for as long as you possibly can (Step 3). This allows you to pay your bills while striving to earn as much excess cash as possible, in order to save and invest it over many years.

B.) Strive to *stabilize* and eventually *reduce* your expenses, in order to live below your means over the long run (Step 2). Reducing your living expenses a little at a time each year provides two advantages: 1) It gives you even more money to save and invest with so you can grow your investment nest egg faster and; 2) It makes it easier to replace (or surpass) your monthly expense amount with passive income **(PI)** later on. Thus, you want A > B over the long term. This requires living below your means much of the time. The person who makes $50,000 a year and saves $500 each month is doing better than someone making $500,000 a year but spends it on lavish liabilities and only saves $20 each month.

C.) Invest your savings in safe, semi-diversified, moderate growth asset classes (Step 4). Monitor your investments as often as you feel necessary, but don't go into "*worry mode*" by checking every hour. Set up a self-managed or fully managed brokerage account. Create a "watch list" of stocks, so you can see how they perform before you buy. To set up a watch list, go to Google or Yahoo finance, key-in "how to set up a stock watch list", and follow the simple instructions. It only takes a few minutes and provides up-to-date feedback in real time. You can then monitor it daily, weekly, monthly, etc., as needed.

Therefore, you want Investment Income (C) to become consistently *equal to or greater* than your expenses (B) over time.

In other words, when ***{C – B => 0}*** on a permanent basis, you become FF. This means all your expenses are being paid by your passive and portfolio investments (non-job), and you are left with either a zero balance each month ($0), or something left over - like $100, $300, $1,500, etc.

It's technically not bad if you're left with zero dollars each month. That's because a zero dollar figure simply means you've successfully paid all your bills (including fun time and taxes) using all available investment and retirement income for that month. If you have money left over, so much the better. The FF cycle repeats itself each and every month so that income is generated automatically to pay bills whether you work or not. When the FF formula (C - B => 0) is consistently achieved on a weekly, monthly, and yearly basis, you are permanently FF as long as you adequately maintain it.

As a recap, asset classes you can consider for an FF investment fund include but are not limited to: Investment grade bonds, indexed mutual funds tied to the S&P 500, U.S. Treasury bonds, growth stocks, dividend stocks, bank CD's, and credit union CD's. My credit union began paying between 2% and 3% as of 12.28.2018, but then reduced it in mid 2019, due to the Fed's rate reductions that have been extended into 2020/2021 and beyond. Underlying this disastrous policy (for savings) are unrelated COVID-19 excuses and the ballooning U.S. national debt that now stands in excess of $26 trillion dollars as of October 2020. For example, my credit union CD rates dropped drastically in late 2020 from 1.75% down to .35%, which is a 500% decrease (five times) in lower passive income! Greed and corruption are basically to blame.

Next, let's look a ***visual*** way to monitor your *Job Income, Expenses,* and *Investment Income* using a ***Graph***.

Using a visual way to monitor the Financial Freedom Realization Point

Another way to summarize your FFRP progress is to plot your Job Income, Expenses, and Investment Income with a graph that visually illustrates all three variables over time using an X and Y axis. All two dimensional (2D) graphs are based on a Cartesian coordinate system using X and Y axes, where X is horizontal and Y is vertical. In this case, ***X will represent time*** in months and years, and ***Y will represent monthly money amounts*** in Euros, Dollars, Yen, Rubbles, Pesos, Yuan, or other currency.

The same three variables from our previous FFRP examples will be used on your FFRP graph as follows:
1) Your monthly ongoing Job Income (Top line). *(Note: Line Jogs are job disruptions)*
2) Your monthly ongoing Living Expenses (Middle line).
3) Your monthly ongoing Investment Income (Bottom line).

When your investment income (bottom line) intersects or surpasses your expenses (middle line), you have reached the ***FF Realization Point***. The key is to hold that steady. Otherwise, you have to make corrections by lowering expenses, increasing investments, and/or go back to work for a period of time.

{Note: The idea behind using a graph is not new or proprietary. It's a common way to express money, math, and scientific relationships that's been used by countless civilizations throughout history}.

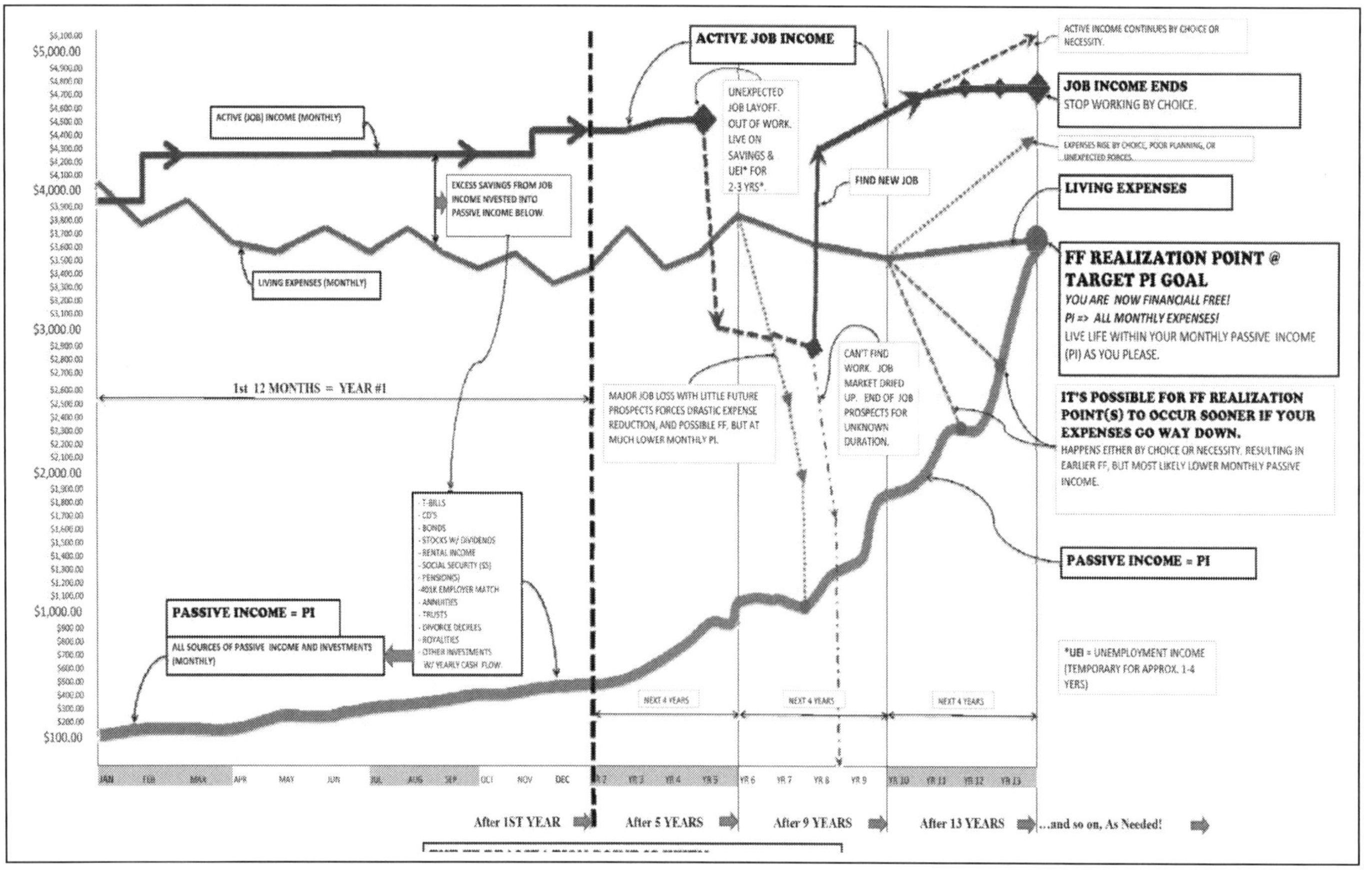

Let's look at the next few pages which explain in more detail how to plot job income, living expenses, and passive income with a graph. The best tool to use is spreadsheet software, like the ones mentioned in previous chapters. If using software is not possible or undesirable, use paper and colored pens. Either way will work. Software has a learning curve, which makes starting out go slow until proficiency and productivity kick in. At that point, it's superior to pencil and paper because changes are quicker and more accurate.

How to express the FF Realization Point using a Graph.

First, plot your Passive Income. Begin by examining your investment results, add-up what you're currently making money-wise each month from all your FF investment sources, and place a dot where the dollar amount (Y axis) and month (X axis) intersect for each month of the year. Do this at least every month. The results are shown in the bottom (green) graph line, starting with a given month.

Next, plot your Expenses each month, starting with January (or another month), and intersect the month and expense amount by placing a dot where the two intersect. For example, find your monthly expense $ amount (on the Y axis), and then intersect that with the corresponding month (on the X axis). Do this each successive month, and then connect the dots by drawing a line between them. This will plot your true expense curve over time on the graph. You can do this on a spreadsheet and have it automatically graph the chart, or just enter X&Y values directly in the spreadsheet and draw lines between the dots. Label the expense graph line as *"Total Monthly Expenses"* somewhere on the line.

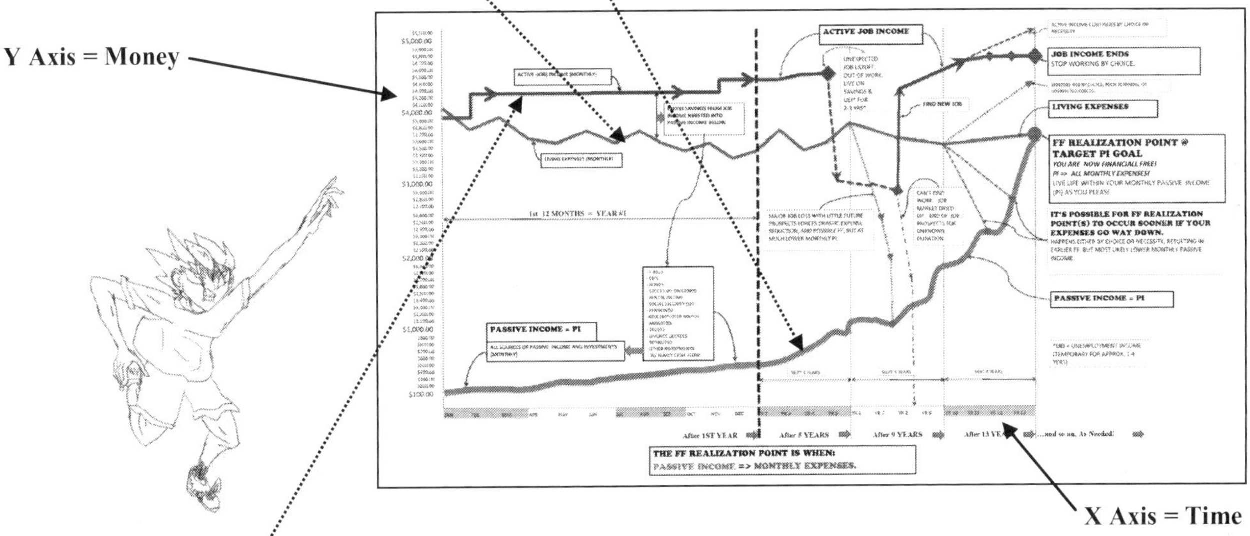

***Finally, plot your Job Income** each month*, beginning with January, or the same beginning month used for expenses and passive income. Find your income $ amount (on the Y axis), and then intersect that with the corresponding month of the year (on the X axis) – just like you did for expenses. Do this for each month, and connect the dots to form a graph line – just like you did for expenses.

Label this income graph line as *"Total Monthly Income"*. Look at the graph. If your income line is HIGHER than your expense line over time, then the difference is positive, and that becomes your savings, or excess cash flow you can use to invest with. If your income line is LOWER than your expense line, then the difference in your cash flow is negative, and that becomes a deficit, or negative cash flow.

If your income stays lower than expenses for too long, it could become an unsustainable situation. In that case, you have to use savings, borrow money, increase income, reduce expenses, or a combination of all four. The inevitable conclusion to prolonged negative income is insolvency. In that case, your monthly income is chronically low, and/or your monthly expenses are too high.

If the income and expense graph lines spike up and down erratically each month, with some months positive, and some negative, cross-check your monthly P&L report for exact ***income or expense*** figures that might be the cause.

For W2 wage earners, your income should be fairly steady each month. For entrepreneurs, part-time workers, gig employees, 1099 professionals, and business investors, your income can vary widely throughout the year so income spikes and drops are common. The basic goal is to aim for a gradual increase in Job and Investment Income, while simultaneously decreasing Expenses over time. Easily said. Harder to do. The only way through is to *begin your FF work now, stay focused, and don't give up*. Action is the antidote to helplessness and fear.

More Tips on making a Graph to visually express the FFRP.

Choose a different spacing if you need more room to write. Use different colored lines for monthly expenses and monthly income. Label the ***X axis*** (horizontal direction along the bottom) as ***Time,*** using months of the year. Show at least three (3) years worth of time, using individual letters for each month, such as J,F,M,A,M,J,J,A,S,O,N,D. Leave several (or more) line spaces between each month. {Use multiple graphs for more years}.

Label the ***Y axis*** (vertical direction on the left side) as ***Currency Amounts***, such as Dollars, Euros, Yuan, Pesos, Rubbles, or Yen. Leave several (or more) line spaces between each currency amount on the graph. Label them from the bottom of the graph to the top, starting with $100, and progressing in $100 (or more) increments toward the top, along the *LEFT* vertical edge of the graph.

For example, starting at $100, and using $100 dollar increments, the left side would begin with $100, then $200, $300, $400, ...all the way up to about $5000. For higher monthly income values, use a higher increment value, such as $500 increments between lines. For example, starting at $100, progress in 500 increments to $500, then $1000, $1500, $2000, $2500, $3000,…up to $8,000...or higher as needed.

Note: The next page illustrates the three graph lines to plot on your Graph - *investment income, expenses, and job income*. It doesn't matter what order you do these in. For example, you could plot job income, then expenses, and then investment income. The results are the same.

The FF Realization Graph is a visual reminder – just like a heart beat on a hospital monitor – of your exact monthly cash flow and the overall trend your income and expense pattern is headed.

Review your progress at least monthly. Periodically save your graph results as a JPG, DNG, TIFF, or PDF on your computer, tablet, or phone so you can see it quickly whenever you want.
If you resorted to making your graph with paper instead of software, keep the original safe but make a copy and hang it up on a wall in an area that's reasonably private and frequented by you...like a walk-in closet, bedroom, kitchen, home office, or garage.

FF Realization Point - Enlarged Summary View

The enlarged graph below shows the 1st year through the 13th year, along with all three major FF graph lines. The amount of years will vary for each person.

1) Active Job Income (monthly)	**-**	***Top line*** *(blue)*
2) Living Expenses (monthly)	**-**	***Middle line*** *(red)*
3) Passive Income (monthly)	**-**	***Bottom line*** *(green)*

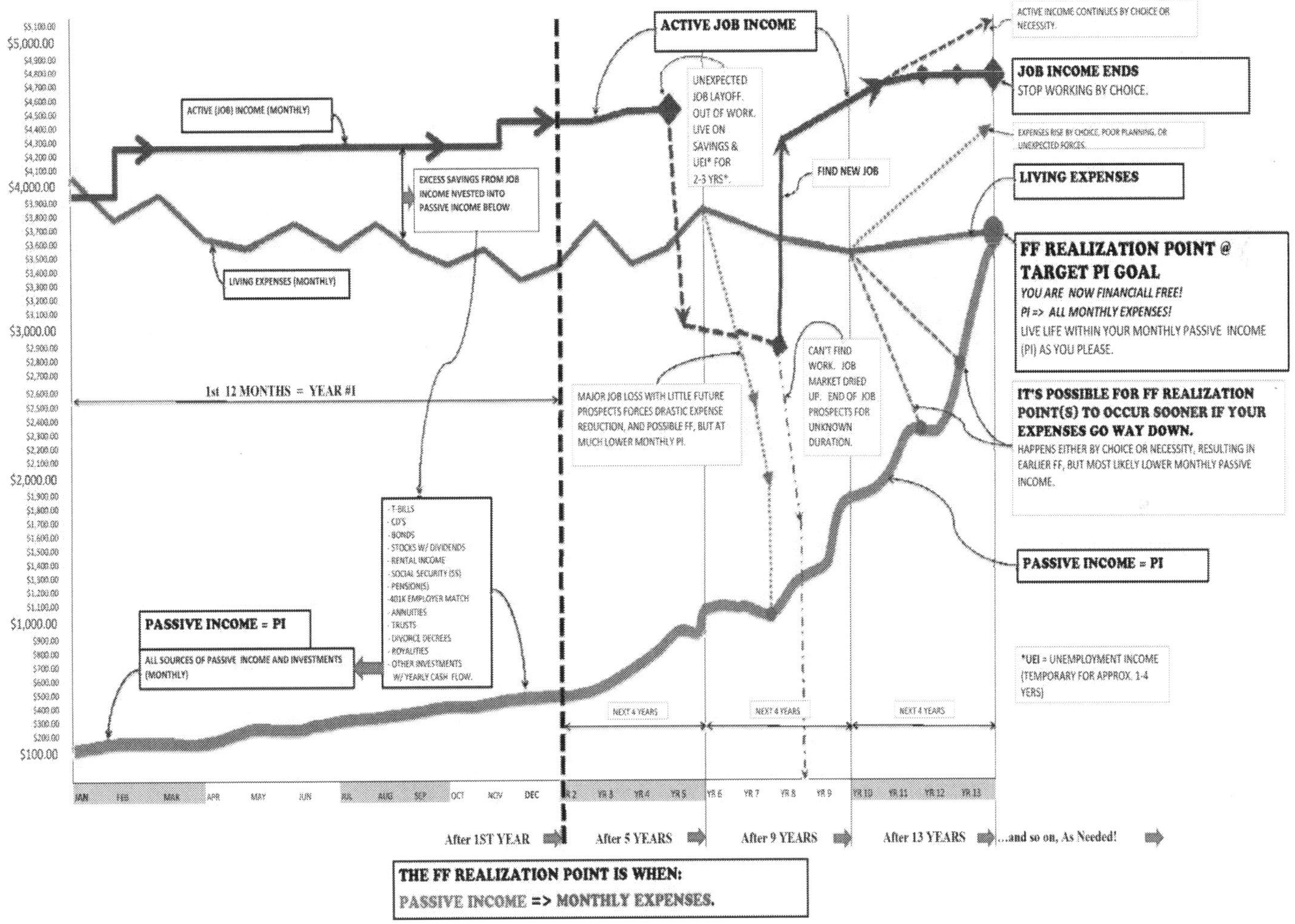

> The FF Realization Point Graph visually shows: ***When*** you become FF.

Maintaining Financial Freedom

There are Four (4) critical things you must do to maintain Financial Freedom once you've gotten there:

1.) **Preserve Principal.** For the most part, don't touch the underlying principal amount of your core investments, except for real emergencies. This is the goose that lays the golden egg (i.e.; the goose that automatically generates interest, dividends, capital gains, and/or rental income). In extreme cases of financial hardship or severe economic down-turns, you might have to sell certain assets or use some savings to pay bills and live off of. I had to do that for several years following the 2008 housing collapse and global financial crisis with about 50% of my investment portfolio. I eventually re-built it back-up. That ordeal took over half a decade to get through.

2.) **Monitor Expenses regularly**. This means creating a realistic income and expense budget (including money for unforeseen expenditures) and staying within those budget parameters each month. This is one of the hardest parts of FF. In some months, expenses will exceed income. Once you conquer spending, and your income stabilizes, the other parts fall into place. Record all income and expense receipts and strive to eventually use a spread sheet or relational data base software.

3.) **Stay aware of Interest Rate fluctuations** ; (i.e. The Cost of Capital, or COC). This is especially important when interest rates drop or rise drastically. You need to ensure you're still covered with enough passive income to automatically pay all your expenses. Monitor your portfolio as needed, but don't obsess over daily stock gyrations. Review assets and make adjustments periodically. A possible starting point for asset allocations for young people and parents might be 35% stocks, 35% bonds, 20% real estate, and 10% cash. For people approaching 50+ years of age and older, those percentages might be adjusted to 20% stocks, 10% bonds, 25% CD's, 25% real estate, and 20% cash. But remember this: These are recommended and "estimated" percentages based on various experience outcomes over many decades. People will argue left and right about exact percentages and asset classes to use. Study and learn all you can, seek advice from multiple sources, then follow your gut.

4.) **Separate "Needs" from "Wants".** How? First determine your essential needs for living and what that's costing you. Essential needs include a blend of things in various degrees, like rent, mortgage, taxes, food, clothing, spiritual worship, fun, rest, transportation, family, your spouse or partner, your kid's (or your own) college education, medical care, and saving for retirement. Then think about your wants and pleasures with this question: "What are the pleasures in life that I spend money on beyond my basic needs above?" As long as you can afford them, "wants" are not destructive to maintaining your FF. But buying things that seldom get used, or funding vacations with credit card debt, translates to wasted money and debt that eats up your principal cash. Thus, by doing a "Needs versus Wants" reality check, you learn to prioritize money expenditures. It teaches you how to consciously separate them, instead of acting out sub-consciously when a buying impulse kicks-in. There's nothing wrong with spending your FF money on "wants", as long as it doesn't undermine your FF nest egg and monthly investment income.

Let's look at a few examples of life's basic "want" versus "need" cycle from the perspective of history. Owning stuff or buying pleasure is only part of the game. Power, greed, revenge, lust, character, pride, ethics, and vision play big roles too.

Maintaining Financial Freedom - *Your Character and Spending habits are Key.*

Madoff	*How much more do you want? $170 Billon dollars wasn't enough for this Wall Street shyster who pretended to invest people's money and lied unremorsefully about their rates of return. His name? Bernard Madoff. He made people think they were earning 12% APR in his bogus investment firm. Instead, many people lost everything. He seldom invested their money at all. Instead, he spent it paying older investors with new investor money while supporting his lavish lifestyle. It was a classic Ponzi scheme. Ironically, he got away with this massive $170B scam for over 30 years until his fraudulent financial empire came crashing down in December of 2008. He's now in prison for the rest of his life. No amount of money made this arrogant con artist satisfied.*
Enron	*Enron had it all: Visionary leaders, dedicated and skilled employees, massive cash flow, strong market share, and industry respect. Then they lost it all in 2001. How? Over spending and fraud. Beneath the surface of outward success lied massive corruption, greed, and arrogance. Fearful of telling the truth about their overspending and losses in the energy sector, they lied to Wall Street investors and their employees about hidden "off-balance sheet" liabilities. After years of success, the end came quick and hard. Enron went bankrupt, employee savings were destroyed, and human lives were devastated or lost. It was the largest U.S. bankruptcy up to that point until WorldCom and Lehman Brothers took that title soon after in 2002 and 2008 respectively.*
Amazon	*Jeff Bozos, founder and CEO of Amazon.com, didn't set out to be the richest man in the world. Instead, he saw a need and filled it by changing the way things were sold and delivered using the Internet. His vision transformed society Money flowed naturally into his life as a byproduct of that inspired idea at the dawn of the Web in 1994.*

To maintain FF, *you have to know* ***how much you spend*** *and* ***what you really need****.*
How? Once you're FF, ask yourself: "How much of my spending is a need versus a want?" Do this by analyzing your spending habits and honestly answering the soul searching questions below:

1. ***Was it a want or a need? Both are OK, but separate needs from wants and stay within your budget.***

2. ***If you decide to keep spending on certain "wants" in retirement, could you still afford it? If so, fine. If not, make adjustments and don't procrastinate in taking action.***

3. ***Could some living expenses go away once you stop working for a living (i.e.: commuting), thus lowering your living expenses? If so, save a portion of that money for later, and enjoy some of it on a few pleasures now.***

4. ***How much lasting satisfaction do you receive relative to the money (and time) you spend on wants? As long as it's your money, you can afford it, you're experiencing joy, no one's being harmed, no laws are broken, and your FF nest egg is not in jeopardy, then enjoy your life when you make those purchases. If not, stop making those purchases and save the money!***

Maintaining Financial Freedom

These thought provoking real life examples and questions are fundamental in all money matters - whether business or personal. The reasons are straight forward. Some spending is fundamental to survival. A certain amount of spending promotes growth and enjoyment. But most excess spending is optional and self-induced. ***Only you can control "you",*** and that means only ***you*** can control your own spending. When you become FF, you need to know why you're spending on things beyond basic necessities and certain pleasures. That engages your character and ethics as much as your self control and honesty. Thus, your physical needs, emotions, desires, fears, pain, hopes, faith, hobbies, family, fun time, friends, lovers, kids, and life goals are wrapped-up inside every buying decision you make in some way.

These questions will help clarify and integrate your earning, spending, investing, purpose, sense of fulfillment, and appetites, so you can better differentiate between needs and wants when you're FF. Spending money will always involve choosing between "essential needs" and "wants". That's part of being human. The trick is to develop awareness about it. If you spend more one month, spend less the next.
To gain mastery over this, visualize having *three* buckets of spending money, all of which add up to your total FF monthly budget. One bucket is for absolute living expenses. It must always be funded first. The second bucket is for fun, hobbies, and pleasures which is money remaining after bucket #1 is funded. The third bucket is for things that won't matter if you lose a little money. That should be the smallest bucket.

Bucket #1. Money for absolute living expenses. *Always first!*

Bucket #2. Money for fun, hobbies, pleasure. *Always after Bucket #1.*

Bucket #3. Money you can afford to splurge, waste, or lose. *Always last! Always smallest.*

Understanding ***why*** you spend money, and ***what*** you spend it on, helps you discover the *right amount* with enough practice and time. This in turn helps you maintain financial freedom with greater joy, confidence, and consistency.

SPENDING, Never Satisfied, HORDING...then....DYING.

Which one will YOU choose?

Hording & dying?

or...

Satisfied & Living?

SPENDING, KNOWING WHAT'S the Right Amount...then...ENJOYING life. Continuing to save, sharing your gift, and giving back.

Doing What You Love Most in Life.

Financial Freedom empowers you to realize both your "sole" and "soul" purpose in life. It's about finding your calling and doing what you love. That in turn helps provide you with a real and lasting quality of life. But, you may find your calling in life early on or in other ways. Some people find their passion in life through their careers or other life endeavors. Retiring makes little difference. What matters most is your health, loved ones, financial security, and the quality of the life you live. To define "quality of life", a meaningful and measurable definition is needed. Essentially, it boils down to this: Your quality of life is directly proportional to the amount of time you have left on earth, the fulfillment you attain, and the choices you make.

You trade your time to make money in order to sustain a reasonable degree of shelter, food, clothing, transportation, health, social engagement, and enjoyment. It also includes the time you trade every day in order to save money for retirement (FF).
In sum, it's the amount of life force you have already traded for money in your life, plus the time you will spend in the future - up to the unknown moment of your death. Remember: this includes saving enough money to fund your financial freedom for the estimated (but unknown) remaining years you have left on earth.

Any amount of money over and beyond the base amount necessary to fund your financial freedom each month is technically not needed. Excess FF investment income becomes extra spending money, or more cash that can be plowed back into the FF account, which in turn generates more savings and investment income. That means more passive income (PI). Also, it can and should be socked away for rainy day emergencies or sudden shocks to the economy. As mentioned before, think of the great depression of the 1930's, the savings and loan crisis in 1987, the housing and financial crisis of 2008, and the COVID-19 world-wide pandemic and economic crisis during 2020/2021.

Life is full of exciting choices once you follow your dreams. Along the way, master money, invest wisely, and then just do what's fun and inspiring. Avoid jealous and negative people. Your feelings will give you clues. Listen to them. Believe that it's possible, even before you see the results. Then, do the work, and do it to the best of your ability.

Do what ignites your inspiration. Share it with others. Do things that give you joy and contentment. Soar like a hawk. Avoid shame based thinking and institutional dogma. Listen to your heart-felt dreams. Pray and meditate on wise direction, harmony with others, and achieving your life's goals. Always listen to, trust, and follow your instincts - especially when external clues are vague, but your feelings are telling you something else. Somewhere within all these parameters lie the keys to your destiny.

To soar like a hawk, follow your heart.

Ask yourself: "Am I making a living I enjoy"? If so, fine. If not, make changes. Then, get more serious about becoming FF.

Separate your ego from your work title. That will help free you to find your calling in life. It could be your existing career. Or, it may be something else.

Along the way, be diligent about mastering your money, staying healthy, and learning to invest wisely.

Consider these Issues when Seeking Purpose and Joy in Your Life:

A. Ask yourself: "Am I spending my time (or making a living) that, while not necessarily perfect, is aligned with my long-term goals and aspirations?" If the answer is yes, fine. Keep going. "Or, am I lying to myself and dying a little bit inside each week just to chase money and pay bills?" If the second answer is true, make a plan for your life and then work hard on doing something about it. Reading books like this is the first step.

B. To find your purpose in life, look for clues where: *You feel content and joyful; Your skill level is very strong; There's a real need for your skill; You can (if you choose) earn money providing that skill in a way that supports your lifestyle, or you can do it for pure pleasure; People benefit from your skill; Your skill is not easy to acquire and is respected (competitive advantage). You're full of energy.*

C. Separate your ego from your work and wages. This helps open-up endless options for increased opportunities. Your true identity does NOT have to be bound to what you do to make a living or where you worship. Cutting the bonds between "*who you really are*" versus "*what you do for a living*" or "*where you worship*" will free you to make more fulfilling choices. This applies to organized religion as much as your job. The difference between organized religious groups and spirituality is hotly contested and is seldom agreed upon - ever. I learned this first hand in my early twenties. I asked my pastor at a Baptist church what he thought I should do for a career. Without asking me anything about my background, goals, or skills, he emphatically said " go into the Christian ministry". I did just the opposite and followed my ambition to become an architect and entrepreneur. I am so glad I did. A few years later, he was thrown out of his position by his own church due to feuding factions within the ministry. That story of narrow minded selfish dogma repeats itself throughout history and continues today. Honor your faith, but remember this: God made you unique and gave you dreams and feelings. It's up to you to make them a reality by being true to yourself. Don't be defined by some else's beliefs or agenda. God speaks in mysterious and gentle ways, not through dogma and coercion. Intuition, feelings, and instincts are inside us for good reason.

D. Time is precious. Everyone has an unknown finite amount of time left in their lives. Determine how you want to spend those precious hours, days, months, and years right now while you still can.
No one thinks of more money on their death bed. Rather, time is what becomes most precious.
The above issues are meant to help you be true to yourself. *Honesty* and *facing reality* are two of the best friends you can have. No one can nurture and protect them more than you.

Live Life Your Way when You're Financially Free. *The options are limitless.*

01 Pursue your true passion. Forget about age stigmas. Society is a poor judge of people's age versus their capabilities and character. Follow your own path and listen to your heart. It takes guts.
02 Delve into your hobbies or charity work. Look into non-profit entities that you could join.
03 Spend more time managing your stocks, bonds, real estate, or other investments.
04 Have meaningful conversations with your soul mate, close friends, or family members.
05 Spend more time with your kids, grand kids, spouse, best friend(s), or pets. Make new friends.
06 Play a musical instrument. Hone your craft. Listen to classical, jazz, rock, country, or pop music.
07 Write a poem, article, or book. Publish your work. Teach others. Consider pro-bono work.
08 Start a new career (but don't spend your FF money on it. That's untouchable).
09 Read more books and become a subject matter expert. Jog, swim, walk, or ride a bike.
10 Go back to school and learn more. Get or finish a degree (but only if it's financially feasible).
11 Invent something! Start a business! Don't touch your FF nest egg however!
12 Create jewelry. Write computer programs. Build models. Engage in drawing, photography, or art.
13 Travel the state, country, or world. Do a budget first and stick to it closely. Travel is expensive.
14 Play Golf, Practice Kung Fu. Do Yoga. Visit beautiful forests, beaches, mountains, or deserts.
15 Enter your prized pedigree dog (or other pet) in a city, state or national pet contest.
16 Donate your time to help people less fortunate than you.
17 Engage in part-time or full-time work, but only if you like the challenge and want the extra money. Even when you're FF, there's nothing wrong with working when you enjoy it.
Nth Your Choice. The possibilities are endless. Can you think of one now? _______________
Nth Write down some dreams: ____
Nth Write down some goals: ____

CHAPTER 6

Getting Through College Wisely...

...with Little or No Debt. (Your Child or Yourself)

Getting Through College Wisely...with *Little or No Debt*

(Including Elite or Ivy League Universities for Your Child or Yourself)

Most parents deep down want their children to succeed in life. But talk is cheap and good intentions are easy. Realizing that dream requires years of hard work on both the parent's and the child's part. It requires consistently good parenting, getting high grades in K-12 school (especially middle and high school), getting a college education, and ultimately establishing a paying career.

Getting a good college education means finding a direction and passion that your child can potentially prosper from. That means earning a good salary and having a satisfying job. It's a matter of getting admitted to the best accredited universities possible.

This in turn requires meeting minimum college admittance requirements, and that (ideally) requires preparing your child to get top grades from middle school through high school. It also requires scoring high on the SAT or ACT exams, completing a lengthy admission application, and typically writing an exceptional statement of intent. Admission interviews are also involved.

Off To College.

That's the basic formula, but only a small portion of the population knows how to work that formula. Many people will end up in some category that falls short of that ideal, including myself when I was young. I had to find college success in other ways, and so can you. There's hope and opportunity in every situation and economy. Alternatives to elite college admission are discussed later in this chapter. But if you want the secret to maximizing your child's (or your own) chances for top college admission straight from high school, read on.

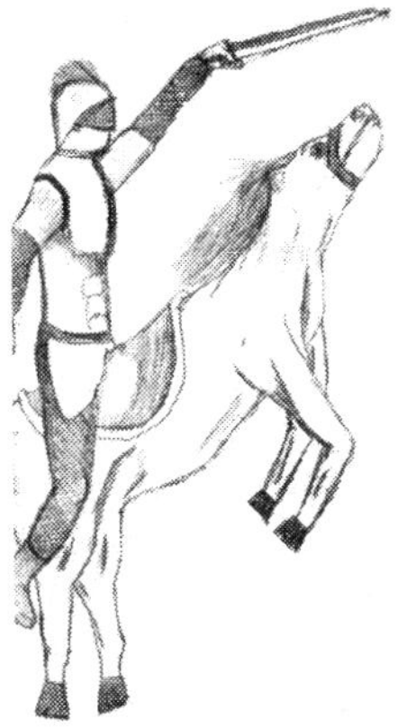

While most parents want their kids to get the best education possible, many don't know how to prepare them for it. Worst still, some parents pay lip service to the merits of getting good grades and a college education, but do little - if anything - that helps their kids translate academic study into meaningful college admission. It boils down to healthy parenting. Parents have to guide, mentor, hold accountable, and prepare their kids *every week* if they want them to get the best education from a top-tier university.

Always be aware of one simple truth: Many so-called colleges and universities are mediocre educators that charge very high prices. They will gladly take your hard earned money whilst overcharging and under delivering.

Your future depends heavily on education...

...especially the College you choose and how much you pay for it!

There are basically two categories of parents; 1) Those that do the hard work of parenting to raise and properly prepare their kids for higher education, and; 2) Those who either don't know how, are incapacitated, or simply don't want to. The good news is there is hope for just about everyone living in the United States and many other countries, regardless of what kind of parents you had (or have). I had hard working parents who had decent mid-to-upper class income during the mid 1950's to the late 1970's. However, they were wrapped-up in their own ambitions and drama to adequately guide and prepare me or my sisters academically. This had more to do with them being self-absorbed than anything else. They had the time. They had the intelligence. They had the money. There were a few exceptions, but in general, they simply had no desire to take the time and guide us academically toward higher education during our K-12 schooling years

My father, who was driven but often divisive and jealous, never said a word when I told him I got admitted to a top architectural university. Eventually he reached out after I was enrolled and later graduated, to congratulate me for doing it on my own. I was fortunate to have internal drive, some talent, goals, and a work ethic. That's partially what helped me to get admitted to, and graduate from, a top-tier architectural school in the Western United States. Years later, I earned an MBA degree - which while not from a top-tier college - was from a respectable California state university. I paid cash and got loans for all my college education costs. Fortunately, the tuition I paid during the 1970's for my five year undergraduate degree in architecture, and later in the 1990's for my master's degree in business and technology, was quite reasonable relative to the skills I learned and earning power it provided. The importance of this fact is especially acute today because of skyrocketing college costs. It's much more expensive in today.

My college education began four decades ago and ended over two decades ago (with large gaps in between while working full time). Since then, college costs have soared exponentially - especially over the past two decades - and are now outrageously high at all levels except K-12 and community college. But even there, corruption is alive and well. Property owners and developers get hit with outrageously high property taxes and building fees which unfairly subsidizes students and funds the vast majority of unionized faculty and administrator salaries, benefits and pensions.

When combined with my state licenses to practice architecture, building construction, and real estate sales, both college degrees furthered my earning ability and professional status in the fields of architecture, post secondary teaching, technology, and real estate. Without them, I could have been a mediocre draftsman or a low-paid rock musician, which was my other career alternative in 1971 upon grading high school. The odds were ten million to one of making it as a rock star, so I focused on getting college educated and licensed. The point is I escaped feeling hopeless by deciding to get a college education from a school of architecture that was ranked among the highest for my major, and was also sensibly priced. This occurred in spite of not having healthy parenting in my childhood. You can too if you want it bad enough and put in the time and hard work. But first, let's look at an overview of the ideal methods and strategies to help get your child (or yourself) a top-tier education and potentially pay for it with as little-to-no debt as possible. Other college strategies will be explained later in the chapter.

The idea that one's child will one day be successful, rich, and happy looms in the hearts of all caring parents. Omitting "rich" out of the equation leaves the "successful and happy" objectives - which are the most important. Defining "rich" is nebulous and will yield many answers - some true and many false. One definition of rich is: "If I am healthy, then I am wealthy." Why? Because no price tag can be put on good health, and from a healthy body and mind springs hope and ideas that can make you money at any age and in any economic cycle - good or bad. How much money we end up with is another matter. But the general idea is to have enough cash saved-up so it can automatically generate more cash during your retirement years. Done right, this allows you to live comfortably without having to do any work for hire. Historically, the proven ingredients that contribute to personal wealth generation are:

A good college education + a steady paying job + skill + hard work + timing + taking measured risks + integrity + who you know...and occasional luck.

Which College should I apply to?

What do they specialize in?

How much will it cost?

How good is their reputation?

How good is their faculty and curriculum?

What accreditation board do they use?

Not all wealth creation requires a college education or every ingredient above. Lot's of millionaires were created on less. But generally, a college education is the surest route to greater career success for most human beings. And, the better the college, the better one's chances of success - assuming a person works hard after graduation, takes calculated risks, and develops a lasting career that's aligned with their passion and skills. More on that later. Right now, let's first focus on ***two*** major hurdles in getting your child (or yourself) the best college education possible with attractive financing.

The first hurdle is getting ***admitted into the best university for your chosen field***. The second hurdle is ***paying for it wisely with as little debt as possible***.

College costs remain outrageously high and have been increasing unchecked for decades. Course books are high priced too. Why? Because college demand is so strong that universities experience entitlement and corruption from continuous massive cash flows. This often occurs regardless of how well they perform or how fair or realistic the price is. They take advantage of that power by regularly increasing tuition virtually every year throughout campuses across America and other industrialized nations. Typically, 5% to 10% annual tuition increases are common. That's the reason college tuition doubles every ten to fifteen years. Colleges receive these massive cash flows from tuition, government grants, government backed loans, property taxes, and huge donations - which they politely call "endowments." Colleges would still have tons of money even if they froze tuition for years at a time. If all this greed wasn't bad enough, most colleges (besides *"for profit universities", or FPU's)* successfully lobbied the legal system and enjoy "tax free" status even though they operate billion dollar empires that mirror commercial enterprises. Al Capone had another name for this: A tax-free highly profitable racket.

The wise way to get educated is going to the right college without crippling debt.

As of this writing, top-tier private universities in the U.S. charge around $250,000 to $300,000 for a four-year undergraduate degree. In some situations this includes tuition, housing, and food. In other cases it's for tuition only. For medical, law, and PhD students, the price tag is often higher. Mid-tier private colleges, state universities, and for-profit colleges raise their tuition costs regularly, despite vast differences in quality.

For example, a well known for-profit college called The University of Phoenix (UOP) charges about the same (*sometimes more, sometimes less*) as many city, state and private colleges. Yet, it is not a campus-based setting like a traditional university and typically scores lower in accreditation and reputation. Universities like this - known as "for-profit universities", or "FPU's" - issue school loans that are typically government subsidized. Tax payers end up footing the bill when student loans are defaulted on. The university keeps the tuition because the government backed the loan. Student loan debt in the U.S. is at an all time high. Currently, over $1.7 trillion in total student loan debt exists, according to the U.S. National Debt Clock.Org, which gathers its information from the Federal Reserve. That figure includes government backed loans, private bank loans, and parent borrowing. The ease of having the Feds pay for student tuition results in FPU's admitting almost anyone. Completed course work from colleges like UOP are generally not recognized by traditional colleges and universities. This becomes a major impediment and financial setback when transferring courses from an FPU to a traditional college or university. My wife experienced this first hand when transferring out of UOP to a California community college.

College is essential. But, you must go to the "right" university, and pay for it wisely!

Don't fall on the sword of excessively high college loans - especially from lower-tier schools.

College costs have been rising across the nation unabated. Some have doubled or tripled from just a decade ago - especially since the great recession of 2008-2012. Even if your kid is brilliant and you do all the steps to get admitted, what happens to that sky-high college bill that becomes due (in full or by a payment plan with interest) soon after gradation? Paying back $60,000 over ten years is hard enough. Paying back $300,000 dollars can be a living nightmare - especially if one's annual salary is between $40,000 to $70,0000 like a vast number of college graduates. There are ways to fund college that make sense, but they must be relative to your *earning power.* For example, President Donald Trump graduated from an Ivy League school - namely the Wharton Business School at the University of Pennsylvania, known as "UPenn". Three of his kids also went to UPenn, two of which attended the Wharton Business School like he did. Mr. Trump likely had to pay full retail for their tuition costs, but it was well within his earning power as a billionaire to do so - even with three kids plus himself. Therefore, it was *relative to his (and his father's) vast earning power* even at $250K per child. That made it the right college at a reasonable price.

I couldn't afford to pay a fifth of the $265,000 to $300,000 (and climbing) it now costs for tuition, room and board at an Ivy League or elite university. Yet, our youngest child was admitted to an Ivy League university and graduated debt free within six months after graduation. Not only was he admitted to the Wharton Business School, (Class of 2016), he was also admitted into Wharton's prestigious Huntsman Program where only fifty top students from around the world are selected from a hyper competitive pool of bright young minds: twenty-five from within the U.S. and twenty-five from foreign countries. The Huntsman program is like the Navy Seals of the Wharton Business School. Each student usually earns two degrees and must study at Wharton as well as abroad in a foreign country for several semesters.

The "right" college means one that gives you marketable skills, is respected within the industry you major in, and, is priced sensibly relative to the university's reputation and your ability to afford it without staggering debt.

Huntsman students are also required to learn a second language to near- fluency level. My son's chosen language was Japanese. This stemmed in large part from my former travels to Japan during my youth on numerous business trips with my father during the mid 1960's to late 1970's. My father and I shared a deep affinity for Japanese culture, work ethic, education, industrial innovation, quality, and cuisine - all of which were exposed to my son years later. Thus, he began to develop a natural affinity for Japanese culture too. He studied Japanese for four years in high school, plus another three years at Wharton. During high school, he applied for and won a full scholarship to travel to Japan for two weeks. During college, he studied in Japan for several semesters via the international exchange program that Wharton provided within the Huntsman program. He made eight trips in total, each time immersing himself in the language and culture. Today he lives and works in Japan for the Walt Disney Company's Tokyo office and speaks the language fluently.

Prior to sending our son off to college, my wife and I were both working, but our combined incomes were considerably less than a few years earlier due to the housing and financial crisis. Our salaries from both passive and active income was just shy of $100,000 a year. That may sound adequate, but after taxes and expenses, we had to budget every dollar spent. All that was left barely covered a low-to-mid tier college education. No way could we pay for two households and a college tuition price tag that was among the most expensive in the world. Yet, we managed to do so.

The total costs for my son's four year college education approached $250,000, plus travel costs. It rose about 4% virtually every year because top universities are impacted, have wealthy clients (student's parents and donors), and become easily addicted to all that cash pouring in. Our son's tuition started at $48,000 for the first year in 2012, and ended up at $52,000 per semester by 2016. This did ***not*** include housing, food, books, or cross-country and international travel costs.

The breakdown of these costs and how we solved the high price tag dilemma is explained next.

University Tuition = potentially very high $ debt.

College costs are high! Tuition costs keep rising every year, which is absurd given how rich most universities are. At a minimum, universities need to freeze tuition costs. Better still, they should lower their tuition costs, not raise them! Most colleges would never dream of doing this...even if forced too. And that's the problem: unaccountable greed. Other than FPU's, most universities pay no income taxes either. Follow the tuition and it adds up to massive balance sheets, billion dollar endowment funds, and lucrative pensions. Meanwhile, students and parents get hit with run-away costs and high debt.

So instead, you must "***kick debt to the curb***" by taking advantage of "free" money that's available for many four year undergraduate college programs in the U.S. That means scholarships and grants. Thus, "need based financing" is debt free. The wise way to get educated is going to the ***right c***ollege without crippling ***debt.*** But first, you must qualify. How? Read on.

The Wharton Business School is located in Philadelphia on the campus of the University of Pennsylvania, or "UPenn" as its commonly called. When our son Sean graduated from Wharton in 2016, my wife and I had spent $50,000 toward his college costs, plus an additional $5,000 on airfare over four years between Philadelphia and LA during semester breaks and his study abroad in Japan.

"If my wife and I can send our kid to an Ivy League University, with middle class income, and little debt, so can you!"

Edward S. Rickter 2020

The $50,000 we paid UPenn went toward housing, food, and high-priced books, and constituted 20% of the $250K total (before travel costs.) The university paid roughly $185,000, which comprised 74% of the $250K total. That means it was a college gift, and thus, debt-free money. My son took the remaining 6% tuition balance of $15,000 as a loan, and paid it off in less than half a year. Upon graduation, Sean was offered a job with The Walt Disney Company as a financial analyst within their Global Development Division, which oversees all of Disney's global theme parks, resorts, and cruise lines. He was Disney's top pick among seven bright candidates, beating out four Harvard graduates, a Princeton graduate, and another graduate from Wharton. Do you see a pattern here?

When it came to hiring - even entry level financial positions - Disney only interviewed students from Ivy League (or top elite) universities. It was the manifest of words I spoke to him years earlier when he was eight years old: "Get top grades during K-12, then you can choose among the country's top universities. Coupled with a good attitude, that in turn paves the road to exciting job offers from the world's top companies upon graduation".

His salary and sign-on bonus were generous and helped towards tuition debt reduction. But his ability to pay his college debt quickly occurred for additional reasons. During his first year of employment, I allowed him to live rent free at home, provided he created a budget (P&L statement), spent below his means, and focused on paying off the remaining Wharton $15,000 in less than a year. He accomplished that goal in five months. He was debt free soon after graduating, had two degrees from an Ivy League University, and had secured a job from the largest entertainment company in the world. This type of outcome was the very thing my wife and I instilled in him was possible. It started during the time he was attending elementary school around age eight.

Sean's outcome could have resulted in a different college, a different major, a different company, or a different industry. What mattered is my wife and I taught him to believe in himself, aim high, choose the right university, work hard, be respectful, and learn to manage money. Some kids rebel. Other's take heed. The outcome is never 100% predictable. But, the odds of success are exponentially increased when both kids and parents work as a team toward a common goal.

First and foremost is this:
Parents need to lead this process by mapping out an eighteen year plan for their kid, and work at it daily regardless of their kid's push-back. It requires more than feeding and housing them. Helping them personally with their homework means everything. Listening without squashing their dreams energizes their souls. It's exhausting and immensely rewarding and the same time. Nothing worthwhile is easy.

When done in a positive and accountable manner, Kids naturally follow a parent's lead. That was the case with our youngest son. But what if parents don't take the lead? Other family members sometimes step-in and take on a mentor role that helps fill the gaps of a missing parent. What if that's not the case? What if parents try hard but their kid still rebels? Ultimately, the challenge falls upon each kid (or individual) to take ownership of their own destiny. It's not easy and takes years to realize. But it will work with determination, faith, and hard work. It's something I had to do to get educated properly. "What-ifs" like these will be explained later in the chapter, but in this case, *our son won, my wife and I won, UPenn won, and Disney won.*

This was an American dream come true. He got one of the best business undergraduate college degrees in the world, and did so with a good job offer and relatively little debt. Likewise, my wife and I paid a reasonable $12,500 each year in cash toward his room and board costs, for a total of $50,000, plus an additional $5,000 in travel costs, over four years. Because our incomes were half of what they used to be prior to 2008, we struggled at times. We had to maintain two households while she worked in San Francisco and I in Los Angeles. Spending $50,000 on top of regular living expenses for four years - including a mortgage, rent, property taxes, insurance, food, etc. - is not easy or cheap. But it's still about the same or less as colleges that are orders of magnitude lower in stature than an Ivy League university.

"All American citizens should have access to a great college education without burdensome debt upon graduation".

Benjamin Franklin,
U.S. Constitution co-founder and founder of the University of Pennsylvania (UPENN). 1776

For example, California State University Long Beach where I got my MBA over twenty years ago, cost roughly $2000 per year full-time in 1998. Twenty years later, it's well over three to four times that amount - approaching $10,000 to $15,000 a year for tuition - plus books, room and board. Ironically, that figure is cheap compared to elite private schools or the California University College (UC) system. Talk about a deal! Wharton was a mega deal with unlimited upside life- changing potential! Opportunities like this really exist, but they're kept relatively quiet. You have to look for them.

So, how did we pull off this educational cu'de'ta'? In a nut shell, it took team work, extensive financial research, healthy parenting from *both mom and dad*, budgeting, talking to college admission administrators, attending recruiting seminars, traveling around the country to visit university campuses, and our son's consistent hard work to achieve high GPA and SAT scores during high school. But the affordability part goes back to a seminar we took our son to in 2010 in Orange County, CA, which was being hosted by Wharton recruiters. My son was in the 10th grade at Polytechnic High School in Long Beach, California. His GPA was exceptional, but his faith in himself as a top-tier college candidate was still undeveloped. He felt comfortable with mid-tier colleges, *but* he was unsure about being good enough for Harvard, Yale, Stanford, or Wharton. I knew otherwise because as an adult, you gain perspective and experience. H*e was good enough* and probably just as good as the best applicants out there. What I was stymied over was how we could ever afford the high cost of an elite college education, short of taking on massive debt.

Somehow, I felt an answer might come, but I wasn't sure how. The answer unfolded during that seminar. The true story behind that life-changing moment will be explained soon. But first, know that all families have struggles and drama. You have to accept it as normal, even if you think your situation is abnormal. Our situation was no exception. There was plenty of drama and struggles to deal with.

Because we were a blended family, raising each of our three kids had different outcomes. My wife had a son prior to our marriage who I raised from the age of eighteen months. I had a daughter prior to marriage who was raised by her mother until age eighteen. Our youngest son graduated from Wharton. Our oldest son was seldom interested in education. My daughter, who earned her bachelors and masters in psychology, obtained her degrees during her thirties. Despite her mother's insistence and contrary to my advice, she wasn't ready for college immediately after high school. After half-heartedly enrolling at Cal State Fullerton, it wasn't long before she dropped out. She moved in with my wife and I for the next five years and began pursuing a successful career in professional modeling and acting that lasted ten years. Both our oldest kids from prior relationships were head strong about their future life direction, regardless of our attempts to influence them. Figuring this all out in real time wasn't easy or spontaneously obvious. It took lots of battles and therapy to understand that we were a family, but we were all different too.

Sean was the youngest and only child between us. I was forty and my wife was thirty five. This was considerably old to be having another kid, but the fact remained my wife wanted a child between us. She was right. I had put it off too long for selfish reasons related to building my business. It was now or never. The upside was our parenting skills had improved and we both had fairly good income. And so, on October 17, 1994, Sean was born. By 4th grade, he began demonstrating a strong propensity in drawing Yugio art, which is a stylized from of cartoon characters popularized in Japanese comic books and videos. By 5th grade, he was becoming exceptionally good at it. He created his own characters and soon advanced to writing and illustrating his own comic books. My work colleagues saw his cartoon art work pinned on the wall of my office and couldn't believe it was created by a nine year old child. Sometimes I couldn't either.

One summer when he was nine, I made him date and scan all his art work to my computer for fear that his inspired hand drawn creations might get lost with the passage of time. He moaned and groaned, but I told him it was for his future benefit, not just mine. It took him several weeks, but he got it done. At the time, it seemed like he might be headed toward fine art school. We would have supported an art career if that's what he was passionate about and exceptional good at - which he was. Ironically, fate turned out different. When Sean became twelve, he put down his beloved pencils and paper and stopped drawing. He'd lost interest after almost seven years of pure passion and joy. He was entering his teens, but to this day it's still an enigma because he loved it so much. However, that's when our "*parent imposed*" *back-up college major* kicked-in. This meant we re-directed Sean's focus toward business. Years later after Sean finished college, the idea for this book sprung up in my head and I decided to use his art work to help illustrate certain concepts and make it more fun for younger audiences. I asked him how he felt about using his art work in my book (with full credit). He was happy to oblige. Upon graduating 5th grade, I gave our youngest son incentives to get good marks in school, which he seemed to relish. This included gifts and showing him hundred dollar bills with the caveat: "If you get excellent grades, graduate college, and get a good job, you'll have them too. Lots of them.

This meant Sean (and us as parents) had three important steps to endure that lasted ten years:
1) Study hard and get top grades in elementary, middle, and (especially) high school.
2) Major in something he loved and could earn money doing. If unsure, then a "parent-imposed" standby major was selected. That meant a business degree since it could be used in virtually any industry around the globe in any type of economy - good, bad, or uncharted; (i.e.: COVID-19).
3) By 9th grade, enroll in an advanced high school scholastic program (like *CIC or *PACE), pick a foreign language (Japanese), enroll in a sport (track), and focus on straight "A's".

> ***Important Facts:*** *Most colleges start tracking GPA's from 9th grade. College applications must be submitted by early-to-mid year of 12th grade. It's imperative to get your kids ready for high school, ideally starting from elementary through middle school. That means working hard on their homework and getting consistently high test scores. Parents need to be directly involved with their kid's weekly progress more so than teachers, nannies, and tutors. Why?* ***Kids want and need their <u>parent's attention and guidance</u>! That's always been the divine plan. It's the purist way to nurture their hearts and minds!***

To give Sean more incentives, I made a deal with him that paid $50.00 cash for each "A" and $500 for the whole semester if he got straight "A's". "B's" paid nothing. **He needed to focus on A's,** *not B's and C's.* Our father-son "study/reward agreement" gave him extra incentive to push himself harder in ***all*** his classes, not just the ones he liked the most. As in life, people get financial rewards when they work hard and do their best. The third step helped paved the way to being a top contender at an elite Ivy League university because he developed a consistent "A" mentality. Some might call this bribery. I considered it an incentive to reach the top 2% of his class, by simply remembering there's always going to be work and reward consequences in life.

By 5th grade, Sean and his class mates had to make a speech at their elementary school's 5th grade graduation about what they wanted to be when they grew up. Like all ten year old kids, he was unsure what to say and asked me for advice. A young moldable mind was seeking higher wisdom, so I obliged. I suggested something along the lines of: "After I graduate 5th grade, and eventually high school, I want to go to a top university, major in business, and work for a great company. Maybe I'll even rise to become a financial executive or president." I wasn't sure if he'd stammer or forget what to say. Surprisingly, Sean casually walked up to the podium and delivered words to that effect, but in a way that came across naturally for his age. The audience didn't know I coached him. That was our little secret. It worked. The audience let out a collective "whoa". One of his classmates then shouted out "his goal was to work for Sean when he grew up". The remainder of the students had no clue what to say, and expressed cute but mundane goals. They needed coaching.

The message for parents is this: When our kids ask us for advice about their future - help them dream big. That's the time to do it! Don't limit their thinking. One day it just might become reality, and in Sean's case, it did! He simply believed he could do it because as parents we didn't limit his thinking or make him feel inferior. We helped him feel empowered, which in turn strengthened his intellect, character, and social skills. By high school, Sean was hitting his stride. He got all A's (and one B) the last semester of 9th grade, and straight A's throughout 10th and 11th grades. Those are critical years for kids and parents. Most colleges start tracking GPA's from 9th grade forward, and make their decisions for admission in the Fall or Spring of 12th grade.

That's why it's imperative to get your kids ready by middle school to study hard on their homework and tests. Kids will have raging hormones, want to goof-off, and hang out with friends. Parents need to love them unconditionally, but that doesn't mean goofing off is acceptable. Parents have to ultimately hold their kids accountable by giving them very strong boundaries about *when to study, when they get to play, and who they hang out with.* This worked for Sean. It didn't always work for our other two kids who had their own agendas during and after high school. *Maturity happens at different ages, and occurs in mysterious ways*. We love all our kids. Each one is unique. Today our oldest son makes a high five figure income (with barely a high school education) working in HVAC construction (Heating, Ventilation, and Air Conditioning). After my daughter realized she wasn't ready for college at eighteen, she followed her heart and successfully pursued her modeling and acting career. It took almost two decades before she completed her undergraduate and master's degrees in psychology (while married).

Pursuing a college education upon graduating high school is the ideal. But it's not for everyone no matter how much parents want it for their kids. Push your kids towards college by mentoring and guiding them. But ultimately, the most you can do is be a good parent, give them your time, hold them accountable, and then "pray" for a decent outcome. It may come directly as you hoped. It may not. It may come later in life. It may turn out as an unexpected outcome that eventually works out. In general however, I see more positive outcomes from good parenting than not. The odds are highly stacked in that favor.

Expose your kids to the names of top-tier colleges when they are young and impressionable.

...Wharton, Princeton, Brown
...Harvard, Yale, UPenn
...Stanford, MIT, Cal Poly SLO, Cal Tech
...University of Tokyo (Todai)
...Oxford, Cambridge
...USC, Notre Dame, UCLA
...Your Dream College

At the college recruiting seminar, I asked two questions about Wharton's tuition costs and admission test scores that seemed to go unmentioned in the seminar.

The story behind the breaking moment of insight at the Wharton recruiting seminar in Orange County, California was soon to unfold. By the end of 11th grade, the time had come for our son to start thinking of colleges. When he was in 7th grade, I had him write down the names of all eight Ivy League schools: *Brown, Yale, Princeton, Harvard, University of Pennsylvania (Wharton), Dartmouth, Columbia, and Cornell University.*

He wrote them down on a piece of paper and pinned it up on the wall in front of his desk at home where he did his homework while our cat studied with him in his lap. The idea was to make him aware of the names of great universities, and plant the seeds of self-esteem so he would feel worthy of applying to them. At the time, Sean didn't know he was that good. Most kids don't.

The list of schools could have also been Stanford, MIT, Oxford, Todai (University of Tokyo), Cambridge, USC, UC Berkeley, The Berkley School of Music, Julliard, NYU, Cal Tech, The Art Center in Pasadena, etc. Many fine colleges exist. The point is to expose your kids to the names of top-tier colleges when they are young and impressionable because kids naturally are inclined to follow directions and soak up good advice. The reverse also holds true. This in turn sprouts forth a greater degree of believing in themselves when they get in high school and have to map-out which college to go to.

It might as well be an elite college rather than a mid or lower-tier university. Even if they don't get accepted, good alternatives exist because many universities have excellent curriculums and industry reputations. Not everyone will go to Yale or Harvard. Various state and private schools offer excellent college educations - at various price points.

Some colleges are outstanding. Some are mediocre. Others are a blatant rip off, like ITT and Corinthian College - both of which went out of business after years of poor instruction, high fees, false advertising, and bogus job placement claims. Shoot for the stars, then scale back if you have to. You'll never get what you truly want if you don't take a chance and do what's needed. Why not try and see what happens? There was nothing for us to lose as Sean's parents either. This is how it happened.

Two Critical Questions and Answers for Top-Tier College Admission

One day an advertisement came in the mail from the Wharton School at UPenn that indicated they were having a recruiting seminar in Orange County, California. It was an hour drive, but far more convenient than flying across country to Philadelphia. Kids in 10th grade are heavily targeted because most colleges mail them out to various high schools and households as part of their "on-site" recruiting process in various U.S. cities.

Remember: 10th and 11th grade are when to start seriously thinking about which college(s) to attend. By the Fall semester of 12th grade, or late Winter the following January through March, students have to send in their college applications. By that December or early January, most colleges make their first round selection announcements. The second round college selections are usually made between March and April of the 12th grade. This occurs like clockwork every year in the United States.

My wife and I decided to take our son to the Wharton recruiting event to size it up. First, there was the usual slide show and movie about how Ben Franklin founded the University of Pennsylvania in the late 1790's, which eventually became one of the eight Ivy League universities on the east coast in the U.S. The seminar soon transitioned to the history of the Wharton Business School on UPenn's campus, after which, they talked briefly about general admission requirements, but very little about specific scores and nothing at all about tuition costs.

The guest speaker from Wharton's Admissions Office was more than happy to answer both my questions. The answers he gave were life changing.

I still had very specific questions that were unanswered - especially tuition fees, loan options, and available grant money. Loans have to be paid back, but grants are free college money that don't require repayment. I took advantage of grants thirty years earlier when I was admitted to Cal Poly University's School of Architecture in San Luis Obispo, California.

After the presentation ended, I decided to walk from the back of the room where we were seated to the front podium and ask the speaker privately my specific questions concerning Wharton's tuition costs, admission test scores, and how the university awarded grants and scholarships.

The two questions I asked were:

1) *"How does Wharton determine how much* ***grant (free) money*** *is awarded to students who get admitted, but whose parents can't afford the high cost of an Ivy League education?"*

2) *"What is the preferred SAT score and GPA that ensures the highest chance of being admitted to Wharton?"*

Those two questions, and the answers to them, changed the course of our son's life. The answer to question #1 was as follows:

Answer to Key Question #1:

Grant money (free cash that doesn't require repayment) is awarded to students based on their parent's "financial status", or in other words, their income. This means that if a child gets admitted to Wharton, (or Harvard, Yale, Brown, or most other elite universities), the cost of "free" tuition money is based on how much income the student's parents make, regardless of the tuition amount.

For example, if the parents make around $100,000 or less, then they are considered "lower income status" and unable to afford the full tuition price. As a result, the university picks up the bill for a huge portion of the total four year tuition price. *The key point here is they help pay the tuition not as a loan that has to be repaid, but as a gift or scholarship that is 100% free.*

Now, another key question to ask yourself is "how much tuition is actually paid for by the university?" The answer to that depends on how much money the parents make, but at about $100,000 annual "gross adjusted income", the short answer is: *the majority of it*! That means about 80% of the total cost of attending an Ivy League college is paid in-full by the university. That will vary up or down, but it's a good rule of thumb. It's also not a loan that has to be repaid.

Which college should I go to? How will my parents (or I) pay for it?

The important thing is that your kid (or you) gets admitted to the college. The money will work itself out with proper due diligence. If parents have higher incomes, then the grant money shrinks and the university expects the parents to pay more out of pocket. All colleges have their own formulas to determine grant assistance, but the figures just stated are real examples from about eight years ago. The cut-off for free grant money approximately begins at salaries in the $250K range and above. That leaves a lot of people who can qualify.

So, if you or your parents are rich, you pay the full tuition price of college with cash or mountains of borrowed money that has to be repaid (i.e.: student loans). Talk to the college's admissions and financial aid departments to get their specific answers to these critical questions. But generally, this is the formula many elite universities follow in the United States. Other countries have various types of financial deals. Be direct and ask them specifically.

"Need based college financing" is a great blessing and life-changing opportunity within the higher education system - especially at elite U.S. universities. It's the main reason most great colleges have such large endowments, which are pools of money given to them by rich people, corporations, and various organizations backed by wealthy donors. All of that endowment money is in addition to regular tuition fees, book sales, housing fees, and food services that universities generate revenue from.

Two Key Questions you MUST ask all Colleges are:

1) ***"How do they determine how much grant (free) money is awarded to students who get admitted"***

and ..

2) "What is the preferred SAT score and GPA that ensures the highest chances of being admitted?"

University endowments are used in large part to help pay college tuition costs for students whose parents cannot otherwise afford to pay the full retail price. That included us, and a lot of other hard working middle class folks. I knew at that moment that our son had a very strong chance of not just getting admitted to a top-tier university, but that my wife and I would have tremendous assistance without debt financing. Furthermore, our son would be able to graduate with little or no debt. He just needed to get in.

My wife and I still had a sizable amount of remaining tuition to pay for with cash - about $52,000 over four years - but it was low in percentage terms. Our tuition share equated to about 20% of the total costs ($260,000) to attend Wharton. It was going to impose a strain on us, but it was totally worth it and within our means as long as we both generated our current income, established an accurate budget, and stuck to it religiously.

Furthermore, the costs were spread out over four years. We refused to take out loans or use our retirement money to fund our son's college education. We also refused to have him take on excessively high debt after graduation. A little debt maybe - like 5% to 15%, but no more.

As it turned out, our son graduated from Wharton with 5.8% debt ($15K) and paid it off in less than half a year. The $245K balance ($260,000 - $15,000) was paid in full by both UPenn and my wife and I; (UPenn paid about $193,000 and we paid $52,000). What I learned at the seminar was a wake-up call for me, and a message to all parents. Make every attempt to attend these college marketing events when your child is in 10th or 11th grade. It's a small investment of time with a huge return. It equates to unlimited opportunity for your kids and tremendous financial help for you as parents. If you don't receive notices in the mail by 10th or 11th grade, call various universities and ask for their admissions department. They always have student and parent tour days each semester and are happy to answer questions.

Later I'll address how to find and get admitted to a college if you or your child lacked academic preparation in high school. In that case, additional preparation is required before applying to a desirable four year university. That was my situation, and it still yielded success in my forty year career as an architect, real estate developer, technology entrepreneur, and educator. I've taught and mentored many students and adults who are in the same situation.

The elite college route is a noble ambition. But not everyone does the proper academic preparation required to attain it because they either don't know how or they haven't had their minds exposed to it's wonderful potential later in life.

A top-tier college degree helps tremendously in achieving success in life, but it still requires more than just your degree once you graduate. You also have to work hard, continually develop new technical skills, take risks, have integrity, and never stop honing your communication skills.

The answer to Question #1 was:

Need-based grant money = free tuition money that doesn't require repayment. It is awarded to students based on their parent's "financial status", or in other words, their IRS verified annual salary.

This means that if a child gets admitted to Wharton, (or Harvard or other top university), <u>the final cost of tuition is adjusted</u> based on how much income <u>the student's parents make,</u> not the retail price set by the college.

The answer to Question #2 was more straight forward, but equally critical. It provided the specific admission targets for our son (and us as parents) to aim for. The desired GPA is 3.5 to 4.0 or higher, and needs to be from an advanced or accelerated high school program like *CIC or *PACE.

** See page 126 for definitions.*

There are scores of people who are widely successful with degrees from various colleges, and some without any college education, largely because of *who* they are. Think: Andrew Carnegie, Henry Ford, Jack Welsh, Larry Ellison, Bill Gates, Steve Wozniak, Jonny Carson, Jerry Seinfeld, and countless others. It's good to shoot for the moon, but you also need college backup plans. So, between the summer of 11th and 12th grades, we took our son to various college campuses in the U.S. prior to him making a final decision. This gave him a sense of what it was like to actually be on campus and get direct answers from the school's tour representatives.

We took him to Wharton, Stanford, Columbia, NYU, UCLA, and few others. It was the surest way to get accurate admission answers and gain a feel for the campus vibe. Harvard, Yale, MIT, and many other top universities were equally good, but his focus was quickly narrowing down to business, and Wharton was rated number one in the world out of 100 undergraduate business colleges according to a Financial Times (FT) survey back in the 2010 / 2011 timeframe. The FT is a widely read business and financial news publication in England that's similar to the Wall Street Journal in the United States.

Answer to Key Question #2:

The answer to the second question provided the specific admission targets for our son (and us as parents) to aim for. Wharton's desired GPA range was around 3.75 to 4.0 (on a 4.0 scale), and 4.5 to 5.0 (on a 5.0 scale). The 5.0 scale includes advanced or accelerated high school academic programs like *CIC or *PACE. For example, Poly High School's CIC program uses a GPA range from 1.0 to 5.0, which Sean's GPA was tied to.

Naturally a high GPA means a student is doing very well, but it's still not necessarily straight "A's". Our son's GPA was 4.7 (on a 5.0 scale), and even that wasn't perfection. But it remained excellent and was well within Wharton's coveted GPA range for admission. The competition is fierce. You need every edge you can get. That's why I pushed him the hardest in high school to get straight A's in10th and 11th grades. He got mostly "A's" in 12th grade, except for two B's, which I let slide since he was admitted to Wharton by then. Equally important were the courses themselves. The "right" courses included four rigorous years learning a foreign language, advanced mathematics that included four semesters of calculus, three years of an intense sports activity, community service work, and ideally, some form of U.S. or foreign travel. As for SAT tests, Wharton's preferred scores were as follows: on a scale of 1 to 2400, 1800 was the lowest, 2000 was good, and 2200 and up was virtually a slam dunk to rise to the upper echelons of Wharton's admission list.

This is the basic formula to follow for receiving top consideration at most elite universities in the U.S. and other *G8 countries direct out of high school. It's a tremendous amount of hard work and takes incredible determination and tenacity. *The way to get through those challenges and obstacles is to stay focused on the end goal = the prize = the final reward.* This is what motivates and empowers *all* champions in life.

Summary of the Key Steps to Top-Tier College Admission

In the construction industry, there's a term called "Critical Path Method", or CPM. CPM is a project management technique that isolates the essential steps necessary for completing each building task prior to beginning the next one. The critical path (steps towards final completion) for getting the best college education possible for your kid - even when you think you can't afford it - are summarized below. Concentrate on getting prepared first, then tackle the money part second. Money flows to those who are prepared.

1) Infant to young child ages (1 - 6)

Praise your child's inquisitive nature and small accomplishments when they are between the ages of one to five years old. During this time, they'll go through the "terrible two's", where a child discovers the ability to say "no", and their ego awareness begins to develop. Don't spoil children by letting them do anything they want. You may create self-entitled obnoxious adults. Love them, but give them firm boundaries. That often means telling them "no" back without feeling guilty.

From five on (kindergarten), it's critical to have them on a regular schedule of fun time, rest time, and learning time. Avoid excessive television, internet, and cell phone usage. Help them discover passions and talents by exposing them to things like drawing, musical instruments, games, sports, reading, math, models, building blocks, and other arts and sciences. Praise their accomplishments and gently help them learn from their mistakes. As they get older, raise the bar by increasing your level of expectation, but don't break their spirit. Mistakes are how we learn as human beings - especially during childhood - and even in adulthood. Too many American managers are poor leaders because they're poor mentors. Expecting perfection and punishing subordinates for occasional or inevitable mistakes, instead of helping them learn and grow from those mistakes, is a primary reason. This does not mean tolerating continual incompetence. A negative mentoring mentality is largely rooted in childhood. So is a positive one. Jack Welch - the legendary CEO of industrial conglomerate General Electric - understood the principal of effective leadership and healthy mentoring exceptionally well.

2) Young Child through middle school (7 - 12)

At home, foster your child's talents. If they don't seem to have any, keep placing things in front of them and see what they take to. In elementary school, get them used to doing homework right after they get home from school. Give them a quick snack and a short amount of free time, then find a good study spot in the house and teach them that homework is an essential part of growing up and becoming a success in life.

Every so often I would flash hundred dollar bills in front of my son's eight year old beaming eyes so he could physically see the manifestation of what the fruits of honest hard work and a good education can yield. His face would light up as I asked: "Would you like to have these hundred dollar bills?" He'd immediately say "yes". Then I'd say: "Good. One day you will. But first, you have to get your homework done, get high grades in elementary, middle, and high school. Then you'll have the greatest chance of getting into the best universities. From there, you'll have the best choices of establishing a career with a good company that pays you a decent salary and inspires you to work. After that, the hundred dollar bills will begin to flow nicely."

I'd always leave the door open to self-employment, and say "one day you might even start your own business like I did", but I'd always preference it by saying "that is a path that requires a lot of work, risk, and experience before jumping into it." In most cases (not all) , you need to work for well managed companies first before you know how to start, run, and sustain your own company.

Self-employment is extremely hard and most people delude themselves when entering into business for themselves. I did it for ten straight years fulltime, and another twenty years part-time - and was profitable virtually every year. But, it often required many twelve hour days and every ounce of my intelligence, energy, and net worth. Why did I do it? Because I was passionate about technology, profitability, quality, building, and teaching. I was raised by entrepreneurs and probably have it naturally in my blood. But I also worked for large corporations for over twenty years. There are pros and cons to both career paths. Being exposed to both was highly beneficial.

As a way to reinforce strong study habits during 3rd to 5th grades, I'd reward my sons with skate boards, musical instruments, and Yugio cards (which they were crazy about). When Sean got four "A"s and two "B's" in 5th grade, he earned a trip to the skateboard shop that summer and got to pick out a custom skate board. Then he got to enjoy it all summer long. When my oldest son struggled in 12th grade due to poor study habits, I took him to a music store and promised I'd buy him a keyboard synthesizer he wanted, if he would focus and get his high school diploma. He worked extra hard, graduated, and got a keyboard too. When given for the right reasons, gifts instill a healthy study-reward balance for kids. During this time, explore different ideas about what they like and don't like about people and the environment around them. Ask them what they would like to be when they grown up. Help them dream. This helps them connect dots to their highest feelings of self-worth, inspiration, and passion. From that springs forth their true calling in life. It doesn't always happen overnight. It may not happen at all for periods of time. In that case, keep your child focused on home work, tests, and social skill development. That's enough for all kids. Asking them about the things they love is like planting seeds of hope and inspiration in their young and impressionable souls.

By middle school (ages 11 - 12), teenage years arrive and hormones kick in. These are rough waters for some kids and parents. If you spend quality time with your kids in prior years, they will typically not rebel as hard, and those waters will be less turbulent. Parents that spend little time with their kids by pawning them off on nannies and others to help them with their homework, or who are overly critical of their behavior, will probably encounter more turbulent waters and rebellion once kids go through puberty and become young teenagers. That was my experience because I lacked healthy parental guidance and dealt with the frustration of a dominant and punitive father, so I rebelled. It was my love of architecture and music that gave me purpose and inspiration, which guided me toward a career goal in my mid-to-late teenage years. Not terribly late, but I'd probably have a Harvard degree had mom and dad spent more one-on-one time with me and my sisters guiding us and explaining the benefits of a top-tier college education during middle and high school. We were bright and eager to learn, but ultimately, like most families, we were clueless about how to harness the tremendous benefits of higher education. Fortunately, I found my own way to achieve it. My two sisters never did

3) High School years (13 - 18)

Between 9th and 12th grades is when universities officially keep track of your kid's grade point average (GPA). Good GPA's are extremely important for admission to high caliber universities. That's why it's critical to instill a strong study regiment in your child during elementary school. A good GPA (on a 1-4 scale) would be something starting at 3.3 A very good GPA begins at around 3.5. Great ones are 3.8 and above. The best of breed are up to 5.0 on a 1-5 scale. Once in 9th grade, the GPA clock starts ticking and the race to top-college admission is on.

Below are the key sub-steps to maximize top-tier college admission success:

a) Set the bar high for grades. A's primarily; B's minimally; nothing lower than a B.
b) Make every effort to enroll your kid in an accelerated academic program (PACE, CIC, etc.)
c) Create a safe home environment for your kid to come home to, study, and feel nurtured.
d) Make strict rules about study time. No friends, cell phones, or goofing off during study time.
e) Check-up on their homework every day. Give your time to them as much as you can. Even fifteen minutes of your time can make a huge difference to their homework progress.

f) Enroll your kids in a sport they feel comfortable with. Both my son's loved track and field.
g) Give your child freedom to pick a career path. If they don't know, see Items i) and j) below.
h) Avoid degrees that are near worthless in the real world. Do reality checks with other people.
i) If all else fails, push your kid towards a business degree. They can expand that infinitely.
j) Other degree choices like medicine, architecture, engineering, the arts, teaching, and others, are still solid choices. But make sure to research pay scales by interviewing people who work in those industries when possible. Don't rely solely on college or high school counselors.

k) Find out what the beginning and top pay scales are for a chosen degree and career path.
l) Make a list of at least five great universities. Set the bar high. Don't feel unworthy of the best.
m) Call universities and make appointments to visit their campus with your kid.
n) Around 10th grade, begin SAT preparation. Pay for SAT study courses ($800 to $1000) if needed. I did and it raised my son's SAT score (which he took twice) from 1900 to 2200.
o) Partake in after-school community volunteer activates. My son helped Japanese kids with their grammar, and later was selected for two all-paid trips to Japan during high school.

p) Between Fall and Spring of 12th grade, help your kids apply to at least three top colleges.
q) By December of 12th grade to the following Spring, final college admission and rejection letters are sent out. This is the deciding moment you have been preparing and waiting for.
r) Wait, pray, but expect anything. Know that you and your kid did everything humanly possible. If rejected from your favorite college choice, examine the others. If rejected from all, read the next chapter on how to get into college if you don't make it by 12th grade.
s) If accepted, rejoice. Begin immediately setting up the financing arrangements. Call the financial aid department of the college immediately after receiving acceptance. Parents will need to fill out complete financial background information, including tax returns, wage statements, a balance sheet, and an income statement. This will determine a parent's (or your) "financial need", which in turn determines free tuition assistance.
t) Apply for FAFSA, which stands for *Free Application for Federal Student Aid,* and is a U.S. federal government student loan program. Don't use FAFSA as the primary means to fund college. Use it as a backup for partial tuition only. Why? Only the application is free. The money isn't free and has to be paid back with interest. It will be tempting initially, but the down side is massive tuition debt that can last for years - even decades - after graduation. Debt is like an avalanche: It builds slowly, and then crashes suddenly. College debt will be on top of other debt after graduation, like car loans, credit cards, and mortgage loans. You may not qualify for a house loan later on unless your other debt is paid off, or your salary increases drastically. Just ask any college graduate who is strapped with a five or six figure college loan what they've experienced trying to qualify for a home loan or rental property since graduating college. The answers are often horrifying.

u) After submitting necessary financial documents, wait for the college to send you the actual tuition cost breakdown - including tuition, books, housing, and food. Examine the results and compare them to your cost expectations. Most colleges require 1st year freshman to live on campus in dorms and eat at the college cafeteria. From the 2nd year to 4th years (and beyond), housing and food choices become optional.

v) Review the college's proposed financial outcome. If parent income is typically at or less than $100,000, look for the following ratio: 80% to 90% grant (free) money, 10% to 15% out of pocket money to be paid by parents, and about 5% by your kid in the form of debt they will have to pay back after graduation. That would be considered "good debt".

w) If you get close to those figures and get this far - *rejoice*! This is the American dream.

x) Parents making between $150,00 to $200,000 may still get some type of grant money.

y) Parents making roughly $250K or more will probably have to pay most or all college costs.

z) During 12th grade, make sure your kid still gets top grades and doesn't slack off. Help them prepare for leaving the nest and remind them it's natural to feel a little home sick at first. It will soon pass and they'll be excited to study hard, learn amazing things, and make new friends.

Once kids get to college, don't get sentimental about how homesick your child might initially become. *Huge mistake!* Instead, tell them they are in the best place on earth right now, and that a million other kids are dying to take their place. They *will* get used to it! In time, they will like it and thank you. It passes like a fever.

Homework time.

A word of advice once Your Kid (or you) becomes accepted by the University.

Once they get to college, don't get sentimental about how homesick your child might initially become. Mothers often struggle with this more than fathers. Stay focused and firm. Tell them they're in the best place in the world right now, and that a million other kids are dying to take their place. My son had a short spell of remorse shortly after beginning his first semester at Wharton. He was actually considering leaving and applying to Stanford instead.
I calmly said: "NO WAY! You worked way too hard to get in, and so did we."

She ended up going to another college and lost that once-in-a life time opportunity to graduate from a world renowned business school.

She needed to grow up, not be coddled.

I reminded him that he was in the *best place on planet earth* at this exact moment in time, and that it was a once in a lifetime opportunity for his promising future career in life. Thoughts of regret would soon die down. Fortunately, he listened, trusted my guiding (but firm) response, and soon felt at home during his freshman year at the University of Pennsylvania, twenty five hundred miles away from mom and dad and California heat waves.

I've heard of horror stories when parents caved-in to their kid's whining and natural homesickness immediately after starting college. Then they let them drop out and throw away the opportunity of a life time. Don't do it! Huge mistake! Make them stay and get through their natural bout of homesickness. It's like a rite of passage - especially for kids entering a large academic institution like an elite University. It eventually passes like a fever .

Ninety percent of kids get through this occasional bout of temporary anxiety. Don't be like the student who was admitted to the Wharton Huntsman program along with my son, but got overwhelmed by peer pressure and anxiety her first month on campus. She complained to her parents and they allowed her quit. She ended up going to another college and lost that once-in-a life time opportunity to graduate from a top-tier Ivy League business school. She needed to grow up, not be coddled.

Remember...
It's OK to play hard, but only after you STUDY hard and finish ALL your homework!

Say goodbye to bad habits, unhealthy food and selfish individuals.

Keep focused (not on obstacles), but on the final goal. That's your great reward.

The Reward

The way to get through your challenges and around your obstacles is to stay focused on the end goal = the prize = the final reward. This is what motivates and empowers all champions in life. Exceptions always exist, but in general, parents are the ones responsible for setting their kids straight when irrational fears take hold during their first year at college. It's normal to feel a little home sick and intimidated at first. That's when they need to hear the voice of experience and reason the most.

Irrational fears fade quickly when you're realizing your destiny. Before long, college becomes an exciting adventure toward a life-long dream that's being realized. You and your child worked hard for eighteen years to get to this point. Don't throw it away on understandable, but momentary home-sickness. Seize the golden opportunity in hand. All that hard work and preparation will pay off a million times over. The final reward is a highly respected degree from a top-tier university, job offers from industry leading companies, and the ability to pay for it without staggering college debt.

Graduation Day! Class of 2016, The Wharton School of Business.
University of Pennsylvania.

The way to get through your challenges and around your obstacles is to stay focused on the end goal = the prize = the final reward.

This is what motivates and empowers all champions in life.

The final reward...
Two college degrees from an Ivy League University with only 5% debt that was paid in less than six months after graduation.

A job offer as a financial analyst was extended from the Walt Disney Co. Sean accepted the offer and became a dedicated employee in the Magic Kingdom.

Sean Rickter on Graduation Day. Wharton School of Business. Huntsman program, UPENN. Class of 2016.

Let's briefly review the realities of what's involved in the elite college admission process from the perspective of what our son experienced on a day-by-day basis.

By now, it's evident that getting admitted to a top-tier university straight from high school involves years of early planning and hard scholastic work. There's a relatively small percentage of students who make it each year, which means there's a huge percentage of high school students that don't . That's why it's imperative to have alternatives to non-elite universities. The details of choosing among alternatives to non-elite colleges will be explained later in this section.

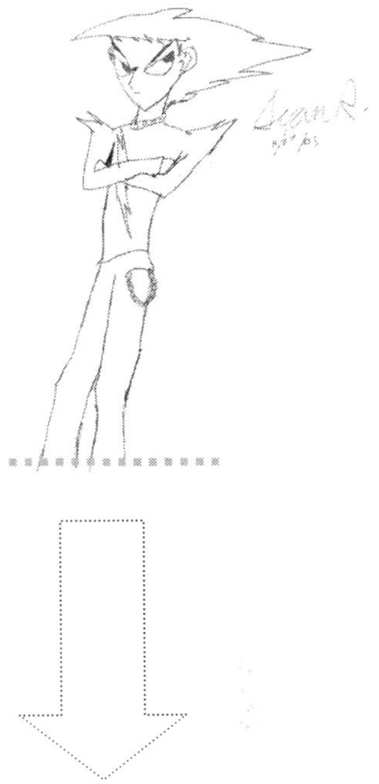

Let's recap the realities of what's involved in elite college admission. Adding to the rigors of an advanced high school curiculum is the fact that it must all come together by the Fall or Spring semester of 12th grade. That means the earliest application submittal date is around November of every 12th grade academic year, or early Spring at the latest. Think about that for a minute. As a parent, your kid, (or you as a student), must have a high GPA solidly in place since ninth grade (preferably "four-point" something or even higher), score very high on the SAT, and be enrolled in a high school accelerated academic program like *PACE or *CIC. All of these requirements entail advanced courses and extensive amounts of study time on top of regular classroom hours.

If that wasn't enough, there's more to add to the above requirement list. This includes learning a foreign language, participating in an after-school sports activity for at least three years, community volunteer service, and various electives for at least two to three years. Sean liked running, so he picked track as his high school sport. He wasn't sixteen yet and couldn't drive. Therefore, my wife and I had to drive him around town after school every week for practice track meets, and then on weekends for city-wide track competitions. We waited several hours each time he practiced running miles of grueling distances and competed against other high schools. He would get up at 7:00 am, walk a half mile to the bus stop, and then head to high school for math and other advanced courses. When school ended each afternoon, it was time for three hours of after-school sports running five miles a day. Sean would then come home, eat, study for three to five hours, sleep, wake up, and repeat the same regiment all over again the next day.

This continued for the next four years like clockwork. For his foreign language, it meant hours of grueling study time learning Kanji characters, just to be able to read, write, and speak Japanese at the most basic level of proficiency. Then there was community service. He won two all-expense paid scholarships to travel to Japan as a student ambassador for Long Beach for a local trade organization between Yokkaichi, Japan and Long Beach, CA. He ended up with four years of Japanese in high school, (followed by three more years at Wharton), for a total of seven intense years studying Japanese. He now speaks Japanese fluently on a daily basis, but getting there took long, hard work.

Advanced high school programs are critical for college admittance straight from 12th grade.

Otherwise, kids should go to junior college to make up lost course work before re-applying to a four year college. That's what worked for me and countless others.

*However, going to college straight from high school is the best route **IF** all your kid's "academic ducts" are lined up.*

The four years of Japanese he studied at Poly High School, combined with his trips to Japan, were an added bonus on his Wharton application. There was also an additional community service activity that *Poly High School required seniors to perform. For our son, it entailed raising money (by cold-calling on local businesses and asking for money) to fund a "lasting school project" for the high school. We ended up helping him select a sitting bench (park bench) project that was made from fiberglass and plastic composite materials. Therefore, it would never need painting, rot, cause splinters, get attacked by termites, or be too heavy to install. It required $700 dollars uninstalled. These projects become a permanent and visible donation from each graduating class.

As I gave my son Sales 101 lessons, the money slowly trickled in. To help him get a bigger donation, I took Sean to an Italian delicatessen my family has frequented over the past fifty years called the Santa Fe Italian Importers, in Long Beach, CA. I'd never met the owner, but I had a long history with the store and took a chance he'd be willing to speak with us in person. Despite my initial concern of looking like solicitors, the owner happily agreed. I briefly told him how much we loved their delicious pizza and Italian sandwiches, and our patronage spanned three generations in my family. I quickly moved on to our reason for meeting with him, and then turned the floor over to Sean.

The deli store owner listened attentively while Sean delivered his rehearsed sales pitch. Without any hesitation, the owner gave him a generous donation of $100 toward the project, but with one condition: the owner wanted Sean to send him a picture when it was done. Two months later the bench was completed, and Sean delivered a finished picture to the store owner as promised. It was a valuable lesson in sales, and a lasting "bench-mark" for my son's high school graduating class of 2012. Sales may seem easy or appear frivolous, but it isn't. Without sales, the world would stop functioning. Just think back to the 2008 housing and banking collapse, or more recently to the economic meltdown in 2020 caused by the COVID-19 crisis. In each case, the sales of many goods and services completely shut down. The economic fallout was disastrous.

Parents and students who've experienced this kind of high school academic rigor and preparation for elite college admission (straight from high school) can attest to the incredible work involved. They could undoubtedly add their own stories to the above list of activities which helped their kid stand out to college admission committees. Extra activities like math tutoring, SAT tutoring, sports lessons, music lessons, debate teams, choir, etc., are all examples of the money parents spend, and the time kids must commit that's over and beyond regular class hours. Our son was no exception.

High school advanced program examples are shown below:

***PACE** = *Program for Additional Curricular Experiences*

PACE was created in 1975 to provide an authentic and rigorous secondary school opportunity to advanced students, and the program has continued to meet this lofty goal throughout its forty three years of existence at Long Beach Polytechnic High School. (PHS website)

***CIC** = *Center for International Curriculum*

*CIC emphasizes an Honors college prep curriculum with a global approach infused into each course. Since 1982, CIC has prepared students for university admission and successful global careers through a unique variety of *AP, Honors and Accelerated courses, including Japanese and Chinese. (PHS website)*

***AP** = *Advanced Placement*

Advanced Placement (AP) is a program in the United States and Canada created by the College Board which offers college-level curricula and examinations to high school students. American colleges and universities may grant placement and course credit to students who obtain high scores on (AP) examinations. (Wikipedia)

** Long Beach Polytechnic High School is nationally known as the Home of Scholars and Champions. Every student at Poly becomes a part of the Poly family, united by a 113-year tradition of excellence" (PHS website). College admissions for past Poly High School grads include Harvard, UPENN (Wharton), Stanford, USC, UCLA, UC Berkeley, MIT, Princeton, Brown, Yale, and a host of other top universities. High GPA's within the PACE and CIC programs are a primary reason.*

I paid $800 for his SAT tutoring, which raised his 2nd test score to 2200. He was in two after-school activities - choir and track - which took weekly time commitments over and beyond his CIC program during the course of four years. He was pushed to the limit, and we as parents were worn thin. Caring parents voluntarily do this in addition to earning a living, working on their marriage, raising their other children, dealing with personal issues, and enduring the stress life demands each day. The point is this: Getting into a top university straight from high school isn't easy and shouldn't be taken lightly. Nor is everyone ready. But it's still very attainable and the life-long rewards are "beyond incredible." However, that ideal scenario doesn't always happen, which begs the next question: *What about all the kids and adults who don't fall in this ideal category?*

The answer is: There's still plenty of hope and opportunity for getting a good college education that serves you well in life and doesn't cost a fortune. I know this first hand because I was one of those individuals.

As a prelude to the upcoming section on "Alternatives to Elite Colleges", the following example shows how a viable college education can occur long after high school graduation. The benefits transformed my career.

Getting into a top university straight from high school isn't easy, nor is everyone ready.

Therefore, you need viable college alternatives. I certainly did and eventually I found the ones that worked for me!

Find your own path by listening to your inner voice and pursuing your heart's desire.

My parents had a turbulent marriage and divorced by the time I was in 11th grade. Neither one gave me much of their time or academic guidance as to how I should approach college during high school. I was alone in my own world of drawing, playing guitar, and building model railroads. My only alternative was reaching down in my soul and deciding what turned me on in life. Playing guitar was at the top, followed by building things. I had some exposure to *Architecture, Engineering, and Construction* (AEC), along with manufacturing, from working at my father's lucrative but highly chaotic manufacturing business in West Long Beach CA during the 1960's. I'd also admire all the buildings and bridges when we went to places throughout Southern California. I'd sit in the back seat and mentally analyze the forms, colors, textures, and massive loads they supported as I gazed at them. Becoming a skilled guitar player by age eighteen was also weighing on my choices, having started at age ten. I was in various amateur rock bands during junior high and high school, but musicians were notoriously flaky, and being able to earn a consistent and enjoyable living as a licensed professional began to have more appeal than dealing with psychotic musicians, drug addictions, and unscrupulous promoters. Combining business acumen into my future also seemed important. Someone was controlling all that money in order to build those huge projects. Financial questions were always looming in the back of my mind; *"How much did that building cost? How much did the architect and contractors make? Did the architect and engineers lose money? Were there any lawsuits?"* After three years of architectural classes at Wilson High School, I got turned on to the idea of becoming an architect, which later led to real estate investing and property development. The term "developer" means different things in different industries. In the AEC industry, it means to design, engineer, construct, and finance the buildings you build. Thus, the term "developer" means to design, build, and own your properties. While music was a voice that reached deep into my soul, architecture and owning real estate became very intriguing.

Winning third place in a city-wide high school architectural design competition provided needed confidence, especially when I beat a snobby rich kid whose father was a prominent architect in LA. His jealous look told me maybe I had some talent and work ethic that even privileged kids like him had to contend with. But other than straight A's for three years in Mr. Copeland's architectural classes, I had a poor high school GPA and lacked essential high school courses like calculus and a foreign language. I also lacked advanced academic courses. Without any voice of reason or someone to help me peek into my future, my limited experience at age sixteen remained "*playing lead guitar in rock bands, not earning a 4.0 or 5.0 GPA.*" By age nineteen, a professional career in rock music was a serious consideration. But as I saw many bands disintegrate, live in poverty, or die young from drugs, I hedged my career bets and decided on a path that entailed 5 years of architectural school, 3 years of internship, and 2 years of state license exams. Like many professions licensed by the California Department of Consumer Affairs, it's a career path that easily takes eight to ten years for licensure. Since doctors, lawyers, and CPA's had similar journeys, I figured why not go for it Besides, it's the end reward that counts. And so, it came to pass. In 1983, three years after graduating, I became a licensed architect in the state of California.

Music remained a large part of my life. Going to concerts to see live rock, jazz, and flamenco artists who were exceptionally creative and famous was exciting. Bands like: *The Who, Cream, Jethro Tull, Iron Butterfly, The Grateful Dead, The Doors, Yes, Al Dimeloa, Chick Corea, Paco De Lucia*, *Chicago, Grand Funk Railroad, Styx,* and countless others, inspired my guitar playing. Famous musicians came and went. The one's that lasted and achieved wealth were exceedingly rare. The same goes for "glory minded" architects. The odds of becoming rich and famous as a rock star or world- renowned architect are a hundred million to one, if not higher. It's not a lack of talent or hard work that creates those odds. It's the insanely competitive nature of those businesses, coupled with exceedingly low pay scales, that requires beating out the other 99.99 million competitors every day. That leaves room for just a handful of stars at the very top. The rest either starve, find a competitive advantage, or go into other fields. Many outstanding professional musicians and architects I met made very little money. That didn't work for me. I needed a competitive advantage and found it by leveraging technology and business acumen with my architectural degree. As it turned out, I was able to build custom homes, acquire a fantastic guitar and amp collection, and do whatever I please each day while my expenses are paid with passive income. Working in corporate America, and later as an owner of a real estate development and technology training business, helped me become financially free by my late forties initially, and permanently by my early sixties. It's a fairly typical retirement age for most people, so "*what's the big deal?*" The big deal is this: *I didn't begin my FF journey until around age forty, which proves there's hope for many of you right now who are in the same boat.* Thus, like many people, I started my FF savings fund later in life, which only amounted to several thousand dollars after I was already half way through my theoretical life expectancy.

What matters is *I got started*, and *so must you*. Had I not started on my FF quest, I could easily have ended up like my high school band buddy who became a professional drummer, toured the country playing in big concerts during the 1970's, didn't report all his income during good years, and today earns about $3000 a year playing insufferable pop music at $50 a gig, and receives $250 a month from Social Security. His paltry income forces him to rely on his ninety year old mother's Social Security check to prevent him from being thrown out on the street. He and his third wife enjoy being married. He's now in his late sixties. He's still a superb drummer. He still smokes pot like a factory. And, he still lives below the poverty level. Retirement ages vary widely, but I am not *retired*. I am *financially free, and choose to work when I want*. That's a big difference. My FF age, though not young or early, provided a satisfying life style that beats working sixty hour weeks or schlepping in grid lock traffic every day. The point to this personal testimony is that having a passion in something you love can turn into a viable career. I overcame poor high school performance and a lack of parental guidance during my high school years by having a goal that inspired me, making up missed high school classes at a junior college, and then transferring to a state university that was a top contender in my major. Luckily, it was priced fairly too. *It can and will come true for you too*, if you want it passionately enough, follow your heart's desire, and create a plan to get there. Don't just think it - *feel it.* Then set a plan in motion and *do it.*

To their credit, my parents give me more than just food and shelter. Both were entrepreneurs and charismatic, which I soaked-up heavily. In spite of being forced to work Saturdays and Summers for my domineering father while simultaneously watching my mother pawn us (kids) off on baby sitters as she created a fashion business and hid her infamous drinking problem, there were valuable experiences lodged within that chaos. It was her idea to buy me a guitar for Christmas when I was ten, which I was totally smitten with. That musical gift turned into a life-long passion and hobby that I still enjoy to this day. I was exposed to construction, manufacturing, and business throughout my youth, which greatly benefited my future career in building. Parents have strong influence on all of us, pro and con. None the less, after high school, I was on my own financially. I paid 99.5% of my architectural college costs, and later, 100% of MBA tuition. At Cal Poly SLO, I took federal Sally Mae loans (and grants), and paid them all back over ten years at 3% interest. All my college degrees were from California city and state colleges. The one exception was an international summer course where I studied architecture and music at the Ecole De Beaux Arts' in Paris France. This required persuading my moody Brooklyn New York father to kick in two months of room, board, tuition, and air fare for a very reasonable cost at the time. But as usual, I had to give him something in return. It was basically two like-minded opportunists haggling for money invested and a rate of return. It constituted a fraction of what I paid myself for college, but was an appreciated gift none the less.

My mother was equally magnanamous. By now, my parent's turbulent marriage had ended in divorce. Shortly after I was admitted to Architecture School, I asked her for a little financial help. She begrudgingly handed me five hundred dollars with the loving condition that I pay her back every penny immediately after graduation. I was thankful for any help, but I later realized both my parents had plenty of money to pay for most if not *all* of my college education back in the mid-to-late 1970's, not just token amounts. University tuition and housing costs, while rising, were still relatively much lower back then compared to today. Their incomes were relatively high, averaging well into the low-to-mid six figures during a time when the mortgage on their Southern California home in the upper-scale beach community of Belmont Heights, cost less than $300 per month including property taxes! Their combined incomes were many times that amount. Like all people, my parents had their short comings. They withheld their time and money when it came to investing in their children for college. Their career ambitions and alcohol abuse left scars upon the family. Therefore, my best options were to follow my dreams, get a college education, and soak up the best things my parents could offer: exposure to the arts, construction, world travel, and first hand observations on how to (and how *not* to) start and run a business. Everything else pertaining to my future education and career, from high school forward, was up to me. My childhood is not uncommon. History is replete with people who pulled themselves up by their own boot straps despite the dysfunction in their family of origin.

And so, *you too must find your own path by listening to your inner voice and pursuing your heart's desire,* especially when you're in your late teens and early twenties. But even if you're older than that, it's never too late to reinvent yourself and pursue a dream. Too old? Too young? Too socially awkward? Too poor? Too unattractive? Too single? Too married? Too many kids? Too whatever? There will always be an excuse to fall prey to that shames you into abandoning your dreams. Do you want to realize them or not? Finding your calling in life is tantamount to realizing your destiny, even if it takes on new twists and turns. It might happen in your youth. It might happen later in life. It doesn't matter. Colonel Sanders was 66 when he struck gold with his Kentucky Fried Chicken empire. An unexpected career twist for me was teaching information technology and financial literacy. It came as a by-product of practicing architecture, applying IT in Fortune 500 corporations, and developing real estate in California, Idaho, Arizona, and Texas. There was a great demand that needed filling. Earning money teaching vital industry software skills that I had mastered in business was both lucrative and personally satisfying. I enjoyed mentoring and helping hundreds of engineers, architects, contractors and college students further their own skills and career goals. This was especially true during the transition from mainframes to desktops, 2D to 3D, and static web sites to Ecommerce. IBM and DEC mainframes once ruled the computer world like huge dinosaurs ready to crush their competition. Before long, Apple II and Macintosh desktops, IBM/Intel/Microsoft based PC's, TCP/IP, Oracle databases, dozens of application software start-ups, and the Internet, created entire new industries. At the same time, the market share for many existing industries drastically shrunk or was destroyed.

Alternatives to Elite Colleges: *When they make sense*

More Ways to Pursue A College Education and get the most for your dollar and long-term career prospects.

The past four decades have been an exhilarating era of educational, technological and financial transformation. It's also been turbulent and fraught with risk, corruption, high costs, and enormous learning curves. Software and hardware sales reps were (and still are) notorious for smoke and mirror tactics. The IT industry evolves, but also remains the same. Technology is a double edged sword that creates and destroys. Technology never stands still. Software updates are occasionally advantageous but often contain looming "bugs" that wreak havoc on our existing applications that were already working just fine. It's always a crap shoot. Many times, measuring software productivity and ROI is a guessing game. Software companies make people think updates are better. In reality, they're often worse and only benefit the software vendors in the form of continual fees from annually paid subscriptions. They make far more money in today's mature software environment renting yearly software licenses versus issuing permanent licenses like they used to.

Like technology, ***choosing among different colleges that are not in the elite category is tricky*** *and fraught with looming pitfalls*. So, how does the rest of society get a viable college education that's reasonably priced when your high school grades are mediocre or mom and dad are absent from the equation? To help answer that question more meaningfully, I've used *real life examples*. The mention of my youngest son's college experience and how he made it into an esteemed Ivy league university was meant to illustrate how important good parenting and early planning are for both parents and kids. Likewise, the mention of my childhood, college experience, and lack of academic parenting are meant to provide hope to millions of others who fall outside the ideal category of "getting accepted to an elite college straight from high school." This latter category of people encompasses a vast number of kids and parents, so it's inclusion is imperative.
In the U.S. and other countries, a state-subsidized college system exists that offers people eighteen years and older, an excellent higher education path that ranges from low to moderately high in cost. In California for example, there are three college systems: **1)** The CA Community Colleges (aka "city" or "junior" colleges;
2) CA State Colleges (i.e. California Polytechnic State University, San Luis Obispo;
3) The UC College System, which is the highest level and stands for: "University of California at...", like UCLA and UC Berkeley. Two year community college degrees are typically less than five thousand dollars. State college prices vary more, but fifty thousand dollars, give or take, for a four year degree is in the ball park. (I paid seven thousand dollars in 1980). A UC college degree (UCLA, etc.) can average up to twenty thousand dollars per year, or eighty thousand dollars for a four year degree. All three of these college choices can and do lead to outstanding career paths by providing two-year degrees (AA/AS), four and five year under graduate degrees (BA/BS), and post-graduate degrees (MBA's, JD-Law, PhD's, et. al). Unfortunately, property owners are getting hit hard all across America in the form of escalating property taxes for state school districts that are funded heavily from property taxes. Political and unionized corruption makes it hard and costly to fight.

A vast majority of California colleges that have enormous campus settings, solid reputations, and well established curriculums are accredited by what's called "WASC", or the "Western Association of Schools and Colleges". However, many colleges and schools are ***not*** WASC accredited. WASC accreditation is a coveted credential. In general, WASC accredited colleges in California are well recognized by other colleges and companies throughout the country. This becomes critical when transferring to other colleges or applying for competitive jobs. WASC is the same accreditation board that issues accreditation status to all three California college systems, including elite CA universities like UCLA, UC Berkeley, as well as mid- level state and junior colleges. Most people are unaware that many colleges have questionable accreditation status. Some colleges deliver mediocre education and have unrecognized accreditation status. I know this for a fact from both attending at, and teaching within, the CA college system at the junior and state college levels, as well as teaching at private universities and privately owned business that offered post secondary education, including my own business. There are hundreds of small, privately owned post secondary schools and colleges, with and without accreditation. The quality of education varies drastically. So do their reputations and tuition costs.

To get into a good four-year college, you may need to start with an accredited junior college. When seeking a two or four year college degree, and you need to make up missed high school courses, a good starting point is a Junior College (JC) that offers two year degrees (AA/AS). Some JC's now offer select four year degrees. Reputable career colleges with proven track records are also worth exploring, but you have to perform careful due diligence to avoid colleges that over charge, have corrupt academic standards, and poor reputations. Specific examples of what to watch out for are explained later.
A college's accreditation is important and becomes even more so later on. Begin with these major thoughts in mind: Junior colleges, aka community colleges, offer good-to-excellent (and sometimes poor) college course material equivalent to the first two years of just about all four year colleges - from mid-tier to elite. Second, they are low in cost and good in value. California is a high cost of living state, but the community college system is extremely low priced for the education received. For example, a typical four unit class (like many that I taught at Rio Hondo College between 2010 and 2016) costs about $150 per semester, or approximately $38 dollars per unit, plus books, parking, food, and housing. For a full course load of 18 units, that works out to about $684, compared to many times that amount at state and private universities. Furthermore, there are no entrance exams or qualifications for admission, other than being 18 years old, having a high school diploma (or equivalency certificate), and legal residency. Places like Long Beach City College, Rio Hondo College, Santa Monica College, and Skyline College have both good and bad course offerings and instructors in the arts and sciences. Once an AA or AS degree has been achieved, either full time or part-time, and providing certain requisite courses have been taken, admission to a California State university is almost guaranteed. Admission to a UC University, while more difficult and competitive, is still a strong possibility if your GPA is strong and you score well on entrance exams. The major exception to an automatic transfer process are university degrees from coveted schools that have extremely high demand, such as schools of business, engineering, architecture, law, medicine, information technology, the arts, politics, and communications. Because these schools are in high demand by students, who in turn, are in high demand by industry, admission standards are tougher and require more vetting via tests and interviews.

One example is the School of Architecture and Environment Design at Cal Poly State University in San Luis Obispo, CA. To begin, you need a strong design portfolio, some industry experience, and solid referrals. That alone can take three or four years to obtain. Then you must endure an in-depth interview process, complete a rigorous admission application, and pass an entrance exam. I knew a spoiled USC student who quit that college because he coveted Cal Poly's reputation in architecture even more than the esteemed reputation of USC. I roomed with a pompous straight-A architectural student who was initially rejected and had to apply twice to get admitted. Cal Poly's rejection rate is close to 90%. Thus, ninety students are turned away for every hundred that apply. Harvard's MBA Business School rejection rate is about 93%, resulting in only seven out of every hundred applicants that get admitted each year. Cal Poly SLO's 10% admission rate stems mainly from the fact that the AEC profession consistently hires Cal Poly (SLO) intern architects and engineers because of their practical technical skills which are rooted in extensive math and engineering principals, not just abstract design theory that by itself is almost worthless to the real-world professions of architecture, engineering, and construction.

Unfortunately, what's sorely missing from Cal Poly SLO and other American *under and post grad AEC colleges*, are courses in *business, construction costs, and building codes*. The vast majority of AEC educators in the U.S. fail their students miserably by omitting these vital fundamentals. Invariably, this traces back to rigid teacher unions and out-of touch tenured professors who's entitlement is only surpassed by their incompetence in the classroom. Instead, they remain ignorant and arrogant in the isolated world of academia, protected by self-dealing unions and complacent deans. It's a business model that serves academia and their generous pension funds, but severely short changes students.
I only had a few good teachers who had solid industry experience and/or were passionate about truly helping people learn. But as a general practice, schools and colleges tolerate far too many pathetic instructors, including Cal Poly SLO, CSULB, Rio Hondo College, and many K-12 school districts.

This deficiency is ubiquitous throughout the U.S. It's one reason I began teaching technology and financial literacy courses. The need was overwhelming. The "old school model" of teaching architecture cripples a student's future. A better way is desperately needed. Replacing incompetent instructors from the classroom with experienced and licensed professionals, and removing corrupt or incompetent deans and administrators is a huge first step forward. Utilizing instructors with real-world experience who know how to command a classroom and engage students to learn real-world problem solving skills translates into higher employability and career success. Incorporating business fundamentals, financial realities, and building codes into the curriculum, not just fantasy design exercises that are utterly worthless in real practice, is the next needed step. Unfortunately, it's extremely difficult to make these kinds of changes because of entrenched academic bureaucracy, tenured professors, and union protections. Academic corruption is rampant. It's alive and well, even at Cal Poly where I graduated, Rio Hondo College where I taught part-time as an adjunct instructor for six years, and at scores of other schools. In spite of this, some city, state, and private schools attempt to address these deficiencies. But other colleges and esteemed four year universities refuse to because deans and faculty ignore their importance in industry, which hinders each student's chance of future employability and cripples their knowledge in industry.

I had students with college degrees attend CAD and construction estimating classes I taught at Rio Hondo Community College (and also at my privately owned school), simply because those courses were not offered at their university. These courses were essential to their major and tantamount to getting hired by industry. What happened? Inept administrators and instructors? Corrupt teacher unions? Tenured entitlement? Unaccountable faculty? All the above? I witnessed this numerous times. One example was a bright Asian female student who already had her four year college degree from Cal Poly Pomona's Regional Planning Department (RPD). When I asked why she was enrolled in my junior college drawing course, she stated: "Cal Poly Pomona's RPD didn't offer (CAD) drafting courses to City and Regional Planning majors." Thus, she never had one drawing course during four years of college and couldn't draw a thing! Self-serving academic polices allowed deans and faculty (with and without tenure) to willfully omit subjects that short changed her education. Why? Because professors and deans had no interest or mandate to teach them, even though the regional planning and AEC industry relies heavily on drawings and expects students to have this knowledge at graduation. In the AEC world, technology, business fundamentals, construction, and drawing should be taught to every student, at every college, regardless if professors want to teach them or not. It's not about the school's agenda. It's about industry and the student's future.

Always encourage your kids - and yourself - to Dream Big. That's not the same as daydreaming or having your head stuck in the clouds.

How to buy a Rolls Royse: My son had a dream to own a Rolls Royce since he was eight years old. Instead of telling him he could never afford it, I took him to a Rolls Royce dealer in Rancho Mirage, CA, and let him feel, look and touch one up close. Then I told him the following: "You can afford just about whatever you want once you are financially literate. One day *you will be able* to afford this car.

But you have to do it the smart way. **That means study hard, get a college education, and establish a good paying career.** Then, buy it used so half or more of the deprecation (cost) is drained out of it. Pay all cash and spend no more than 15% or less of your *after-tax annual salary*.

Even then, make sure the price you pay is below dealer auction price. Then, you can not only afford that car, you will drive it for free (less maintenance) and might even make money when you sell it".

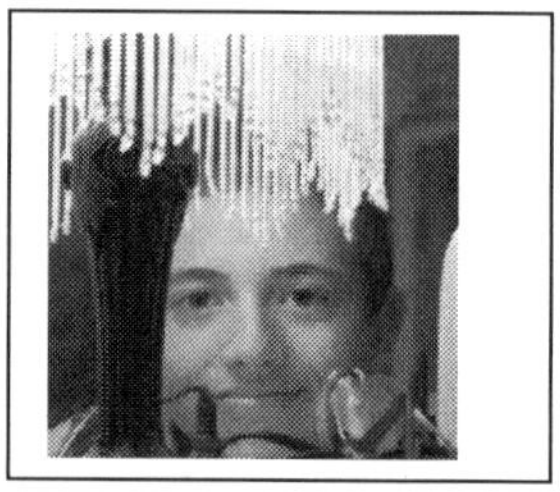

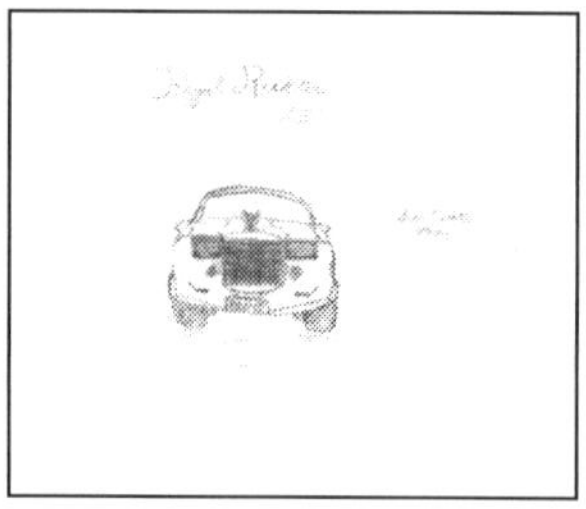

Dream big - like a Rolls Royce. But pay wisely!

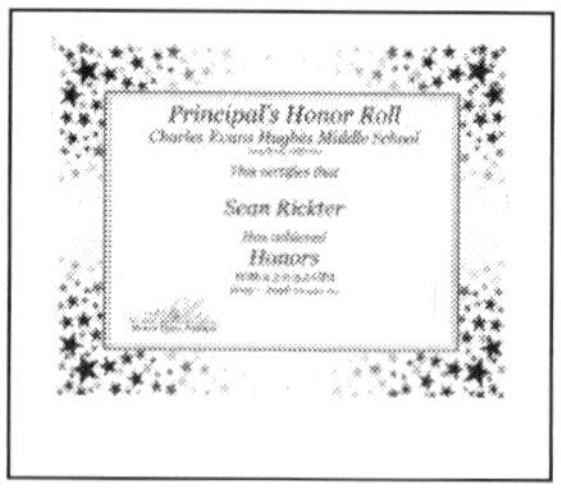

Another example was a bright female student who graduated from the University of California at San Diego, which offers a similar City and Regional Planning Degree, yet failed to provide planning majors with any courses in drawing, either by hand or with CAD software. This is akin to mal-practice since 99.9% of the built environment is drawn with CAD software today. The point is: many AEC college graduates experience this kind of academic mal-practice and are forced to attend the community college system to learn high demand industry skills that certain four year colleges stubbornly refused to offer. It cheats students and is grossly unfair to property owners who pay taxes for public schools and city colleges that end up subsidizing this form of academic mal-practice.

The State School Argument

Many two-year and four-year state colleges have gained high status as academic institutions, and compete very well against top-tier universities when placing their graduates in industry. To find the best ones, you have to gather all the information and suggestions you can find - including high school counselors, college counselors, teachers, working professionals, companies, plus current and past students. Don't rely solely on one individual or source, no matter how convincing it seems. Time and again, as an adjunct instructor and licensed AEC professional, I cringe when I hear students explain how they're planning to attend such-and-such four-year college, simply because their high school or junior college counselor told them to do so. When I asked: "what other colleges did they mention for you to consider?", the answer was usually none. At that point, I pull them aside and give them other colleges to look into. Why? Because I know from living long enough, going through the education system, working in AEC and IT, and lots of research and reading, that while some colleges are good, many more are not. What matters most is the university's overall *academic standing and industry reputation* - not how easy it is to get admitted, obtain a student loan, or how close it is to home. As a potential college student or parent, never rely completely on school career counselors. Listen to their advice, but compare it to other sources mentioned above. Especially listen to former graduates and accomplished professionals who have at least three to five years of experience working in that industry.

Below is a starter list of sources you can use to begin checking out colleges, their rankings, and their costs:

The college admissions office
Various Internet searches on "annual university and college rankings"
Bloomberg/ Business Week Magazine's annual college rankings
Financial Times (Annual College Rankings - world-wide)
Wall Street Journal
U.S. News & World Report (Annual College Rankings - U.S.)
Employees of companies you want to work for
The Deans and assistant Deans of universities you are considering attending.*

*{Side note: Prior to applying to my desired university, I asked to met with the assistant dean at Cal Poly, SLO. He agreed to meet with me and said architecture school was tough to get into. He also said it was a notoriously low paying profession. I took his words to heart, but still wanted in. I got admitted, graduated, got my license, and then later got an MBA and leveraged technology and business acumen with my architectural background. I made far more money as a real estate developer, broker, educator, and technology entrepreneur than just being an architect. It was far more rewarding and a lot more fun too}.

Make a list of other sources you can think of to check out a colleges' industry reputation, accreditation, tuition costs, and grant money policy. Then, rank the colleges in order of choice.

1. 1st university choice
2. 2nd university choice
3. 3rd university choice
4. 4th choice
5. 5th choice
6. ________
7. ________
8. ________
9. ________

... and so forth...

Private "For-Profit Universities" (FPU's): *Tread Carefully*

The material on the following pages in this section of the book is based in large part on Internet research from sources that include Wikipedia, CNN, the Associated Press (AP), and other established media outlets over the past decade. Condensed excerpts are also presented based on both personal experience and summarized press statements that pertain to the ethical, financial, and legal issues surrounding the academic operations of various FPU's.

Private, "*For-Profit Universities*" *(FPU's)* have been around for many decades. Most FPU's have no real college campus. Instead, they operate out of rented freeway-close office buildings and hotel conference rooms. They have little or no admission tests. GPA thresholds (from prior transcripts) can range from 2.0 and above, or lower. In general, most FPU's admit anyone that will pay. FPU's such as the University of Phoenix (UOP), DeVry University, ITT Institute, Corinthian College, (and others) typically have lucrative profit margins. Unfortunately, it usually doesn't stem from offering a rigorous academic program, viable accreditation, excellent instruction, or high brand value like traditional universities with real campuses and solid reputations. Quite the opposite is often the case. One FPU co-founder wrote a book on how and why the college he co-founded in 1976 had strayed so far from its noble academic roots (UOP).

What FPU's *do* offer is easy admission and quick access to government-backed student loans so people can get started immediately on a college degree. Unforntunally, some FPU's have low placement rates, overpriced tuition, condensed curriculums, and inconsistent instructional quality. Over the past ten years, many FPU's have been under government investigation for fraud and corruption. Some went bankrupt. I personally know people who have attended FPU's (and their close cousins known as "Trades Schools") who received post-secondary educational courses lasting from six weeks to four years in length. The end results vary widely.

Some FPU's and trade schools teach viable industry skills that don't always require a four-year college degree. For example, electricians, various construction trades, health care technicians, automotive mechanics, and information technology (IT) techies often successfully find employment by being hired from FPU's, trade schools, and community colleges with six month certificates or two year degrees. It can be "win-win" if the schooling provided skills that helped lead to their employment and the tuition costs were relative to the school's standing among industry and academia; (i.e. Harvard vs. a state college vs. a junior college vs. a trade school).

I also know people that enrolled in FPU's who were already employed in industry but lacked a four-year college degree. That group of student prospects didn't want to spend the time and endure the testing required for admission to a regular four-year university. They usually lacked any formal academic background besides high school and were unlikely to engage in the academic rigor of making up missing high school course work at a junior college, or taking (let alone scoring well on) rigorous college admission tests like the SAT, GMAT, LSAT, GRE, etc. At best, this made them suitable for a FPU or other school that accelerated the process of getting a college education that may or may not entail a four year college degree. At worst, it made them ripe targets for unscrupulous practices by unethical FPU's, trade schools, and other schools of prey.

My wife decided to experience the FPU route. In the beginning, all seemed fine. But after repeatedly receiving poor instruction and high tuition bills, she realized she was getting ripped-off.
At that point, I guided her on how to transfer over to the California Community College System and earn a two-year AA or AS degree. She was furious when she learned most of her courses were not transferable. Other than one or two low level UOP courses, none of her courses (out of a dozen or more classes), were transferable to the California junior or state college system. The rest were unrecognized and became an utter waste of time and money.

My wife was sold the full "bill-of-goods" by UOP, whose academic accreditation during that time was *not* WASC. Instead, it was another accreditation board that most state and private universities in California do not recognize beyond a few low-level transfer courses. UOP's accreditation is simply not acceptable to colleges and universities with WASC or equivalent accreditation. What makes it inferior? For starters, things like no admission tests, tolerating ultra-low GPA's, condensed course curriculums that are not transferable to regular colleges, and shorter semesters than WASC accredited colleges offer. Some FPU's have been accused of engaging in profit-driven sales gimmicks that are disguised as "friendly" admission practices. This in turn has lead to student lawsuits, government crack-downs, and college closings.

Generally, FPU's will admit almost anybody to their "non-campus" rented classrooms as long as students can pay tutition. If a student can't pay cash or use their own debt financing, the FPU quickly pedals tuition debt in the form of tax-payer backed student loans. Still, many people attend these schools, work hard, and experience various levels of career success after graduation. But other students refuse to study hard, don't pay back their loans, and get away with poor academic performance because they were never vetted properly in the beginning by the trade school or FPU. This brings down the level of academic quality for everyone else. This is especially problematic when team projects are required for majors like business, law, healthcare, communications, psychology, and other majors with high degrees of student collaboration.

What is accreditation? Why is it important?
The purpose of college accreditation is to enforce high academic standards consistently across qualifying colleges and universities. Not all accreditation boards are equal. A school or college that simply says "their college is accredited" means little if it's not an accreditation board that's recognized and used by the best colleges and universities in that region. Some accreditation boards tolerate lower academic standards than others. Therefore, it's critical you know who's accrediting the school or college because it directly affects the caliber and reputation of the degree you get once you graduate and/or seek employment.

Many trade schools, colleges, and other post-secondary educational choices are nothing more than opportunistic companies preying on people's ignorance about the true differences between a viable accredited college education, and a mediocre one that's over priced! That's one reason why they can't get accredited by WASC or other boards with the highest standards.

***WASC** = Western Association of Schools and Colleges. WASC is one of six official academic accreditation boards for public and private universities, colleges, and K-12 schools in the U.S. Its jurisdiction includes CA, Hawaii, Samoa, & Guam.*

Other states in the U.S. have similar accreditation boards with different names. But essentially they should have the same (or higher) academic standards that WASC has for schools and colleges located within its jurisdiction. You can find more information by doing Internet searches on accreditation boards within the U.S. Then ask the college admissions office what accreditation board that school or college uses. Cross-check that answer by finding out what accreditation board the best schools, colleges, and universities use within that region of the country.

I experienced some forms of this "watered-down academic mentality" while earning my MBA degree at California State University, Long Beach (CSULB), which *is* WASC accredited and notches above UOP. But FPU's take the concept of tolerating dead-beat students to new heights. For them, the money typically comes first. Furthermore, FPU tuition costs are often outrageously high and not commensurate with their lower academic status. In my wife's case, UOP was charging her almost $10,000 per year in 1999 to take college courses for their four-year condensed business degree. Since then, UOP tuition costs may have leveled out or come down slightly. The web site "Collegetuitioncompare.com" shows UOP's 2020 undergraduate (4-year) tuition at $9,552 per year, and their 2020 graduate tuition at $16,752 per year. Back in 1999 when I was employed by DIRECTV as an Internet software architect, UOP was interested in hiring me and a fellow DIRECTV employee as part-time evening IT instructors. We got to see the inside workings of their academic "modus operandi": *low instructor pay, cookie-cutter curriculum, inadequate length courses, and expensive tuition relative to better accredited universities.* We both decided *not* to work for UOP and turned them down.

Another example involved a recently failed for-profit college called ITT Institute, which had twenty six campuses in the U.S. ITT had been providing CAD (computer-aided design) courses for several decades and always seemed to be hiring. I had mastered CAD technology years earlier and decided to give them my CV and a copy of my recently published book on advanced 3D CAD, known as "BIM", which means "*Building Information Modeling*". Six months later in the Spring of 2012, I was teaching CAD and BIM regularily at Rio Hondo College in Whittier, CA, when I received a call from ITT offering me a part-time instructor position located in one of their newly opened offices in Marina Del Rey, CA. The part-time instructor gig fit perfectly with my teaching schedule. During the interview, I noticed ITT's class rooms were well equipped with the latest hardware and software technology, and their office location was situated in a large modern commercial building with attractive architecture. It appeared the school was well positioned to offer technology courses in a first class setting. However, once I peeled back more layers, my gut began telling me a web of deceit was about to unfold.

During the hiring process, I quickly began to witness their unscrupulously low student admission standards, questionable student placement rates, greedy management, and the way they exploited their instructors. I wanted the job but toiled all weekend with mixed emotions about their ethics. The answer came by following by gut. I turned down their job offer the following Monday. It became clear why they were constantly advertising for instructors. They exploited part-time faculty with unpaid tutoring policies and demeaning practices. They admitted grossly underperforming students, and then expected instructors to telephone dead-beat students that ditched and return to class. All this was on the instructor's own time. This charade kept their overhead costs low while ensuring the school's federally back tuition revenue kept pouring in. Four years later, ITT Institute was forced to close down all its' U.S. campuses in the Fall of 2016. They ended up going out of business after the federal government refused to guarantee any further student loans due to fraudulent marketing and pathetic academic standards. A year earlier, Corinthian Colleges - another Southern California "sham FPU" - also went bankrupt for the same reasons: *weak academic standards, inflated tuition, and fraudulent marketing.* Karma was chasing them.

In 2016, ITT Institute shuts down due to the increased federal crack-down on FPU academic fraud. The Fed's stopped all future ITT government-backed student loans, forcing ITT to close-down within days.

Moral: Don't believe everything you're told when listening to marketing pitches by FPU's.
Many lie about placement rates and over charge for tuition. ITT was a classic example.

The University of Phoenix: A successful FPU with a noble educational beginning that began in 1976. As the twenty first century arrived, UOP's student and share holder complaints marked much of its' educational reputation over the past decade. Time will tell how things unfold.

- A co-founder of the University of Phoenix, John D. Murphy, wrote in Mission Forsaken (2013) about the school's deterioration from a provider of working adult continuing education programs (in 1976), into a money making machine whose *sole criterion for admission was eligibility for federally funded student loans.*

- In 2000, the federal government fined the UOP $6 million for including study-group meetings as instructional hours: (Study groups are conducted by students only. No teachers were ever involved).

- University of Phoenix students owe more than $35,000,000,000 in student loan debt, the most of any U.S. college. *That's BILLIONS, not millions, of tuition debt, with various default rates.*

- Some critics of for-profit higher education have alleged that Apollo Education Group (the company that owns UOP) and the University of Phoenix "prey upon veterans". Since 2009, the University of Phoenix has received $1.2 billion in federal money issued through the G.I. Bill.

- In 2014, the US Department of Education's Office of the Inspector General demanded records from the University of Phoenix and its parent company Apollo Group - going back to 2007 - in relation to marketing, recruitment, enrollment, financial aid, fraud prevention, and student retention.

- In October 2015, the U.S. Department of Defense suspended the university's ability to recruit on U.S. military bases or receive federal funding. {U.S. Senators John McCain, Jeff Flake, and Lamar Alexander protested the suspension}.

- In 2015, the University of Phoenix lost 50,500 students. To avoid a complete crash of their stock price, Apollo Education Group (APOL) sold itself to a group of private investors when UOP shares plunged 75% in 2015.

- In 2016, stockholders of Apollo Education Group filed a class-action lawsuit against UOP, arguing that the company withheld information that led to significant stock losses.

- In 2016, under President Obama, the federal government began cracking-down hard on for-profit schools - especially the University of Phoenix, Corinthian Colleges, ITT, and DeVry. (Refer to the next page).

More student complaints, law suites, and financial woes: Burlington College, Corinthian College, DeVry University, ITT Institute, Education Management Corporation.

- In 2016, Burlington College closed its doors five years after its president Jane Sanders, wife of U.S. Senator Bernie Sanders, saddled the college with millions in bank debt due to an expensive property purchase. Jane and Bernie Sanders have been under FBI investigation at various times, with inconclusive findings. Ms. Sanders bought the land to expand the school 's campus, based on increased enrollment projections she believed (hoped) would occur.
  As president of Burlington College in 2010, Jane Sanders secured a $6.7 million loan from People's United Bank, which the college used to purchase a 33-acre lakefront property for the school. The seller was the Catholic Church, which allegedly needed the money to pay legal fees related to sex abuse charges against the priesthood. The school's enrollment never increased as much as Jane Sanders had hoped, and Burlington College eventually went broke. They permanently closed their doors in May, 2016. School officials cited excessive debt related to the land purchase during Mrs. Sanders reign, as the primary reason for going broke.

- In 2017, Senator Bernie Sanders from Vermont - the same state where Burlington College existed - was subject to federal scrutiny for allegedly pressuring the People's United Bank into making the loan to Burlington College during his wife's tenure as president (2004-2010). Findings have been inconclusive.

- In 2015, FPU Corinthian Colleges collapsed and closed all its campuses after being fined $30 million by the federal government for overstating their graduate job placement rates.

- In 2015, DeVry University was sued by the FTC for false graduate placement rates and deceiving new students. One example involved a DeVry graduate business major who couldn't find work in his major's professional field, and ended up working as a restaurant waiter. DeVry counted that as a valid job for their business school's placement ratings.

- In 2016, another for-profit college fails completely - *ITT Institute* - due to the increased federal crack-down on FPU academic fraud. The Fed's put a complete stop on all future ITT government-backed student loans. ITT closed down completely within days. ITT had been in business for several decades. Once ITT lost their main funding source - government-backed student loans (i.e. tax payer money) - it ended their *for-profit academic business scam* overnight.

- In 2015, the second largest for-profit college - Education Management Corporation (EMC) which operates 110 schools in 39 states - was forced to pay almost $96 million to settle four lawsuits related to fraudulent recruiting and student deception. They also had to give back an additional $103 million in student loans to the students who were scammed by the college.

As stated earlier, my wife's higher education pursuit included both an FPU and eventually junior college. She started out with UOP in the same way as her co-worker, namely with no admission test or GPA requirements. She was also reimbursed for most of the tuition by her employer at PWC (PriceWaterHouseCoopers). But when my wife retired from PWC after ten years of employment, I saw the writing on the wall. My wife, however, didn't see the storm brewing. No more PWC subsidies meant UOP's high tuition was coming straight out of our bank accounts. In four years, she would have racked-up almost $40,000 in school debt, and ended up with a lower accredited four year college degree. She already had $15,000 in UOP school loans, and that figure was climbing. I finally got her to understand the accreditation process, and steered her toward Long Beach City College (LBCC), which offered nearly the same (two-year) courses for a fraction of the cost. Plus, LBCC was WASC accredited. That meant my wife could transfer to Cal State Long Beach, Berkeley, or San Francisco State (and many other CA state-owned universities) upon completing her AA degree requirements at LBCC. She finally saw the light, quit UOP, and transferred to LBCC.

She transferred to Skyline Community College in San Mateo county, where she graduated in 2016 while working in the financial district in downtown San Francisco. She was admitted to San Francisco State University in early 2017, but had to post-pone that option once we move back to LA four months later when her job was eliminated. But her hard work was done and she could reapply to any number of state or private universities later on. She also avoided excessive college debt. The Skyline College AS degree was WASC accredited and substantially lower in cost than two years at UOP: ($4000 compared to $20,000; (50% of 40,000 = $20,000). She was also reimbursed by her former employer (Marsh and McLennan) for most of the tuition. Win-Win.

**Note:*

"In four years, she would have racked-up almost $40,000 in school debt, and ended up with a lower accredited four year college degree. Instead she got her fully WASC accredited two-year AS degree and acceptance to San Francisco State University for much less!"

**Regarding my Wife, just prior to quitting UOP, and instead, enrolling at Long Beach City College and later Skyline College to get her AS degree.*

If you're considering "for profit colleges", ask these (3) critical questions before you make any decision:

1. ***WASC (or equal) Accreditation? Y/N?***
2. ***Tuition Costs - High? Fair?***
3. ***Reputation within the industry you will work in, and among other academic institutions?***

Make sure you get specific answers to each question. Then, compare them carefully to the competition.

DeVry University: What the Fed's and former students have to say about another well known FPU.

As the worst FPU's and trade schools get caught, fined, or closed down, others continue or spring-up. Some are sold to new owners. On October 1, 2018, the Associated Press (*C.Binkley and R. Lardner)* published an article related to the sale of DeVry University, and thousands of student complaints: "The Trump administration gave a tentative green light to the sale of DeVry University to Bradley Palmer, chairman of Connecticut-based Palm Ventures. DeVry has an annual enrollment of about 46,000 students and faces thousands of fraud complaints filed by students." The article further stated: "If the DeVry deal is finalized, it would be another in a series of recent sales meant to breathe new life into troubled for-profit colleges. Purdue University recently bought the for-profit Kaplan University chain and converted it into a nonprofit to lead the school's online programs. Kaplan agreed to a $1.3 million settlement in 2015 after it was accused of hiring unqualified instructors. Last year, the Dream Center Foundation, a religious charity, purchased three chains from Education Management Corporation, which in 2015 agreed to nearly $200 million in settlements over allegations that it used illegal recruiting tactics."

In 2010, this author personally visited DeVry University's Long Beach, California location. As usual, there was no college campus but instead rented office space near the 405 Freeway and the Long Beach Airport. While speaking to the Dean of Admissions for their business school, I asked about faculty and dean credentials. He stated: "Ph.D degrees are required for faculty and dean positions". When I asked the dean if he had his Ph.D, he answered: "No." That discrepancy is reflected in a long list of student complaints. According to the above October 1, 2018 AP article, the authors further stated: "In an SEC filing on Sept. 17, (2017), Adtalem said DeVry's accreditor, the *Higher Learning Commission*, had approved a transfer of the school's accreditation to the new owner. The December 2017 purchase agreement permits Cogswell Education to walk away if the Education Department receives more than *2,250 fraud claims* from former DeVry students, on or before the deal's closing date. There were approximately 10,275 complaints against DeVry pending review, according to department data, including more than 3,700 filed since January 2017."

And so, the list of high-priced, troubled for-profit universities continues. FPU's are a lucrative business model because it's very easy for students to enroll and become contractually obligated to high tuition costs. This generates massive cash flow for the school, but not necessarily academic excellence for their clients (students). Therefore, know who you're dealing with. Before signing contracts and handing over money to FPU's, trade schools, or any college for that matter, check their reputations thoroughly. In fairness, virtually all higher education providers - including famous colleges and universities we all know - have both good and bad aspects to them. FPU's, however, unlike universities with stellar reputations and massive endowments, are a business model that provides post-secondary education at a relatively high cost, delivers a wide range of quality outcomes, and depends heavily on tax payer-subsidized student loans as its primary source of revenue. Still, even the most esteemed universities charge extravagant prices and don't always delivery quality education.

What's the most important consideration then? What matters most is the university's name brand reputation measured over many decades (or centuries) of graduated students who have gone on to have successful careers in industry. Right behind that are the tuition and living costs. Colleges are definitely not all equal. *Did DeVry deliver education liked they promised?* For many students, the answer was yes if those students graduated with satisfaction, experienced success in finding a job, or furthered their personal goals. But, as the AP article revealed, over ten thousand (>10,000) students have complained about DeVry because the school was allegedly negligent in delivering on its' promises. Over two thousand of those were fraud complaints. Those are large figures and serious allegations. They warrant serious consideration. Therefore, student beware: *Tread very carefully when considering an FPU as your education choice.* Some FPU's continue to help people reach their college education and career goals. Others do not. Remember this: *college education is a lucrative business*. It's entirely up to you to make sure the price is fair, their reputation and accreditation are solidly respected by industry, their placement rates are real, and their instructors and curriculum deliver measurable quality. That's a lot to ask, but if you don't, the consequences can be very disappointing and expensive.

If you're considering a "for-profit college", *Ask all the questions you want, but include* the following ***three*** *(3)* questions before you make your decision:

First, meet with a counselor face-to-face and ask them the specific name of the accreditation board they use. If it's not WASC, or its equivalent in other parts of the country, that's red flag number one. Verify what you hear with web research and personal contact with people who've already experienced the school you're considering.

Second, ask them about all costs, loan programs, and their placement rates in industry. If their tuition costs are close to, or as much as well accredited, top branded "real" universities, that's red flag number two. Compare their tuition to junior and state college pricing as a yard stick for whether you're being "rightly charged" or "over charged".

Third, meet with people in the *industry you are planning to work in.* Ask employees, hiring managers, past instructors, HR personnel, and business owners what they think of a college degree from the FPU or college you're considering. If the college you're considering is substantially ignored by your chosen profession, or it's mentioned with a lot of negative feedback, that's red flag #3. At this point, it's three strikes out and probably time to dump that college off your list of contenders. Many FPU's blatantly advertise online with insidious pop-up ads about their easy admission process. That's another red flag. It won't be easy to get admitted if it's a reputable college. When it's easy to get admitted, then it's usually hard to pay back the high cost loan they stick you with. It's even harder when you can't find work.

In certain situations, there are arguments in favor of colleges like UOP. Even though it eventually became foolish and expensive for my wife, it worked for one of her co-workers. Both of them were employed at PWC, which covered the cost of most post-secondary tuition for employees. My wife and her co-worker easily enrolled (due to low admission standards and no test requirements), and began realizing their dream of earning a four year college degree. For the co-worker, she finally finished after four or five years of part-time college night classes. She wasn't looking for a new job. She wanted a four-year college degree primarily for personal reasons. She remained at PWC armed with a four year college degree from UOP and her existing job. She's been at PWC for several decades now. Since she was already a well-regarded employee, PWC didn't care if her degree was from UOP, Yale, or high school - even though UOP was probably as low on the accreditation list of colleges PWC would reimburse her for. My wife's co-worker would still be employed by PWC, with or without the UOP degree. She did it for personal satisfaction, coupled with the fact that PWC was willing to pay for most of it. Plus, she may not have been accepted into a state or private university without going through a tremendous amount of academic preparation, testing, time commitment, and possibly out-right rejection. Her strong professional work ethic and high school education were her primary credentials. She took advantage of her employer's willingness to pay UOP's tuition costs. She would have also qualified for a government backed student loan had PWC not paid her tuition costs as an employee. This is UOP's and every other FPU's ideal target market.

The aforementioned FPU's are examples of what works and what can go wrong - even if they have a seemingly successful reputation. The best FPU's, trade schools, colleges, and universities help people in ways that are realistically aligned with their careers and finances. The worst are simply opportunistic businesses preying on people's ignorance about a "pretend" college education, versus a viable college degree which is well respected in industry. That's one reason why most FPU's aren't accredited by WASC and other higher-grade accreditation boards. The bottom line is: *some FPU's serve a viable educational need in society. Others do not. No school is perfect. They all have strengths and weaknesses - just like people.* The key take away is this: Learn how to sift out the really bad ones. That means due diligence is imperative. To do that right, do it yourself! Remember, your college degree is a vital and lasting career credential. It stays with you the rest of your life. Typically, you have one shot at getting it right.

High College Debt and High Home Prices Affects Everyone...Especially Millennial's.

High college costs have become a major component of rising inflation in our country. As universities and colleges continue to grab more revenue with annual tuition increases, the inflated costs and massive debt loads are transferred to students. The solution to high college tuition doesn't lie with pandering politicians handing out student debt relief like flu shots. That just lets colleges and universities off the hook and encourages them to keep raising prices. The problem is systemic. Far too many elected officials are financially illiterate and virtually all schools, colleges, and universities are guilty of raising tuition well beyond reason. On the surface, ten percent seems to be the norm and that appears more to be a desired growth rate projected by academic committees and their financial investment arms, than from the principal of "what's a fair price for our clients (students) and in line with the cost of living index".

For now and the foreseeable future, the realistic answer to avoiding high college debt basically consists of three options. Of the three, option # 2) is the best choice for middle class wage earners, while option # 3) is the route the rich have to take. Option #1) is the best solution, but also the most difficult to achieve. *The three options to dealing with high tuition debt are:*

1) Universities need to substantially lower their tuition costs; Extremely unlikely. Requires forced action.
2) Students must find scholarship and grant money that greatly reduces tuition costs or avoids tuition debt all together; This has a good probability of succeeding. Our son's Ivey League education is testimony.
3) Students (and their parents) pay the full retail price; This works if you have lots of cash, planned ahead and saved money over many years, or qualify for student loans and thus finance it with debt.

High tuition costs = high debt = high expenses after graduation = little or no ability to afford a home. This is especially true now (2020), since many recent college graduates in expensive cities can't purchase a home due to excessively high college debt. A recent article from the National Association of Realtors sheds some light on those statistics. According to a recent REALTOR® Magazine article in October, 2018: "mounting student loan debt has been identified as a major factor holding people back from purchasing real estate, based on an annual survey of 1000 U.S. adults." The article further states: "Consumers drowning in student loan debt say that it is delaying their purchase of homes—a concern most often faced by women and millennials - according to the sixth annual Neighbor Works America at Home report".

"Rising {college} costs has prompted overall student loan debt to climb 130 percent since 2008. Student debt in the U.S. has now surpassed ***$1.5 trillion*** dollars and makes up 42 percent of all consumer debt, according to the report. That's a staggering ***TRILLION*** and a half dollars of college debt! Of that, women carry about two-thirds of the total school debt at nearly $900 billion." In a separate study conducted in 2017 by the National Association of REALTORS®, parallel evidence supports the above facts. In addition to rising home prices as a root cause of housing un-affordability, so too is massive student loan debt, which has been increasing rapidly in the last two decades. The article found that eighty three percent (83%) of non-homeowners (from their survey) cited student loan debt as the chief factor in delaying them from buying a house {by up to seven years}.

The report also noted twenty two percent (22%) of people surveyed stated they lived with family and couldn't move out after college due to student loans. Other contributing factors include low inventory, rising property taxes, and high home prices. All combined, consumer debt creates enormous financial pressure on middle class home buyers in achieving the dream of property ownership. A large portion of that is college debt, which creates huge affordability problems later in life. Clearly, getting a college education has become immensely expensive and laden with long-term debt. Make sure you have options and strategies to deal with it. The next and final chapter helps re-summarize those strategies.

Intentionally Blank

CHAPTER 7

Summing It All Up

Summarizing Strategies for the Right College at the Right Price
Making a Mentor List
Ultra-Conservative U.S. Treasury Bonds versus other Low Risk Investment Vehicles, Pros and Cons
Concluding Thoughts about Money

Summarizing Strategies for the Right College at the Right Price.

The purpose of Chapter 6 was to provide *key insights* into the major issues facing kids, parents, and working adults who pursue a college education either straight from high school *or after* they graduate from 12th grade. Either way, using real life examples was meant to shed more light and truth on the often complex and opaque process of finding, attending, and paying for a decent college education in America. This includes many universities in other countries too.

A college education has enormous potential to further your career and financial position, providing the school is reputable, you significantly improve your employment prospects by having a specific degree from a specific college, and the tuition is priced fairly relative to the school's reputation and your ability to afford it. Going to an elite university with a full scholarship is ideal. However, only a relatively small group of people are selected each year who are ready and qualified to be admitted to their dream college by the Fall or Spring of 12th grade. I certainly wasn't and neither are many other people. The important thing is to find your passion. Then look at how that could develop into a career within the context of the current and future job market. Always research colleges thoroughly and never stop asking questions or learning new skills. Be especially careful about *for-profit schools, colleges, universities, institutes,* and other names they bestow upon themselves. You can learn a lot about a college's *true* reputation *from people in industry and by reading college rankings*. Always check their accreditation. When possible, do background checks on teachers and deans. Compare their tuition costs and diligently look for grant money. High debt after graduation can largely be avoided if you or your parents qualify and you make an effort to find grants, especially at elite universities. Some colleges and universities only offer token grant amounts or none at all. In that case, it means paying cash or taking out a student loan. The key is to take on student debt as a last resort, not as a first impulse.

Don't be afraid to ask specific questions about tuition costs and the free grant money that's available to help pay for it. As in my wife's case, it could be your current employer that helps pay. But if you're not paying cash, or your employer won't help, or the tuition is very high because it's an elite college, or your income is not enough to cover full tuition, then you have to find the money elsewhere. Colleges have plenty of money. They just don't want you to question them too much about it. Your job is to find as much of it as possible that doesn't have to be paid back. That can range from 10% to as high as 80% or more. But, you also have to be worthy of this gift by having a high GPA and SAT score. *Thus, find grant money first, then pay cash. Use loans as a last resort.* Keep debt as low as you possibly can. Keeping school debt between 5% to 15% of total tuition costs would be an ideal range. The amount of free tuition versus debt will always vary, especially for masters, Ph.D., and Doctorate degrees. Shop colleges the same way they shop students: *go for the best quality at the best price that you can find.* Then negotiate even more if possible. You might be pleasantly surprised.

Colleges have plenty of money.
They just don't want you to question them too much about it. Your job is to find as much of it as possible that doesn't have to be paid back. That can be as high as 80% or more. Thus, more grants, less loans. This applies primarily to undergraduate degrees.

Note: ***Post graduate degrees - like master's and doctoral programs - have fewer pools of grant money available and typically require more cash or debt to finance them. Thus, grants and scholarships are primarily reserved for undergraduate students first.***

Post graduate degrees - like master's and doctoral programs - have fewer pools of grant money available and typically require more cash, work-study programs, or debt to finance them. Work-study programs include on-campus jobs like tutoring, working in the book store, or helping professors with research projects. It's a great way to help reduce tuition costs that might make a masters or doctorate degree nearly free in some cases. Doctors, dentists, lawyers, architects, structural engineers, and some scientists could easily have $100,000 to $500,000 in education costs after eight to ten years of advanced university courses and state mandated licensing tests. That can take decades to pay off. Some post graduate degrees from elite universities pay for themselves in a few years or even several months with the *right college, degree, company, job offer, sign-on bonus, and careful budgeting.* An MBA degree might be my son's next academic quest down the road. Or, he may remain content with his two Wharton degrees. For now, he's happy working for Disney Japan as a key member of their financial team. Whatever he decides, he completed his GMAT test in the summer of 2018 with a respectable score. GMAT tests are good for five years before they expire and have to be retaken.

There are approximately 5,300 colleges and universities in the United States according to research conducted by the Washington Post (2015) and EducationUnlimited.com (2019). This figure ranges from obscure trade schools to Ivy League universities. Choosing the right one becomes overwhelming very fast. There are elite colleges, private colleges, state universities, junior colleges, various certificate courses, trade schools, and a plethora of "for-profit" universities and colleges. You can attend on campus, off-campus, in commercial office buildings, in hotel conference rooms, on-line, on Zoom, and/or study abroad in a foreign country. For top tier elite college admission, make your academic choices ideally between the ages of seventeen to your mid twenties. Perform diligent background checks on each college to gain full awareness of what you're getting in return for your hard earned money, time, and energy.

Make your academic choices carefully and with full knowledge of what you are getting in return for the time, effort, and money you spend.

If you've already graduated high school, have a job, or have a family, don't let that stop you from pursuing your goals. There's usually a viable educational alternative that fits your age and situation. Just don't rush into getting a degree or certificate because it sounds good, or it's easy to get admitted, or you can get quick tuition financing. Those are red flags! Once a college has been vetted and selected, you've made a huge commitment to your future. The results will last your lifetime. Only you can ask the tough questions that many colleges won't divulge unless you ask them specifically. It's your money, your time, and your life energy. Spend it wisely. You're the customer. It's your satisfaction that must be met, not just the colleges'. Don't feel intimidated or let them bamboozle you with academic non-sense, hyperbole, or attitude. If something seems confusing or doesn't feel right, then it probably is. Do your research, listen, talk to others, learn all you can, ***then trust your gut instincts and take action.*** Get the best degree from the best college at the best price you can. After that, it's up to you to make the best use of it. Try to remain open to new adventures too, even if they fall outside your major. You never know when opportunity knocks and something new, exciting, or lucrative is waiting just around the corner. It certainly happened to me and changed the course of my life and career for the better.

Making a Mentor List: *FF/FI Mentors and Teachers who can Help You...Past and current.*

"You Are Who You Choose to Associate With." History's Entrepreneurs

Every hero has another hero before them who inspired or mentored them. Let's look at some of history's men and women that laid the foundations for society, government, academia, industry, architecture, engineering, finance, law, science, literature, and self-enlightenment. The list captures many prominent financial and strategic thinkers who helped shape the 20th and 21st century. History teaches nothing if we fail to listen and learn from it. It imparts great wisdom when we do. That means you need to read and learn all you can about history and people. If they did it, why not find out how?

Making a mentor list is a missing topic in many financial literacy teachings. *Which sources among so many should you study and what do they offer for your personal quest to FINANCIAL FREEDOM ?* The point here is to avoid thinking there is only one source or book or author to rely upon. It's better to know about many viable FF teachings so you can gain different perspectives from multiple sources, and refer to them when needed.

For example, investing in the stock market involves many choices and risks. This in turn requires careful study from many experienced investors and (true) experts. To maximize your returns and avoid losses, you need to learn about stock investing from more than just one person's perspective. Why? Because *everyone* has a personal bias and different appetites for risk and reward. My personal bias leads me toward conservative, but consistently paying investments. My investment friend is just the opposite. My approach is too slow for his appetite of high risk and fast reward.

Either way, there were mentors who guided and helped both of us. But, we had to make an effort to actively seek them out, study their teachings, and apply those teachings to our individual investing approaches. I studied bonds in MBA school and later read books by well-know stock and bond investors who had a proven track record based on conservative, consistent, long term investing. I generate cash flow each month and sleep well at night regardless of stock market swings. My friend paid to join an online stock club which greatly increased his returns. He earned capital gains in excess of 20% per year over four years, and didn't mind gambling large sums of cash to do so. Even though we both have different biases and chose different mentors, each of us reaped rewards by learning from the experience and expertise those mentors provided.

Whatever your bias is, the fact remains that the potential to lose money on Wall Street is greater than making it. Everyone needs help at times. In other words, everyone needs a mentor to turn too at some point. When you delve deeper into the quest of your own financial literacy, it will ultimately help you attain greater financial strength by providing a 360 degree perspective of your money matters. You can learn as much from failure as you can from success.

Making a Mentor List

The following books can help inspire you to further integrate business, financial, and technical literacy into your everyday thinking. Give yourself ample time to read and absorb them. A few books were written by this author. As for the rest, I have no affiliation or relationship of any kind with any of the authors listed below or elsewhere in this book. The written publications and copyrights of those authors are theirs alone. I simply respect their teachings and career accomplishments and recommend them to others. This is a beginning source of inspiration, not an all inclusive list. Other books and resources exist and will continue to emerge beyond those listed here. This literary compilation, when studied and applied diligently, can serve as an excellent starting point to create a rock-solid foundation of financial wisdom and career insights that will last your entire life.

Industry Leaders, Book Authors, and Entrepreneurs

{A collection of books and resources that can provide FF inspiration and career insights based on real life examples}.

- Ride of a Life Time, Bob Iger, CEO, The Walt Disney Company

- Think and Grow Rich, Napoleon Hill

- Rich Dad, Poor Dad, Robert Kiyosaki with Sharon L. Lechter

- Stocks for the Long Run, Jeremy Siegel, former professor, The Wharton Business School, University of Pennsylvania

- The Intelligent Investor, Benjamin Graham, with Jason Zweig of the Wall Street Journal

- The Most Important Thing, by Howard Marks. Founder and former chairman, Oaktree Capital Management

- The Snowball, Warren Buffett and the Business of Life, Alice Schroeder.

- Straight from the Gut, Jack Welch, former CEO and chairman of General Electric Company

- The Power of Who, Bob Bodien

- The 43 Laws of Power, By Jeffery Green. Lessons in how power shapes our lives and financial well being, as told from real life stories in Western and Asian History over the past 3000 years.

- Modern Finance, Published by Harvard Business School Press. (Part of MBA program at HBS, CSULB, et al).

- Kevin Trudeau, Your wish is your command; Health Cures 1 and 2.

- The Total Money Makeover, Dave Ramsey

- Achieving Financial Freedom *In 5 Basic Steps*, Edward S. Rickter. *Financial literacy fundaments for adults*

- Money Matters for Kids and Parents, Edward S. Rickter. *Financial literacy and college selection for kids and parents*

- The BIM Imperative, Volumes I & II, Edward S. Rickter. *The power of Intelligent 3D Design and Engineering in AEC*

- BTrade Study Guides, Part's A&B, Edward S. Rickter. *Financial Literacy and Trade Course for General Contractors*

- Math Summary Guide, Edward S. Rickter. *Applied Construction Math and Cost Estimating Fundamentals in AEC*

Making a Mentor List

Journals, Magazines, On-line Publications

- The Wall Street Journal, Barron's, Market Watch, Forbs

- Bloomberg/Business Week, Fortune, The Financial Times, Investopedia

- Avoid shallow and negative mainstream media sources

- Learn from other people. Ask them: *How they became successful?* I learned a lot about business this way.

- Add your own list of mentors - from all walks of life and periods of history. The list is endless.

- Go to the Internet and learn about "self-managed brokerage accounts" like E*Trade and TD Ameritrade. You can set up a free IRA, Roth IRA, 401K, or Roth 401K, and then invest in stocks and bonds for less than $5 to $10 a trade. Some trades are free.

- This is in contrast to "managed broker accounts" that may charge additional fees and commissions. For example, before I switched brokers, I had to pay Edward Jones Investments (EJ) $40 a year for each of my two retirement accounts (401K and Roth IRA). They took $80 annually for doing nothing. I later switched to E*Trade, and now pay zero cost to have my retirement accounts held there. I also no longer receive calls from desperate sales agents trying to make quota. Instead, I get free advice any time I need it, when I need it, on my terms, not the brokers. In the past nine years, I've saved $720 in bogus retirement fees just by firing EJ and switching to E*Trade! It was one of the best investment decisions I've ever made.

Obstacles and bullies come in all sizes throughout our lives. Don't let obstacles or bullies get in the way of your dreams. Bullies are just insecure cowards acting stupid. Obstacles are opportunities to grow stronger. Failure is an opportunity to begin again more intelligently. Follow your heart and listen to your gut instincts. Never give up. In time, success will follow naturally.

When life becomes confusing or painful, meditate, pray, talk to safe people, go to the library, visit a book store, or go on the Internet and read about real-life stories of people who worked through their struggles and became successful. Everyone and every family has issues and struggles in life - including rich, powerful, and famous people. How we deal with issues and overcome obstacles determines our success in life - regardless of age or the state of the economy.

Remember: The way to get around your obstacles and through your challenges is to stay focused on your goal. That's what motivates all champions in life.

Making a Mentor List

Investment Books

Below are two examples of investing books that helped this author learn more about navigating the perilous twists and turns of the stock market. These books are listed here because of their proven educational value to this author and countless others. There is no affiliation of any kind between the authors or myself. Everyone wants to make money in the stock market. The key is learning from people that already know how and have proved it over and over.

The Intelligent Investor, By Benjamin Graham. Introduction by Warren Buffett. Chapter by chapter side notes by Jason Zweig of the Wall Street Journal.
Originally Published 1949. Revised publication 2003 by Jason Zweig. First Collins Business Essentials edition 2006. Cost: $22.99

Dr. Benjamin Graham was a British-born American Ivy League economist professor and astute stock and bond investor during the early-to-mid 20th century. Dr. Graham is widely known as the "father of value investing" (Wikipedia.com) and taught one of his prize students - Warren Buffett - how to invest "intelligently" in the stock market over a period spanning eight decades. This book will literally transform your relationship about buying and selling stocks and bonds. The Intelligent Investor (TII) is a brilliant book that teaches the profitable and wise way to invest in securities - especially when building a safe portfolio for FF income.

Ben Graham taught Warren Buffet how to invest on Wall Street the right way during the early part of the 20th century. Mr. Buffet became a billionaire by the mid 1960's and today heads one of the greatest industrial conglomerate corporations on earth - Berkshire Hathaway. As of August 2020, Warren Buffet's personal net worth is around $80B (Investopedia.com). Mr. Graham's teachings greatly influenced scores of other successful investors ever since. He can help you too!

Mr. Graham's writing style is very in-depth. It's packed with step-by-step insights and time-tested investment wisdom. To further clarify Mr. Grahams treasure trove of investment insights, Wall Street Journal columnist Jason Zweig adds chapter-by-chapter summaries that both illuminate and synthesize Mr. Graham's teachings. Together, you get the best of both worlds from these two financial experts.

Stocks for the Long Run, By Jeremy Siegel. Former Finance Professor at The Wharton School of Business, University of Pennsylvania. Published 1994, 1998, 2002, 2008, 2014, 2018. Cost: $40.00 McGraw-Hill Education

This is the perfect companion guide to "The Intelligent Investor". Like Warren Buffet and Ben Graham, Mr. Siegel espouses the merits of wisely investing in stocks and bonds for the long run, and backs it up with nearly 200 years of hard evidence and extensive research. Jeremy Siegel is well known and respected in academia and on Wall Street as a leading expert in stock market investing, research, and financial education.

Ultra-Conservative U.S. Treasury Bonds versus other Investment Vehicles:

Arguments for and against.

United States Treasury Bonds, known as *T-Bonds*, are virtually risk free. A bond is simply a loan. Governments and companies issue bonds in order to borrow money. When people buy a U.S. T-Bond or any other type of bond, they are loaning money to those who issue the bond in exchange for interest income. Like a mortgage or car loan, all bonds have a specific time duration (term) for the bond to be paid back in full, such as 5 years, 10 years, 30 years, etc. All bonds carry default risk and term risk. The riskier the company or longer the pay-back term, the higher the risk. The beauty of T-Bonds rests in the fact that the U.S. government will pay interest and return all principal at a 99.99% guaranteed level. That's as good as it gets in terms of risk-free bond investing. The down side is U.S. Treasury Bonds typically pay a much lower rate of interest compared to corporate bonds, CD's, annuities, real estate, dividend stocks, or other asset classes with higher risk. This is especially true today. While 3% seems low, T-Bonds today have fallen even lower to about 1.5% to 2%. Today, a bond or CD rate that offers 3% still has certain advantages if you have a large enough principal base, the loan duration is short-to-mid term (i.e. 1 to 5 years), the interest is compounded, and there's a very low risk of default. Tying up your money in a U.S. T-Bond for *10 or 30 years* at 1.5% to 2% is very risky because rates may rise higher by then. This means missing out on higher interest income by being stuck with a lower rate.

In comparison, during the late 1970's to the mid 1980's, T-Bonds paid around 10%. Since preservation of principal was virtually 100% guaranteed, people who bought U.S. T-Bonds back then were averaging 10% yields and doing so with essentially zero risk. That's virtually impossible to achieve anywhere on earth today. Yet, because of unique market forces and exceptionally high inflation, it actually occurred for a brief period in U.S. history. Those who knew how unique that moment in time was, jumped on that rare opportunity and benefited very nicely for years to come. Conservative investors who advocated T-Bond investing made good sense at the time. Why risk money investing in the stock market when you can get a 10% return from a T-Bond that's 99.99% risk free and lays the golden egg every month in the form of free cash flow to pay bills? 10% was, and still is, an excellent risk-free, high yield investment return for FF purposes. Unfortunately, U.S. T-Bonds haven't paid 10% in almost four decades. People who experienced the inflation of the early-to-mid 1980's and took advantage of it were both smart and lucky because they lived in an era when they could lock-down a 30-year T-Bond at 10%, or make 18% on a bank CD, simply because of unprecedented high inflation that pushed bank interest rates to nearly 20%. In contrast, 10 year and 30 year T-Bond rates dropped to 2.61% in 2019, and then dropped further to 1.45% as of June, 2020. (Source: U.S. Department of the Treasury). They're slightly up as of early 2021.

Thus, it's essential to consider other investments in order to analyze, select and implement an FF portfolio. Expecting returns using *low risk investments* that are above 5%, let alone 10%, would be extremely unrealistic right now. Why? Returns between 2% to 5% are (generally) as good as it's going to get for the time being using a *conservative* FF investment strategy in a *low interest rate environment*. Seeking higher returns requires more risk, like aggressive stock market trades or real estate speculation. Both offer potentially higher returns. Both come with higher risk of principal loss too. My friend made double digit annual returns (20%) over four years in the stock market, but that's *far from common.* Most people can't do what he does because they buy high and sell low due to panic and fear every time there's a drastic market swing. He's also willing to bet large sums of money. Many people won't do that either. For a FF savings fund, it's wiser to remain conservative and aim for realistic returns that are lower but safer. The remedy to finding investments suitable for FF when interest rates are exceptional low is to *learn more about other investment classes*. This includes growth stocks, dividend stocks, investment grade bonds, fixed annuities, and cash-producing real estate, in addition to U.S. T-Bonds and CD's. From there, you can dive deeper into other ways to *wisely analyze* and *buy* those asset classes by reviewing Chapter 4 and studying the recommended material outlined in this chapter on: *FF Teachers and Masters who can help you.*

U.S. T-Bonds are a viable asset worth considering in your FF portfolio, but I would not recommend them until interest rates begin to rise again. Whether that's a few years away, around the corner, or way down the road is unknown. Eventually it will happen. For example, CD and mortgage interest rates started to rise in late 2018, and continued until mid 2019, after which, they began dropping again after President Trump criticized the Federal Reserve for "hurting economic growth". Political motivation played a role. Stock investors and borrowers felt some of the negative effects of rising interest. But higher rates had a positive effect for holders of CD accounts, annuities, and bonds. There are pros and cons to both sides of the argument.

In early 2020, interest rates dropped drastically as the COVID-19 pandemic gripped the world's economies. 30 year T-Bonds traded at a paltry 1.45% as of mid 2020. You can still do better with some credit union 12 and 24 month CD accounts that began paying 2% to 3% in 2018, then dropped to 1.75% in 2019, and then dropped to a paltry ***.35%*** to ***.75%*** as of December 2020. Ironically, those are better figures compared to interest on bank accounts which pay virtually nothing. A one or two year CD or money market account at .5% is still better than a 30 year T-Bond at 1.45% or 2% because your money is only tied up for one or two years, rather than thirty years! Clearly, the Federal Reserve also benefits from low T-Bond rates because it substantially lowers the interest payments on our nation's unfathomable $28 trillion dollar national debt! The up side is bank loans and mortgages are much cheaper in 2020 / 2021. The downside is savings accounts, bond investors, and annuities have been punished with extraordinarily low returns.

Stock prices are constantly subject to unpredictable market fluctuations, often with little regard to a company's real intrinsic value. This creates an environment that continually poses risk of loss for every investor. In other words, the Stock Market is akin to a gambling casino because the risk of losing money is always present. Another way to describe this is "systemic risk", which means the risk of losing your money never goes away. This stems from the herd mentality of most investors who follow what others are doing instead of spending the time to carefully analyze a company's background to determine its true worth and profitability. The end result is most people lose money by buying when markets are high, and selling when markets are low. Avoiding this kind of irrational behavior requires a proven investment strategy and sticking to it when markets crash or behave erratically. That means ignoring mainstream media hype and remaining disciplined in the midst of temporary turmoil. But how do you do that?

One way to increase the chances of making money in securities is by comparing a company's financials to its stock market valuation. The net book value of a company is its actual cash value indicated on its balance sheet, if it was sold and liquidated into pure cash. This is sometimes called "tangible net worth", because it's a rationally computed dollar value of actual company assets and liabilities, regardless of a company's stock price and market capitalization (market cap) that the stock market often gets wrong. Another company valuation method is called "market cap", which means *market capitalization.* Market cap is a company's total value measured in Dollars, Yen, Euros, Rubbles, Yuan, etc. It's computed by taking the number of shares outstanding (total number of stock shares the company has sold to date), multiplied by the current stock price. The answer equals its *market cap. Thus,* market cap is the cash value of the total company if it were sold and liquidated, just like the first method. For publicly traded corporations, market cap is what irrational stock buyers deem a company's total value is worth minute by minute, day by day, *regardless* of how much net worth, cash, or profit the company actually generates. Thus, net book value and market cap are two conflicting ways (among others) to measure a company's total enterprise value.
How do you solve this dilemma?

One category of investors, known as "*value investors*", attempt to solve this dilemma by comparing the "*net book value*" of a company to its "*market cap*", in order to see how much variance exists between the two. What the fickle stock market says a company is worth, versus what the hard facts from the company's financials indicate, is a proven strategy that can reveal secrets, falsified information, and sometimes hidden *value*. Thus, *value investors* continually look for publically traded companies that are priced right. This typically means their *market cap is trading considerably below the company's actual book value*. This is essentially the strategy Warren Buffet used for decades. Mr. Buffet also likes buying stocks in companies that have "moats around them". This means they have dominate market share due to enormous industry penetration and/or because the cost of entry is so high.

For example, Berkshire Heathway paid a total of $44 billion dollars to buy 100% of BNSF railroad in November of 2009 because railroads are a critical industry in transporting goods within the U.S. economy. Railroads can't be outsourced, there's limited competition, capital costs are very high, and it's extremely difficult to procure land rights across multiple states. The list of successful investors who've adhered to fundamental "value investing" principals is replete with well known names: *Warren Buffet, Charlie Munger, Peter Lynch, David Ackerman, Howard Marks, Benjamin Graham, and many more.* Knowledge can be a competitive advantage. Applying knowledge successfully translates into power. Learning to read a company's balance sheet, P&L statement, cash flow statement, and company management profile is a good example of the ability to make better stock buying decisions. That translates into financial power. To protect your investment, ignore daily market gyrations, herd-mentality stock transactions, and mainstream media hype. Thus, don't sell when the markets are low, and don't buy when markets are at a peak. Instead, look for stocks that are undervalued but solidly positioned to grow in the future, based on astute company financial analysis, brand value, and management strength. Think: Amazon, Exxon, PayPal, Verizon, and various start-ups like Zoom, etc.

The ultimate FF investment goal is to learn to invest in stocks, bonds, real estate, and other asset classes, in addition to T-Bonds and savings accounts, in order to achieve a high enough rate of return to cover all your living expenses. This also includes using pensions and Social Security whenever possible. The key is to maximize your "total cash flow" potential from as many sources as possible. The point in time you become *financially free, or FF*, is when your investment income equals or exceeds your living expenses. Graphically, the FF realization point is expressed by an X and Y axis which visually illustrates the relationships between: *job income, monthly expenses, and investment income, as explained in detail in Chapter 5.*

Basically, the graph's purpose is to help visualize the primary objective of FF, which is: *Save money from your job income, gradually reduce expenses, and invest the excess cash flow from your savings to generate free money, which in turns pays all your monthly expenses automatically.* ***This is called the "FF Realization Point", which is when you become officially financially free.*** Most people look for silver bullets because they don't want to spend the time and energy doing research that involves financial math and critical thinking. Here's a hint of encouragement: finance is largely based on simple arithmetic and the critical thinking involved is mostly common sense. That means an astute 5th grader, if taught properly, could do it. Mr. Graham and his protégé Warren Buffet, along with other investors, loved this kind of endeavor as if it were a secret passage to wealth accumulation. It turned out it was and still is. So, if you want to win more often, make some personal effort to learn as much as you can about a company's current and past financial background before you invest money in buying their stock or bond offerings.

Relying on brokers and financial planners to make most or all of your investing decisions is usually not enough. Sometimes it works. Many times it doesn't. With all brokers, you typically pay various fees and commissions whether you win or lose. What's even worse is being in the dark as to what actually happened when your stocks crash or a bond defaults and you've lost a lot of money. It's happened to me and countless others. Better to learn important company facts yourself before investing your hard earned money in them. The Internet and financial web sites are some of your best friends. The vast majority of publicly traded company financial information is free and available online 24/7/360. Why not use it to your advantage?

My personal investment experience over the past two decades has been a mix of broker types. I started with a major brokerage house (Edward Jones Investments) and remained with them for close to a decade. The first six or so years benefited my financial goals and objectives, but not without problems. I had to fire my original sales rep after he fell asleep at the wheel during the 2008 financial crisis and failed to monitor my accounts which were heavily exposed to the financial sector. I lost a lot of money because of his complacency and entitlement. I replaced him with another sales rep, but high employee turnover within the firm made the next three years increasingly frustrating. No sooner than finding a new sales rep who I could trust and respect, I'd wake up one day and find out by surprise that they had been fired. Some of them were good men and women with college degrees, experience, and integrity. They were simply tossed out like garbage for not meeting sales quotas which were always placed ahead of customer satisfaction. The last several years were absolutely terrible. The firm hired a string of arrogant and overly aggressive sales reps who were under pressure to constantly badger clients for more fees and sales. As things changed permanently for the worst, I fired the firm in 2012 and switched to an online investment brokerage firm (E*Trade). As stated earlier, I've have been satisfied ever since.

If you're already doing well with a financial fiduciary or brokerage firm and you're happy with the results and service you've received, consider yourself fortunate. As long as that remains true, keep going in that direction. But if it doesn't, or you start to experience dissatisfaction and/or chronic money loss, there are lots of other firms and investment choices to choose from. Don't hesitate to switch brokerage firms. By law, they have to abide by your wishes and transfer all your money to whoever you choose immediately upon notification from your new brokerage firm. The Internet, healthy competition, a vibrant economy, the rule of law, and financial regulation, together have made this era in our history the golden age for investing in stocks, bonds, and other asset classes. Whether it be a self-managed E*Trade account or a fully managed brokerage firm, the transparency and availability of *decision-making information* has never been greater.

Concluding Thoughts about Money and the Quality of Your Life

The less money we had as children, or still don't have as adults, the more we fantasize about it. A woman once stated "women don't mind if *their faces* aren't on dollar bills, as long as we get *our hands* on them." But getting your hands on money isn't the only end goal. It's what you do with it, and the caliber of your character, that determines lasting, joyful, financially-free living. Achieving immediate financial wealth seldom ever happens because it's statistically almost impossible. Miracles happen, but it's foolish to rely heavily on quick-riches as a silver bullet to your money problems. Examples include winning the lotto, inheriting a fortune, a business windfall, sudden stardom in sports or entertainment, investment windfalls, dumb luck, a great invention, marrying into wealth, or being borne into wealth. You're lucky and fortunate if any of the above examples include you.

Since instant wealth is nearly impossible for probably 99.8% of the people on earth, other money earning strategies are essential. Partnering with someone who is already rich is a common fantasy and frequent ploy – in all cultures throughout all of history. When it does happen, it often comes with strings attached and involves human greed colliding with unrealistic or controlling expectations. The outcome can be intoxicating in the beginning, but toxic or devastating to one or both parties in the end. If it does result in a lasting and mutually happy outcome, it means either maturity, spirituality, financial priorities, or all three forces were in alignment by both parties. It's possible, but not easy or common. It requires constant effort, significant "human actualization", and selflessness by both sides. In other words, it requires mature, unselfish, and enlightened behavior. This isn't easy, fun, or common as history bears out. Pleasure, security, power, and money are way too addicting when handed on a silver platter. Still, there are other ways - especially if you value your dignity and self-worth.

Technology and the built environment have constantly evolved on earth for at least 10,000 years of known recorded history. Yet human nature hasn't really changed. Greed, power, lust, love, hate, kindness, cruelty, violence, equity, inequity, tolerance, intolerance, racism, bigotry, ignorance, enlightenment, jealousy, envy, rationality, and irrational thinking permeate the human species. This mixture of emotional and unpredictable human nature exists today, and existed long before Cleopatra killed her own brother and imprisoned her father in order to ensure her place on the Egyptian throne. People are naturally pleasure seeking and willful – just like infants. Breaking out of that pattern and yielding to another human being's point of view (while remaining civil but standing your own ground) takes a lot of self-control and strength. It requires a moral compass and rational thought, in contrast to yielding to your pride. It takes inner strength, and that takes time and experience to develop.

Therefore, establishing a financially secure future is like creating a building: *you need a good set of plans*! In financial terms, that would equate to a well thought out set of goals, strategies, and procedures on how much money you earn, how much you spend, and wise investing of your savings. Imagine constructing a large complex home and not having building plans or permits. The entire process would be chaotic from start to finish – if it even got done at all! It could end by someone losing a close relationship at best, or in financial ruin at worst. I've witnesses it many times. Divorce, burn-out, and financial devastation has resulted from poorly planned construction projects for that very reason. Our financial future is more important than the most complex building project, yet most people have no financial plan to guide them through their journey in life. Furthermore, most parents, grade schools, colleges, and job environments seldom teach us how to manage our money. These are the major reasons why the majority of the world's adult population never gets past living from pay check to pay check.

Ignoring character and financial literacy is a primary reason why the U.S. divorce rate often exceeds 50%. It's also why approximately 95% of many business partnerships fail within two years of startup. Everyone has arguments and fights. It's how well we make-up and work through those differences that counts over the long run. Honesty, integrity, humility, ego-strength (not ego trip), doing the hard work, and like-minded character are critical. Therefore, achieving and enjoying FF is as much about understanding and controlling our human nature as it is about wise spending, adequate income, and sound investing. Combining both into a holistic solution - *like two sides of the same coin* - is the key. It's like integrating the unpredictability of human nature with the disciplines of self-awareness and financially literacy. Together, you gain a higher degree of lasting joy and true mastery over your *money* and your *destiny*.

When you begin to understand and apply the major components of financial literacy, you're taking a major leap forward in laying a foundation that will last a lifetime. Once you integrate your income, spending habits, and investing strategies, you're FF plan becomes specific to your lifestyle, skill sets, and risk tolerance. A key ingredient to reaching FF sooner is generating excess savings from your job early in your career so you can start investing that money to generate passive income. Having a financial plan is not enough. You have to *use* your plan! Once you do, you'll never go back to living like you did before. Instead, you will have permanently changed your financial destiny. Commit yourself to achieving emotional, physical and spiritual balance in your life. Avoid those who don't. This will help reinforce the foundation of your FF efforts so you can continuing building upon your financial framework based on the chapters in this book, other readings, and insights you discover along the way.

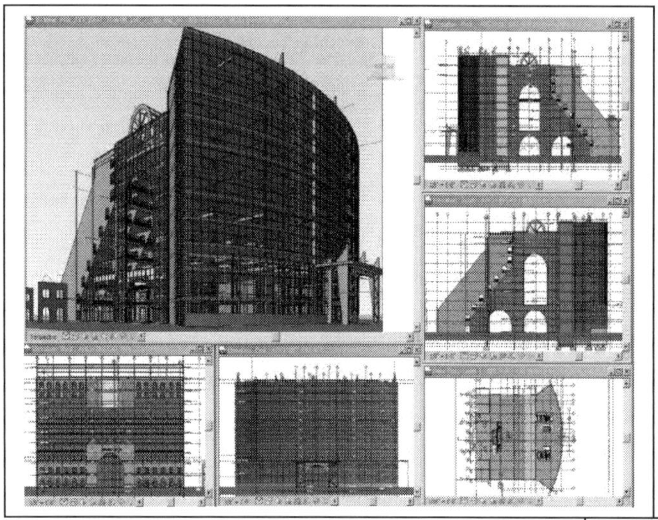

Creating a financially secure future is like designing and constructing a building. Why? Because you need a good set of plans! The alternative is chaos and financial peril.

Just like the 3D BIM generated building design at left, all the views are related, easy to visualize, and can be updated automatically. That translates into greater productivity and profitability. When you use your FF road map, you're doing the same thing by integrating all parts of your life rather than segregating them.

A good financial plan also includes the right education and a paying career.

Live within your means. Maintain little or no debt, other than a mortgage or very short term loans. The reward is more spendable cash and less stress.

Eventually, strive to pay-off all debts.

Financial literacy plus a good and *correctly-priced* college education are critical components to your career and joy in life. No one else will protect the most valuable assets you possess. This includes your time, money, health, skill, talent, ambition, integrity, and dreams. Guard them with all your might.

Upon entering adult hood, build your skills and strive for as little debt as possible. Then, just get out there and do it. Life's choices are ultimately yours alone to make. It takes time to make them wisely. Know that you will occasional make mistakes. When you do, don't be excessively hard on yourself. Society is more than willing to remind you of your mistakes. Many times that includes family. Be aware of other people's agendas. They're often meant to hurt you. Don't dwell too long on past failures. Face your weaknesses, allow a morning period, and be honest with yourself. Learn from your mistakes and from people who have succeeded in both their *personal* and *professional* lives. Be grateful to those who've helped you and let them know you appreciate it. Then, get back up, stay focused, and keep going. Henry Ford said: "Failure is just another opportunity to begin again more intelligently". He also said: "Whether you think you can or can't, either way, you're right". He failed in various business ventures multiple times before starting the Ford Motor Company. Then he struck gold and became the richest man in the country.

Share your passion with the world and create your own destiny. This is my hope for everyone. In so doing, you will set the stage to grow, prosper, and live the life you were destined to live by *being all that you can be*. That will naturally inspire others to do the same. In the end, this is the ultimate gift of freedom we owe ourselves and the civilization we create. It's our birthright. Never let anyone convince you otherwise.

Namaste'.

Study hard, go to a good college, and pay for it wisely. Then, work hard and do what you love most. That's what Warren Buffet did. He once told a class room of young kids to do the same thing. Be all you can be. Strive to become Debt Free and Financially Free! Create your own destiny.

Now...Go forth and make those dreams a reality!

Intentionally Blank

Appendix A

- Sean's Comic Corner
- About the Illustrator
- About the Author

Break Time!
Take a break and read a comic story for fun.

Birthday Christmas Troubles!

Written & Illustrated By Sean Rickter

Later that night...
Morning already
I better water the garden
Wohh

I got it
Thanks
Did you water the garden?
you didn't
Uhh No, but mom-
Ha ha!

Ha ha!
go now mister or your grounded!!!!
as for you, you need to vaccume
if dad were here,
meanwhile

Ahhh! ahhh!
Monster uhh ok
uhh Charlie help please a monster is attacking my house. hurry
theres a monster at Sheldon's house hurry over.
why this early?
come on sis we gotta go!
meanwhile

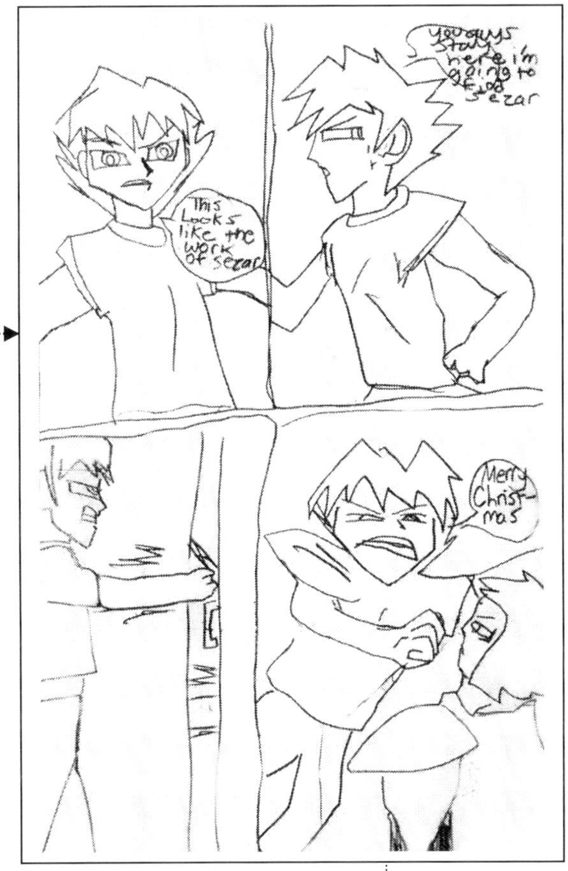

Comic break's over.

Let's get back to financial literacy!

Space to write notes, jot down ideas, express your heart's desire, and take action steps to turn dreams into reality.

About the Illustrator: Sean E. Rickter.
Sean E. Rickter (youngest son of the author) began drawing stylized cartoons and comics as a passion and hobby between the ages of six through ten. He was completely self-taught and created all his own characters and comic stories. Sean's art work in this book represents un-altered versions of his original drawings and comic stories during his childhood years, and had no relationship to this book at that time. Kids are naturally spontaneous, creative, accepting, and inquisitive. Expressing art and mastering your money matters both involve creative problem solving, practice, and inspiration. Combining those qualities in a book intended to teach kids and adults financial literacy fundamentals helped make it a bit more fun as well as educational.

Upon graduating Long Beach Poly High School with honors at the age of seventeen, Sean was admitted into the Huntsman Program at the Wharton Business School, at the University of Pennsylvania in 2012. He graduated from Wharton in 2016 with dual degrees in Economics (Finance Concentration) and International Studies. Sean began his finance career in 2016 and rose to senior financial analyst for The Walt Disney Company at its Burbank, California headquarters. He currently works for Disney as a financial analyst on global projects at their Tokyo, Japan office.

Money Matters for Kids and Parents

About the Author: Edward S. Rickter
Edward S. Rickter is an Architect, Technology Entrepreneur, Real Estate Developer, and Educator. During a life-long journey of designing and constructing buildings, he discover the critical need for technology, financial discipline, and a passion for teaching. This included helping others learn how to achieve financial freedom and the importance of getting a college education that is both viable and sensibly priced. He wants to share that knowledge with you. This book is dedicated to kids and the parents who do the hard work to love, mentor, and raise them.

"If my wife and I can send our kid to an Ivy League University with middle-class income and no debt, so can you!" But...you must do the work and be a parent!
When child and parent both work in unison, the rewards are beyond incredible".

Edward S. Rickter 11.11.2020

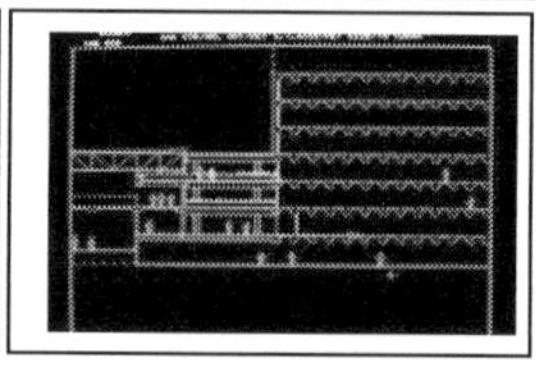

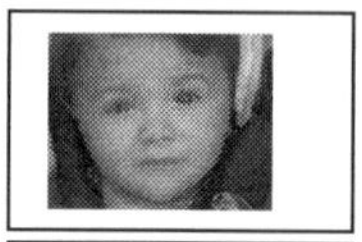

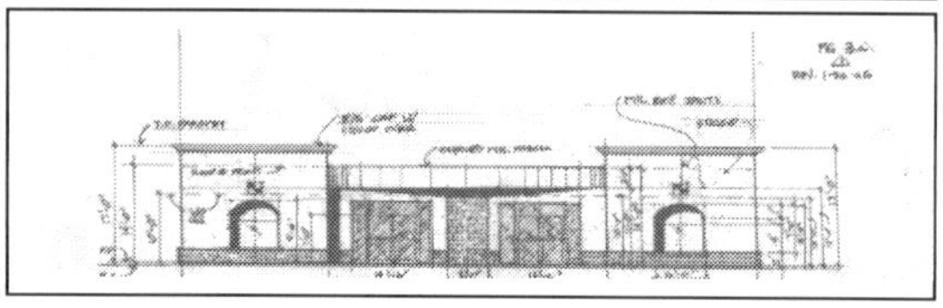

ISBN 978-0-578-67114-7
90000>
9 780578 671147

ISBN: 978-0-578-67114-7

Made in United States
Orlando, FL
04 November 2026

90202943R00092